REDEMPTION SONG

REDEMPTION SONG

MUHAMMAD ALI AND THE SPIRIT OF THE SIXTIES

MIKE MARQUSEE

Seagull
BOOKS
CALCUTTA 2000

First published by Verso 1999

Reprinted by arrangement with Verso

For sale in India and South Asia (Bangladesh, Burma, Bhutan, Sri Lanka, Nepal, Pakistan) only

Cover designed by Naveen Kishore using his photograph of a sculpture by Reba Hore

ISBN 81 7046 173 1

Published by Naveen Kishore, Seagull Books Private Limited, 26 Circus Avenue, Calcutta 700 017

Printed in India by A Das Gupta at Sun Lithographing Company, 18 Hem Chandra Nasker Road, Calcutta 700 010

Old pirates yes they rob I
Sold I to the merchant ships
Minutes after they took I
From the bottomless pit
But my hand was made strong
By the hand of the almighty
We forward in this generation
Triumphantly
Won't you help to sing
These songs of freedom
Cause all I ever had
Redemption songs
Redemption songs

Bob Marley

Contents

Acknowledgements

Many thanks to the following for support and stimulation: Zafaryab Ahmed, Arif Azad, Laurence Brent, Ben Carrington, Liz Davies, Steve Faulkner, John Fisher, Alan Goode, Elliott Hurwitt, Jennifer Macintosh, Jeff Marqusee, Ian McDonald, Dave Palmer, Pamela Philipose, Huw Richards, Rob Steen, Shaun Waterman. Thanks to Anthony Bah of the Ghana TUC and Niels Hooper for help digging through newspaper archives, and to Gavin Browning for photo research. Thanks also to A. Sivanandan and Hazel Waters at *Race and Class*, where I first published my thoughts on Ali, and to Megan Hiatt for attention to detail and care for the language (English and American). Big respect for Colin Robinson, "the Greatest," publisher and friend.

Finally, this book is dedicated to my parents, Janet and John Marqusee, who served their time in the causes of peace and racial justice.

Introduction:

Ali in the Prison of the Present

A strange fate befell Muhammad Ali in the 1990s. The man who had defied the American establishment was taken into its bosom. There he was lavished with an affection which had been strikingly absent thirty years before, when for several years he reigned unchallenged as the most reviled figure in the history of American sports.

Thanks to backstage lobbying by NBC Sports, Ali was cast as the star in the opening ceremony of the 1996 Atlanta Olympics. At the conclusion of the eighty-four-day Coca-Cola-sponsored torch relay, he raised a trembling arm to ignite the 170-foot wire fuse leading to the giant Olympic cauldron high above the stadium. In the control room, Don Mischer, creator of this high-tech, symbolically charged extravaganza, muttered into his headset, "Get ready to help him. Help Ali light it." But no help was needed. The fuse was lit. The cauldron blazed into life. Corporate sponsors, television executives, spectators in the stadium and television viewers in their homes breathed a sigh of relief. Ali had triumphed yet again, this time over his own physical disabilities. Before 83,000 spectators (paying $600 per ticket) and a global television audience which the broadcasters estimated at 3 billion, Ali transcended his illness and his divisive past. The *New York Times* described the moment as the "emotional perfect touch." To follow it up, the organizers played the famous final peroration from Martin Luther King's speech to the 1963 March on Washington. For Atlanta columnist Dave Kindred, the whole spectacle invoked "the world King spoke of on a day a generation ago." King's one-time aide, former Atlanta mayor Andrew Young, was equally enraptured, describing "the presence of Muhammad Ali" as "a symbol of the fact that whether we're Hindu, Muslim, Catholic or Jew, we're all working together."

However, not everyone was at ease with all the symbolic elements of this modern sporting and commercial rite. Outside the stadium, another former colleague of King's, Hosea Williams, led a small protest against the Georgia state flag, which incorporates the stars and bars of the Confederacy, fluttering over a tournament ostensibly predicated on the principles of human equality. It was because of the gap between Olympic ideals and American realities that, thirty-six years earlier, Cassius Clay had flung his gold medal into the Ohio River. And as if to complete this chain of symbolic transfigurations, at half-time during the 1996 Olympic basketball final, with the Dream Team once again confirming American supremacy in the one sport entirely originated in America, Ali was presented with a replacement gold medal by the Olympic boss and former Francoist, Juan Antonio Samaranch.

Ali's Olympic cameo sparked what *USA Today* called "a renaissance for the Greatest." *Sports Illustrated* put him on its cover for a record-breaking thirty-fourth time. *When We Were Kings*, the long-delayed documentary account of his 1974 Rumble in the Jungle with George Foreman, at last reached the screens, introduced a new mass audience to the glories of Ali in his heyday and won him a share in an Oscar-night accolade. It was even rumored that Ali would be nominated for a Nobel Peace Prize in recognition of his "humanitarian efforts." A wave of magazine profiles, television programs, videos and books renewed (and reinterpreted) his fame. Endorsement deals flooded in—$10 million worth in a year. It says a great deal about boxing and about Ali himself that twenty years after his retirement he remained the only boxer able to attract the kind of corporate affiliations routinely offered to stars from basketball, baseball, football or track and field.

Yet during most of his boxing career, the man now being hailed as "an American hero" was far more popular abroad than at home. This genial nineties icon of harmony and goodwill had flaunted a religion that spurned racial integration and repudiated America as a decadent "wilderness." In the name of wider and higher loyalties he refused to serve America in time of war and as a result was threatened with prison, barred from practicing his trade, harassed by his government and condemned by his country's media. At the same time, the very actions that so enraged the defenders of "Americanism" made Ali a symbol of anti-American defiance and the quest for autonomy across much of Africa, Asia, Latin America and Europe.

Like Martin Luther King or even Malcolm X—two other sixties icons with whom Ali enjoyed more than a passing acquaintance—Ali has had his political teeth extracted. It's not surprising. When an icon accumulates as many devotees as Ali has, when it emits such a numinous glow, it becomes irresistible to capitalism. Was there a better figure to help NBC, Coca-Cola and the Atlanta business elite sell the global games to America, and sell America to the world?

It is the fate of all ageing sports heroes to become the receptacles of our sloppiest sentiments. Yet there is something more at work in this strange transmutation of the greatest figure of resistance in the history of modern sport into yet another corporate signifier, to be celebrated, deconstructed, commodified. Ali, we are told, "created his own icon." He has become an American Adam, another Gatsby, and the raw materials from which he invented himself, the collective experiences crystallized in that self-construction, are hidden from sight.

Like many others of my generation, I have my own memories of Ali. As I grew up during the sixties, Ali was a constant presence, one of the few links between the twelve year old full of innocent enthusiasm for competitive sports and the eighteen year old full of world-weary radical rage. After moving to England in 1971, I discovered that Ali belonged not to America but to the world, and that he was adored by different sections of the population for different reasons. Later encounters with sports fans and political activists from Asia and Africa confirmed that Ali had built himself a genuinely global constituency, embracing many who loathed boxing and the values associated with it.

The only time I saw Ali in the flesh was at the Frankfurt Book Fair in 1976. He had come to town to promote his new autobiography, *The Greatest*, and was at the pinnacle of achievement and celebrity. He was immediately encircled by a vast crowd of well-dressed admirers clamoring for his autograph, a rare phenomenon at a jaded international affair of this type. I joined the crowd and waited patiently with a small slip of paper in my hand. Close up, Ali seemed physically immense, but strangely motionless amid the throng. Later I took the precious slip of paper on which the great man had scrawled his name back to my hotel room; it disappeared the next morning, presumably appropriated by one of the hotel's *Gastarbeiter* staff. Nothing else was missing.

What possible justification can there be for adding yet more to the millions of words already in print on the subject of Muhammad Ali? The easy answer is that on a subject as multi-faceted as this, there can be no last word. But as the years of Ali's incandescence recede into the distant past, there is a more compelling reason for reconsidering him. The Ali offered up for veneration in the 1990s is not the Ali of the 1960s, and the image of the 1960s that is celebrated or damned in the 1990s is a mere caricature of the original. In both cases, a complex and contradictory reality has been homogenized and repackaged for sale in an ever-burgeoning marketplace for cultural commodities.

In the nineties we have been told that the causes and complaints of the sixties are redundant, that the conflicts that once surrounded Ali have been resolved. Somehow the rights and wrongs of the hard choices he made have been declared peripheral to his legacy—as if racism and warfare, Islam and the West, personal identity, black leadership and the use of US military might in the poorer, darker countries were yesterday's issues, no longer pertinent, no longer divisive.

The capacity of our rulers to appropriate even the most refractory figures of resistance never ceases to awe, but we should remember that the process is never complete. Ali continues to mean different things to different people, and the various meanings are by no means all compatible. In many parts of the world, including within black America, and not least among black youths who have grown up long after his departure from the scene, Ali stands for values profoundly alien to those which motivated the extravaganza in Atlanta. If we are to reclaim Ali, it is not enough to venerate the icon from afar. We have to get up close.

The Ali story is so extraordinary, with its mythic elements of redemption through suffering, its cycle of trial and triumph, that it has proved and will continue to prove irresistible to chroniclers and commentators. But as we retell Ali's tale, we cannot allow ourselves to be so seduced by its hero that we forget the confusing conditions in which his story unfolded. It could have turned out otherwise. Doubt and contradiction, misjudgement and compromise contribute as much to the making of a hero—at least a hero who is of any real use to the rest of us—as single-minded determination and clarity of purpose. At the core of the Ali story is a young man who made daunting choices and stuck to them in the face of ghastly threats and glittering inducements. This book is about those choices in the context in which they were made.

No other sports figure (and few popular performers of any kind) was so enmeshed in the political events of his time. Ali's entire boxing career was shaped by his intimate interaction with political and social change. This is not to paint him as a political leader, activist or ideologue. In fact, strange as it may sound, Ali was strongly driven by an aversion to leadership, activism and ideology. He resisted political involvement and, at first, rejected the burden of symbolic representation that had been foisted upon black celebrities by both white and black commentators. But such was the alchemy of the man and the moment that he was drawn ever more deeply into politics and found himself becoming ever more symbolically representative. As Frederick Douglass observed, "A man is worked on by what he works on. He may carve out his circumstances, but his circumstances will carve him out as well."

1

The Baby Figure of the Giant Mass

On 25 February 1964, Cassius Clay defeated Sonny Liston to become heavyweight champion of the world. This against-the-odds victory was one of the shocking upheavals characteristic of the era, a surprise that compelled people to reconsider their assumptions. The triumph of the underdog, and with it the confounding of bookmakers and experts, is one of the most visceral thrills sports have to offer; it brings with it a combined sense of disorientation and unsuspected possibility, feelings which were to be intensified by Clay's actions outside the ring in the days that followed.

After the fight, Clay chose to forgo the usual festivities at one of Miami's luxury hotels and headed instead for the black ghetto, where he had made camp during training. He spent a quiet evening in private conversation with Malcolm X, the singer Sam Cooke and Jim Brown, the great Cleveland Browns running back and an early champion of black rights in sports. The next morning, after breakfast with Malcolm, Clay met the press to confirm the rumors that he was involved with the Nation of Islam:

> I believe in Allah and in peace. I don't try to move into white neighborhoods. I don't want to marry a white woman. I was baptized when I was twelve, but I didn't know what I was doing. I'm not a Christian any more. I know where I'm going, and I know the truth, and I don't have to be what you want me to be. I'm free to be what I want.

"*I don't have to be what you want me to be.*" No boxing champion, and no black sports star, had ever issued such a ringing declaration of independence. The next day, Clay amplified his views. In place of his usual ingratiating bravado, there was now a steely and even exultant defiance:

> Black Muslims is a press word. The real name is Islam. That means peace. Islam is a religion and there are seven hundred and fifty million people all over the world who believe in it, and I'm one of them. I ain't no Christian. I can't be when I see all the colored people fighting for forced integration get blowed up. They get hit by stones and chewed by dogs and they blow up a Negro church and don't find the killers. . . . I'm the heavyweight champion, but right now there are some neighborhoods I can't move into. I know how to dodge boobytraps and dogs. I dodge them by staying in my own neighborhood. I'm no trouble-maker . . . I'm a good boy. I never have done anything wrong. I have never been to jail. I have never been in court. I don't join any integration marches. I don't pay any attention to all those white women who wink at me. I don't carry signs. . . . A rooster crows only when it sees the light. Put

him in the dark and he'll never crow. I have seen the light and I'm crowing.

Reactions to Clay's announcement were swift and hostile. The southern-dominated World Boxing Association (WBA) began moves to strip him of his title. His record album, *I Am the Greatest*, was pulled from the shelves by Columbia. A scheduled appearance on the Jack Parr "television talk" show was canceled. Endorsement deals evaporated. Senators threatened to mount an investigation into the legality of the Liston fight. The syndicate of Louisville millionaires who sponsored Clay described him as "ungrateful." With a fine disregard for history, Jimmy Cannon, the doyen of boxing writers, declared that boxing had never before "been turned into an instrument of mass hate. . . . Clay is using it as a weapon of wickedness." Harry Markson, the head of Madison Square Garden, warned Clay, "You don't use the heavyweight championship of the world to spout religious diatribe. We've made so much progress in eliminating color barriers that it's a pity we're now facing such a problem."

Joe Louis joined in the condemnation: "Clay will earn the public's hatred because of his connections with the Black Muslims. The things they preach are the opposite of what we believe." NAACP leader Roy Wilkins echoed the sentiment: "Cassius may not know it, but he is now an honorary member of the White Citizens' Councils. . . . He speaks their piece better than they do." Floyd Patterson told the press he would fight Ali for free "just to get the title away from the Black Muslims."

Other black voices struck a more realistic balance. "Considering the associations and activities of other prizefighters I have known," observed George Schuyler, a conservative columnist, "Cassius Marcellus Clay is picking good company." Jackie Robinson insisted, "Clay has as much right to ally himself with the Muslim religion as anyone else has to be a Protestant or a Catholic." Despite his sometimes "crude" behavior, Clay, Robinson believed, had "spread the message that more of us need to know: 'I am the Greatest,' he says. I am not advocating that Negroes think they are greater than anyone else. But I want them to know they are just as great as other human beings." And a younger man, Leroi Jones, saw even greater possibilities in the new champ: "Clay is not a fake, and even his blustering and playground poetry are valid; they demonstrate that a new and more complicated generation has moved onto the scene. And in this last sense Clay is definitely my man."

Cassius Clay's conversion to the Nation of Islam set him on a path to uncharted lands, and transformed him in the eyes of both black and white. As a young challenger he had been brash and bold, an entertaining eccentric; within hours of winning the championship he had metamorphosed into an alien menace. He dared to turn his back on America, Christianity and the white race. Many black men had been lynched for less. The governors of American sports stood appalled as Clay brought the anarchy of political controversy into their orderly realm. Boxing fans were bemused. And in the black communities, while there was much dismay over Clay's rejection of the civil rights movement, there was also, among many, a mood of pleasant surprise. Whatever else it may have been, Clay's conversion to the Nation of Islam was recognized as an embrace of blackness; in willingly subjecting himself to the vilification that had been the lot of the Nation of Islam for years, he had placed his black constituency on a higher footing than the white audience to whom black performers were normally beholden, and this in itself earned him legions of black admirers.

"*I'm free to be what I want.*" It's often said that at this moment Muhammad Ali "invented himself." Through sheer charisma he brought the old stereotypes tumbling down like a black Samson in the temple of the Philistines. But he did not invent himself out of nothing. In his search for personal freedom he was propelled and guided by a wide array of interacting social forces. Ali's public conversion was one of the unexpected jolts that peppered the decade, opening dizzying vistas of both fear and hope. But as with all such moments, its significance can only be discovered by diving into the river of historical experience which flows into and out from it.

• • •

At root there is something irrational and arbitrary about sporting partisanship. As Jerry Seinfeld once observed, "People come back from the game yelling, 'We won! We won!' No: *they* won; you *watched*." How is it that passive spectators come to feel they partake in someone else's victory or defeat? This leap of imagination, this widening of the definition of the self is a wonderfully human phenomenon, which is why, as Seinfeld realized, it is also a rich vein of comedy.

Shakespeare comments on the irrationality of sporting partisanship—and the dangerous propensity of the masses to read their own fortunes into sporting contests—in his brittle meditation on love and war, *Troilus and Cressida*. Commenting on the prospect of one-on-one combat between the two champions of the Greek and Trojan armies, Achilles and Hector, the statesman-politician Nestor observes to Ulysses:

> Though't it be a sportful combat,
> Yet in the trial much opinion dwells;
> For here the Trojans taste our dear'st repute
> With their fin'st palate: and trust to me, Ulysses,
> Our imputation shall be oddly pois'd
> In this wild action; for the success,
> Although particular, shall give a scantling
> Of good or bad unto the general;
> And in such indexes, although small pricks
> To their subsequent volumes, there is seen
> The baby figure of the giant mass
> Of things to come at large.
>
> (I.iii.335–46)

Modern, secular spectator sports—in the forms of boxing, horse-racing and cricket—first emerged from the womb of parochial ritual and folk pastime in mid-eighteenth-century England. Their midwives were rapid urbanization, the spread of market relations and the growth of an ambitious elite with both time and money to squander. The sporting realm preserved and organized the pointlessness, the triviality of play. The activity unfolding within its boundaries was an end in itself; and the consequences of success or failure in that activity were of a profoundly different order than the consequences of success or failure in other competitive activities—economic, political, military. From the beginning, modern sports commanded a space both apart from and within the society that had given them birth.

Rules for boxing were first codified in 1743. Soon after, national champions were recognized. Newspapers advertised "prizefights" and employed the world's first sportswriters to cover them. Bouts sometimes drew crowds of ten to twenty thousand. They were usually staged under the aegis of aristocrats, who wagered substantial stakes on the results. Prizefighting became a pioneer enterprise in the commercialization of leisure, a trend that has grown to huge dimensions in our own time.

In the early decades of modern sports, gambling offered the principal basis for spectator identification with competitors; the financial investment became an emotional one. But other factors soon entered into the making of sporting loyalties: local, regional, national, generational and racial identities, school ties and individual whims. These give a veneer of rationality to the imaginative act of identification between spectator and competitor, but in one sense it always remains a veneer. The loyalties and identifications are not inherent in the spectacle; the tie between spectator and competitor is a constructed one, and the meanings it carries for either are generated by the histories—collective, individual—brought to bear on a contest that would otherwise be devoid of significance to all but direct participants. Precisely because they are universal and transparent, innocent of significance or consequence, sports became charged with meanings; because they meant nothing in themselves, they could come to mean anything.

Like Shakespeare's Machiavellian Greeks, the Victorians were highly sensitive to the social implications of "sportful combat." They saw that by giving "a scantling / Of good or bad unto the general," sports champions became representatives of larger constituencies. Precisely because "in the trial much opinion dwells," that opinion had to be shaped and guided from above. The Victorian ideology of amateur sports encased the unbridled competitive zeal in which sports are rooted within a higher morality. The egalitarian autonomy that is the presupposition of modern sports was overlaid with the prevailing hierarchies. As a result, competitors were to be judged by criteria extraneous to sports. Winning under the rules was not enough; one also had to uphold certain social and moral conventions. Thus the "role model," that incubus on the back of so many sporting champions, was born out of a need to tame the democracy of sport. It was a means of neutralizing its sublime indifference to social status.

The aristocrats under whose aegis the modern sports revolution was wrought never themselves entered the prizefighting ring (unlike the cricket pitch). Professional boxers were plebeians, performing at the behest of their social superiors. From its beginnings, boxing has been intimately linked with the urban proletariat, but its higher reaches have always been controlled by wealthy elites.

The social rupture that haunts boxing has disempowered boxers and boxing fans; it is one of the reasons why boxing has remained among the most anarchic of major world sports. From its earliest days, boxing has been a honey-pot for criminals, not least because it is relatively easy to fix the fights. During its two-hundred-year existence, boxing has been the plaything of aristocrats, politicians, newspaper proprietors, businessmen, public relations entrepreneurs and satellite and cable television moguls. But the gangsters have been ever present, expropriating fighters, fans and punters alike.

Boxing is not an expression of ghetto criminality or primitive aggression or some innate human propensity for violence, though when a Mike Tyson comes along, it is all too easy to paint it in those colors. The culture of boxing is all about self-restraint, self-discipline and deferred gratification. It is a highly structured response to and safe haven from the anarchy of poverty. The boxing gym is a world of rituals and regimen, mixing co-operation with competition, the hierarchy of skill and experience with the sweaty egalitarianism of the work ethic. Even when boxers leave the ghetto, they take this sustaining subculture with them. It is not boxing itself, but its historically constructed social and economic framework which has ensured the persistence of criminality and exploitation.

Outside the gym, boxers face a daunting gap between supply and demand in the labor market; the rewards at the top of the profession are prodigious, and have always been so, but only a tiny proportion of boxers come within reach of them. Boxing appears to be highly individualistic, but the individuals involved—the boxers—have less power over their bodies and careers, even today, than almost any other sports people. Even successful boxers, with few exceptions, are dependent on the whims of promoters, managers and satellite TV executives. If they are disabled in action, they remain reliant on charity. If they wish to advance towards a title, they must placate a variety of forces behind the scenes. Boxing ability has never been enough in itself.

In boxing, social and moral hierarchies have always been policed with special zeal. Such naked one-on-one human confrontations need to be managed (and packaged) with care if they are to serve as both an avenue of individual advancement and a re-enforcement of the existing distribution of wealth and power. Hence the paradox of boxing, a value-free institution sponsoring a spectacle laden with values.

No one has felt the pinch of that paradox more sharply than the generations of black boxers who have sustained the fight game at all levels. This long history has given boxing a special place in black communities. The triumphs and tragedies of black boxers—dependent on elite white power-brokers to make a living in the ring, expected to subordinate themselves to elite white norms outside the ring—have made black boxing a rich, complex, living tradition. During the first half of the twentieth century, black boxers were the most celebrated individuals in black American life. Their exploits were part of folklore, and they were admired as the epitome of black glamor. If the strangest fact about boxing is that it has not gone the way of cockfighting or bear-baiting, and has somehow managed to survive under the glare of the electronic media, then the next strangest is that it owes its survival in no small measure to the brilliance of black boxers, the people most exploited and brutalized by it.

In the 1950s, Nelson Mandela (a heavyweight) trained regularly at a black boxing club in Orlando, a township north of Johannesburg. "I did not enjoy the violence of boxing so much as the science of it," Mandela explains in his autobiography. "I was intrigued by how one moved one's body to protect oneself, how one used a strategy both to attack and retreat, how one paced oneself over a match." Here, boxing serves as preparation for long-term political struggle. But, for Mandela, the sport's main attraction resides at a deeper level. "Boxing is egalitarian. In the ring, rank, age, colour and wealth are irrelevant. When you are circling your opponent, probing his strengths and weaknesses, you are not thinking about his colour or social status."

Mandela here invokes the "level playing field," a metaphor from sports which has been applied to social, electoral and economic competition. In sport itself, the "level playing field" is more than just an ideological cosmetic, a democratic charade in an undemocratic order. Sports lose their meaning for the spectator—and therefore their place in the market—*unless everyone plays by the same rules, shoots at the same-size goalposts, is timed with the same stopwatch.* The level playing field is the autonomous logic of modern sport. For a contest to be seen as satisfactory, its rules, conditions and conduct must ensure that the result is determined only by the relative and pertinent strengths and weaknesses of the competitors. The objectivity of sporting contests is like the objectivity of a scientific experiment. *To the extent that the extraneous is excluded, the test is regarded as valid.* In boxing, which pits one man's strength, stamina and agility against another's, it was recognized early on that a fight between a heavyweight and a flyweight was meaningless as a test of individual prowess, and therefore unattractive as a spectacle.

The logic of the level playing field gives sports an egalitarian premise, undoubtedly one of the reasons for their enduring popular appeal. The major cliché about race in sports is that sports offer black people opportunities denied them in other spheres. In the autonomous realm of sports, equality reigns. Of course, the level playing field is enclosed within a society that is anything but level. As a result, a host of social forces converge to ensure that, despite its apparent autonomy and indifference to social status, the level playing field mirrors prevalent ideas about social hierarchy, including ideas about race. And when these ideas are challenged from below, the level playing field—or, in this case, the boxing ring—becomes socially contested terrain.

Initially, it was whites who made black boxers into "representatives of their race," declaring that they should be either defeated or excluded altogether from competition precisely because of this "representativeness." In 1810, Tom Molineaux, a black American ex-slave, fought the legendary English heavyweight, Tom Cribb, in East Grinstead. In the nineteenth round, the crowd rushed the ring and Molineaux's finger was broken. In the twenty-third round, Molineaux was dominating. "For God's sake, don't let the nigger win," shouted Sir Thomas Price, prominent member of the "fancy" that followed and wagered on prizefights. "Remember the honour of old England." Cribb failed to rise for the beginning of the twenty-eighth round and Molineaux began to celebrate. Then Cribb's second claimed that Molineaux was hiding bullets in his fists. By the time the black boxer disproved the charge, Cribb was back on his feet. In the thirty-ninth round, Molineaux conceded. Three days later he wrote to Cribb asking for a rematch. "As it is possible this letter may meet the public eye, I cannot omit the opportunity of expressing the confident hope, that the circumstances of my being a different colour to that of a people amongst whom I have sought protection will not in any way operate to my prejudice." The appeal to sporting equality seems to have struck a chord. The rematch, attended by 15,000, was one of the great sporting events of the nineteenth century. Molineaux broke his jaw in the ninth and was knocked out in the eleventh round. Ten years later, at the age of thirty-four, he died penniless in Ireland.

In America, the "representativeness" of black fighters gave their careers, in and out of the ring, a special interest for the black community, and not least among the precariously positioned black middle class. What Manning Marable calls the "strategy of symbolic representation" had been a major strand in the thinking of black American leaders ever since Booker T. Washington dined at the White House. It was thought that the success (and good behavior) of black sportsmen and entertainers would help secure symbolic space for "the American negro" within white America's image of the nation. Successful black performers were thus asked to act as "representatives" in two senses of the word, both as delegates from and embodiments of their people as a whole. Generations of black celebrities, including the foremost black boxers, have wrestled with this ambiguous burden, the burden of making "blackness" present in a white-dominated world. To whom are they accountable? Who "elects" them? And who decides which traits belonging to a particular individual are or are not representative of a whole community? Just what do these "representatives" represent, and to whom?

The black role model compounds the magical contradictions of symbolic representation through sports. The responsibility of the role model is to provide an example to black people of personal success achieved within the laws and customs of the realm. Yet all but a tiny minority of blacks have no hope of achieving such success within those laws and customs. What is more, black sporting role models are mostly male (in the case of boxing, exclusively so). The female black population is assigned a purely passive role; they are not asked to emulate but merely to admire the role models. In reality, they share this impotence with the vast majority of black males. As often as not, the duties of the role model have estranged black sports stars from their popular constituency. By the very fact of becoming a high-profile (and well-rewarded) "symbolic representative" of an oppressed and excluded group, an individual is likely to share less and less in common with that group. And, in a further irony, the more black sports stars remind people of the oppressive realities of black life, the less they are accepted as role models for it.

• • •

When Jack Johnson became the first black heavyweight champion in 1908, defeating Irishman Tommy Burns in front of a crowd of 30,000 in Sydney, a hue and cry went up from white America. Jack London asked when a "Great White Hope" would emerge to reclaim the title. The former champion, Jim Jeffries, who had previously refused to fight black boxers, came out of retirement, vowing to put the black man back in his place. His clash with Johnson drew unprecedented public attention, in America and abroad, and many on both sides of the racial divide were disturbed by its symbolic resonance. "If the black man wins," argued the *New York Times*, "thousands of his ignorant brothers will misinterpret his victory as justifying claims to much more than mere physical equality with their white neighbors." Followers of Booker T. Washington, who deplored Johnson's "boastfulness," warned that "any undue exhibitions of rejoicing on the part of Negroes" should Johnson win would lead to violence by whites. Both whites and blacks saw in Jack Johnson "the baby figure of the giant mass / Of things to come at large" and reacted accordingly, in fear or in hope.

In Reno on the fourth of July 1910, before an overwhelmingly white audience and reporters from around the world, Johnson dominated Jeffries with ease and knocked him out in the fifteenth round. As the news traveled, celebrations broke out in black communities across America; white gangs launched reprisal attacks in the worst racial violence of the decade.

Johnson was the white man's nightmare come alive. Not only did he beat up white heroes in the ring (sporting his trademark grin), he dallied with white women out of the ring and made no secret of it. It seemed that by brute force he had upturned all the conventions of race and gender which governed America. Hated and hounded by the white press, he was ultimately forced into exile to escape a conviction trumped up by the federal government under the Mann Act, which prohibited the transport of women across State lines for "immoral purposes."

Johnson was the most famous black person in America in these years. The wealth, glamor and pretension which the white press ridiculed and deplored exerted a powerful appeal to many blacks. For the most part, the black press celebrated Johnson's achievements; indeed, his fame helped create a new market for black newspapers in the nascent urban black communities. However, his antics made the tiny black middle class uneasy. Washington believed that Johnson had only himself to blame for his troubles with the press and the government, and feared that black people as a whole would bear the consequences of his irresponsible behavior. "It shows the folly of those persons who think they alone will be held responsible for the evil they do." To Washington, Johnson was a wholly unsuitable representative of his people: "A man with muscle minus brains is a useless creature." In fact, Johnson's boxing style was clinically sophisticated; he was one of the first masters of scientific, and therefore largely defensive, ringcraft. And he was quite capable of speaking for himself, even if what he said upset others. "White people often point to the writings of Booker T. Washington as the best example of the desirable attitude on the part of the colored population," Johnson noted in his autobiography. "I have never been able to agree with the point of view of Washington." He preferred Frederic Douglass, he said, because "he faced the issues without compromising."

In response to the publicity surrounding Johnson's marriage to a white woman, anti-miscegenation bills flooded state legislatures. W.E.B. Du Bois observed that this was one issue on which black and white appeared to be "in complete agreement." Behind this consensus, Du Bois saw the hypocrisy of an America perversely divided—and united—by the color line. "Let those people who have yelled themselves purple in the face over Jack Johnson just sit down and ask themselves this question: Granted that Johnson and Miss Cameron proposed to live together, was it better for them to be legally married or not? We know what the answer in the Bourbon South is. We know that they would rather uproot the foundations of decent society than to call the consorts of their brothers, sons and fathers their legal wives. We infinitely prefer the methods of Jack Johnson to those of Governor Mann of Virginia."

Du Bois was one of Johnson's few prominent defenders, not because he admired the boxer, but because he was alive to the grotesque double standard that informed the criticism of him. He accepted that "there is still today some brutality connected with boxing," but wryly noted that "certainly it is a highly civilized pastime as compared with the international game of war which produces so many 'heroes' and national monuments." He ridiculed "publications like the *New York Times*" which "roll their eyes in shivery horror" every time Johnson defeated a white man. "Why then this thrill of national disgust? Because Johnson is black. Of course, some pretend to object to Mr. Johnson's character. But we have yet to hear, in the case of white America, that marital troubles have disqualified prizefighters or ball players or even statesmen. It comes down, then, after all to this unforgivable blackness." To Du Bois, Johnson was representative in so far as he was a black victim of white racism.

Johnson based his own defense on his rights as an individual, not a representative. "I want to say I am not a slave and that I have the right to choose who my mate shall be without the dictation of any man," he insisted. "I have eyes and I have a heart, and when they fail to tell me who I shall have for mine, I want to be put away in a lunatic asylum." In 1915, weary and demoralized after years of exile, Johnson fought the latest white hope, Jess Willard, in Havana, where he was counted out in the twenty-seventh round. In his autobiography, Johnson claims he deliberately gave up the title because he had been led to believe it would ease his return to America. In the end, he returned five years later and served a year in prison.

Looking back on the sensational career of the first black heavyweight champion, the writer James Weldon Johnson lamented the boxer's lack of "culture" and compared him unfavorably to his predecessor, the legendary Peter Jackson, "whose chivalry in the ring was so great that sports writers down to today apply to him the doubtful compliment, 'a white colored man.'" Yet Weldon Johnson also recalled that "Frederick Douglass had a picture of Peter Jackson in his study, and he used to point to it and say, 'Peter is doing a great deal with his fists to solve the Negro question.' I think Jack, even after the reckoning of his big and little failings has been made, may be said to have done his share."

No black fighter was given a shot at the heavyweight title for twenty-two years after Johnson lost it. Throughout the twenties, Jack Dempsey refused to meet black challengers, yet hardly a sportswriter in the country thought this compromised the credibility of his claim to be "world champion." When Joe Louis emerged in the early thirties, his handlers were determined to learn from Johnson's bitter experience. Louis was given lessons in table manners and elocution; he was told to go for a knockout rather than risk the whims of racist judges; he was told never to smile when he beat a white man and, above all, never to be caught alone with a white woman.

Louis was groomed as a role model for black America, inoffensive but dignified, respectful and respected. The symbolic burdens that this would involve became apparent in his first fight in New York City, against Primo Carnera in 1935. At the time, Mussolini was engaged in highly public preparations for his invasion of Ethiopia. Although neither Louis nor Carnera had said anything about the issue, they were seen by many as representatives of Africa and Italy respectively. Fears that rioting might break out among the fans led to a pre-fight announcement urging all concerned to view the bout solely as a contest between two individuals and nothing more—surely one of the most futile exhortations in the history of sports. Louis finished off the hard-hitting, Mafia-backed Carnera in the sixth round.

It was not only Louis's demure behavior that made him acceptable to the white establishment, it was also the peculiar politics of the times. He won the heavyweight crown in Chicago in 1937, in front of a crowd of 45,000, half of whom were black. But the year before, he had been beaten by a German, Max Schmeling, in a fight that had been hailed by Nazi ideologists as a triumph of Aryan supremacy. The rematch at Yankee Stadium in 1938 was at the time the most widely followed sporting contest in history and a huge event in the life of America's black communities. Louis was made aware by the press, the churches, the president of the United States and the Communist party that knocking Schmeling's block off was his duty to America, the cause of anti-fascism and "the Negro." Any remaining doubts were removed when Nazis picketed his training camp.

In "High Tide in Harlem," Richard Wright described the Louis–Schmeling fight as "a colorful puppet show, one of the greatest dramas of make-believe ever witnessed in America . . . a configuration of social images whose intensity and clarity had been heightened through weeks of skillful and constant agitation." But this layer of drama was not entirely extraneous to the sporting nature of the contest itself. The level playing field offered laboratory-like conditions in which to test the theory of Aryan supremacy. Louis's victory, like Jesse Owens's at the Berlin Olympics in 1936, was a "scientific" repudiation of that theory and was seen as such by millions. When Louis demolished Schmeling in two minutes of the first round, the symbolism was intelligible to all, because it emerged from the egalitarian presuppositions of modern sports. "That was freedom day," recalled Andrew Young. Like many of his generation, his early "consciousness as a black person came almost entirely from sport."

This time blacks could celebrate without fear of reprisals. Louis may have whipped a white man, but that white man was a German and, what's more, a symbol of the Nazi regime. Louis was fighting for America, or at least for the liberal America of the New Deal. For once, "Americanism" and anti-racialism were congruent. Louis was praised everywhere as "a credit to his race"—not merely because he had excelled in the ring but because he had vindicated "the American way" at a critical time. For the American elite, Louis was a means to rally popular support for a war against Germany and Japan. For American Communists, and partisans of the Popular Front, the Schmeling–Louis bout was a contest between "fascism" and "democracy." On the night of the fight, Communists organized "Joe Louis radio parties" in black communities. Both the Communists and the elite emphasized the "dignity" with which Louis represented his people and with which he had elevated the hitherto despised sport of boxing.

In 1940, a group of black artists closely associated with the Popular Front came together to create "King Joe," a musical tribute to Louis. Count Basie composed the music, Richard Wright wrote the lyric and Paul Robeson sang it. What's intriguing about "King Joe" is its emphasis on Louis as a creation of black America.

> Lord, I know a secret, swore I'd never tell,
> Lord, I know what makes old Joe hook and punch and roll
> like hell,

Black-eyed peas asks cornbread what makes you so strong,
Cornbread says I come from where Joe Louis was born.

And there is also a suggestion that the Louis white America knows is not the whole man:

They say Joe don't talk much but he talks all the time
Now you can look at Joe, but you sure can't read his mind.

Wright also noted that "what old Joe does at night, lord, sure ain't done him no wrong." Memories of what had happened to Jack Johnson were still alive in the black community, and Louis's fans there were only too aware how any expression of sexuality would be construed by white people. As Langston Hughes put it, "the gossips had no 'they say' to latch onto for Joe."

Joe has sense enough to know
He is a god.
So many gods don't know.

Louis re-enforced his standing as a role model—for white America, for the black middle class and for much of the left—by enlisting for military service in World War II. Langston Hughes, who a decade before had asked, "What's America to me?", now held the champ up as an example to all Americans:

Joe Louis is a man
For men to imitate—

When his country needed him,
He did not stall or fail.
Joe took up the challenge
And joined up for the war.
Nobody had to ask him,
"What are you waiting for?"

While in the army, Louis fought ninety-six exhibition bouts for American troops around the world—all of them serving in racially segregated units. He received nothing more than his ordinary soldier's pay. He dedicated the entire proceeds of one fight to the Navy Relief Fund, even though the navy was widely known as the most racist branch of the services. Louis did everything the white establishment asked of him and still ended up broke and humiliated. The federal government pursued him for back taxes; at one point, he had to take to wrestling to drum up cash. Louis looked in vain for a role in retirement commensurate with the glory he had enjoyed in his days in the ring. His spell in management, including time in Sonny Liston's camp, was a failure. He struggled with drug addiction. In later years, he hobbled around Las Vegas, paid by casino owners to greet the high rollers.

The contrast between Johnson and Louis haunted the black fighters who followed them. There seemed to be only these two stereotypes for black sportsmen in America: the "bad nigger" and the "Uncle Tom." Both Johnson and Louis, of course, were subjected to critical scrutiny never lavished on white champions, and both were defined by white perceptions. It was a polarity constructed by and for white people, and did a disservice to the complexities of both men, but it was nonetheless a polarity to which black people were compelled to respond. And in that response, they argued out the terms and conditions under which black people could survive—or even advance—in white-dominated America.

• • •

> In a remote village in the north of Ceylon many years ago, a group of boys, playing truant from school, crowded into the village bakery to look at their first wireless. The owner twiddled the knobs with a flourish, showing his audience how he could bring the world to his doorstep. And suddenly he stopped—at an English song—though he understood not a word. A man was singing what sounded like a song of his people, a song that sounded so much like their own—and he sang as though the big heart of the radio itself would break. And they all fell silent, as though in prayer. I was one of those boys.
>
> *A. Sivanandan*

No one knew better the complexities of serving as a public representative of an oppressed people than Paul Robeson. In 1922, after a path-breaking career in college football, he was briefly touted as a possible black challenger to Jack Dempsey. After consulting with friends and family, Robeson decided against the idea. The whole image of prizefighting, he felt, was unsuitable for a future leader of black America. Instead, he continued his law studies, supplementing his income by playing football for Akron. Professional football was a game of low pay and low prestige in those days, which was one reason it did not operate a color bar like baseball. (In a move upmarket, blacks were barred by the owners in 1934, and readmitted in a trickle only in the fifties.)

In 1927, after his Broadway triumph in *The Emperor Jones*, Robeson took on the role of a thinly veiled Jack Johnson in a play called *Black Boy*. The white press was offended by the subject matter and panned the play in racist terms; the black press disparaged its simple-minded hero as a stereotype. Robeson found himself caught in what was to become a familiar vice. As one of Du Bois's "talented tenth," he had long seen himself as a member of the black vanguard. As he overcame obstacle after obstacle, forced breakthrough after breakthrough—in sport, scholarship, singing, acting—he wrestled constantly with the ever-shifting demands, from both white and black, of his representative burden.

In December 1943, Robeson, with a delegation of black newspaper publishers, lobbied the major league baseball owners to drop the color bar and admit black players. Commissioner Landis introduced Robeson as "a great American." The owners listened to Robeson in silence, applauded his speech, then did absolutely nothing to meet his demands. For all the talk of a "double victory" over fascism and Jim Crow, World War II ended with Jim Crow entrenched in both the United States Army and major league baseball.

In 1945 Howard University awarded Robeson an honorary degree and he beat out Joe Louis for the NAACP Spingarn award. At the height of his fame and prestige, he was considered the most illustrious American black man of his time. But Robeson was also growing more intransigently political, speaking out in ever stronger terms for colonial freedom and against racism. Even more controversially, he denounced the Cold War and called for friendship with the Soviet Union. As anti-communism gripped the country, Robeson found his professional opportunities restricted. The day after Jackie Robinson's first major league base hit, Robeson's performance in Peoria was banned by the city council. In 1948, following the defeat of Henry Wallace's third-party bid for the presidency (of which Robeson was a national co-chair), J. Edgar Hoover ordered his agents to intensify their surveillance of the singer. In the next few months, eighty-five of Robeson's concert dates were canceled. In February 1949, he departed for Europe. In Britain, every concert was sold out, and he was welcomed as a hero by the labor movement. In Paris, he addressed the World Peace Congress, a Communist-organized initiative which had attracted 1800 delegates from 60 countries (among them Du Bois and Picasso). Robeson attacked those he believed were fueling hostility between the United States and the Soviet Union. According to the Associated Press, Robeson declared, "It is unthinkable that American Negroes would go to war on behalf of those who have oppressed us for generations against a country which in one generation has raised our people to the full dignity of mankind." Though Robeson claimed he had been inaccurately quoted, he never disavowed the gist of the argument, which was to lead to his obliteration as a public figure in the United States. As his biographer Martin Duberman observed, "The showcase black American had turned out not to be suitably 'representative' after all—and it became imperative to isolate and discredit him."

Much of the American press took Robeson's reported remarks as proof that the "Communist fellow-traveler" was a traitor to his country. A *New York Times* editorial declared Robeson "mistaken and misled" and urged him to return to using "his great gifts" in the concert hall, a course of action denied him by the blacklist, which he could only escape from by recanting his political views. The State Department, alarmed at sympathy for Robeson in the foreign press, prevailed on Walter White of the NAACP to issue a formal statement. "Negroes are American," White insisted. "We contend for full and equal rights and we accept full and equal responsibilities. In event of any conflict that our nation has with any other nation, we will regard ourselves as Americans and meet the responsibilities imposed on all Americans."

White, like leaders of other established black organizations, feared that by implying that blacks were disloyal—or worse yet, pro-Communist—Robeson's comments would set back the drive for full integration in the American system. "There's a sort of unwritten law that if you want to criticize the United States you do it at home," observed Bayard Rustin. "We have to *prove* we're patriotic." Rustin convened a meeting of nationally known black leaders at which a "Robeson does not speak for us" campaign was agreed. Statements denouncing Robeson were issued by Adam Clayton Powell, Jr., the A.M.E. Zion bishops, Mary McLeod Bethune ("American Negroes have always been loyal to America, they always will be") and others. The very forces, both white and black, which had decreed Robeson a "representative of his race" and which had lauded his every achievement as a symbolic breakthrough for all black Americans were now insisting he represented nobody but himself. In an attempt to deny Robeson authenticity, Roy Wilkins even went so far as to declare, "Robeson has none except sentimental roots among American negroes. He is one of them, but not of them."

Despite the vituperation, in parts of the black press there was a sneaking admiration for Robeson; he had blurted out what so many blacks thought but would not dare to say. "There is hardly a Negro living in the South who, at some time or another, has not felt as Robeson expressed himself," said a North Carolina paper, "unwilling to lay down his life for a country that insults, lynches and restricts him to a second-class citizenship."

On his return to America in June, Robeson confronted a hostile press corps at LaGuardia airport. "I happen to love America very much," he told them, "not Wall Street and not your press." At a welcome-home meeting organized by the Council on African Affairs, Robeson reiterated the sentiments which had already all but terminated his professional career in America:

> I defy any part of an insolent, dominating America, however powerful. I defy any errand boys, Uncle Toms of the Negro people, to challenge my Americanism because by word and deed I challenge this vicious system to the death. I'm looking for freedom, full freedom, not an inferior brand. . . . We do not want to die in vain any more on foreign battlefields for Wall Street and the greedy supporters of domestic fascism. If we must die, let it be in Mississippi or Georgia. Let it be wherever we are lynched and deprived of our rights as human beings.

The *New York Times* reported this speech under the headline, "Loves Soviet Best, Robeson Declares." The Hearst papers carried front-page editorials entitled, "An Undesirable Citizen" and announcing "it was an accident unfortunate for America that Robeson was born here." The *Amsterdam News* called him a "selfish fraud" and Communist dupe.

In response to Robeson's "disloyal and unpatriotic statements" the House Un-American Activities Committee (HUAC) held hearings in July at which prominent negroes were asked to voice their dissatisfaction with Robeson. Alongside the stream of FBI informants and professional anti-Communists who denounced "the voice of the Kremlin" and "the black Stalin," there were also academics, businessmen, NAACP and Urban League officials, not to mention the president of Fisk College. But the star witness was without doubt Jackie Robinson, then in his third and most successful major league season and already, along with Joe Louis and Robeson himself, one of the best-known blacks in America. He had just topped the All-Star poll and was batting .360 when he received a telegram from the chairman of HUAC inviting him to "to give the lie" to Robeson.

Like Robeson, Robinson was a college-educated all-round athlete and scholar. In the army he had stood up to a racist officer and faced a court-martial for his pains. The Dodgers' owner, Branch Rickey, had chosen him not only for his athletic ability, but also for his articulate, calm demeanor and self-discipline. Unlike Robeson, he was committed to the capitalist system and the Republican party. He subscribed to the American version of the ethic of personal success, but was also a dedicated "race man" and always would be.

On 18 July 1949, in a committee room packed with press, radio, film and television crews, Robinson read out a statement he had prepared with the help of Rickey and Lester Granger, head of the Urban League. Robeson, he insisted, had a "right to his personal views, and if he wants to sound silly when he expresses them in public, that is his business and not mine." He was careful not to claim any representative mandate, while at the same time questioning Robeson's. "I can't speak for any fifteen million people any more than any other one person can, but I know that I've got too much invested for my wife and child and myself in the future of this country, and I and other Americans have too much invested in our country's welfare for any of us to throw it away because of a siren song sung in bass." This was what the politicians and the press wanted to hear. Few noted the caveat Robinson was careful to attach to his declaration of loyalty. "Negroes were stirred up long before there was a Communist party and they'll stay stirred up long after the party has disappeared—unless Jim Crow has disappeared by then as well." Just because blacks would always fight for America against foreign foes didn't mean that "we're going to stop fighting race discrimination in this country." But, he added, "We can win our fight without the Communists and we don't want their help."

The *New York Times* reported Robinson's statement on the front page and praised it in an editorial ("Jackie Robinson scored four hits and no errors"). Eleanor Roosevelt followed suit in her syndicated column. The black press put a different spin on the story. "Lynchers Our Chief Enemy Jackie Tells 'Red' Probers" was how the *Philadelphia Afro-American* reported the story. Other black papers printed letters and cartoons depicting Robinson as a white man's "stooge." Robeson himself claimed there was "no argument between Jackie and me" and insisted he would not "be drawn into any conflict dividing me from my brother victim of terror." Later that summer, Robeson's concert in Peekskill, New York, was attacked by right-wing vigilantes. The American Sports Annual deleted his name from its honor roll of football all-Americans for 1917 and 1918. By the dawn of the fifties, Robeson had been airbrushed from American popular consciousness.

Stripped of his passport, chronically ill, depressed and discouraged, Robeson nonetheless found the strength to deliver a sizzling indictment of the guardians of "Americanism" when he himself finally appeared before HUAC in 1956. "You want to shut up every Negro who has the courage to stand up to fight for the rights of his people," he told the congressmen. When they asked him why he didn't move to Russia, he answered, "Because my father was a slave, and my people died to build this country, and I am going to stay here and have part of it just like you. And no Fascist-minded people will drive me from it. Is that clear?" Openly contemptuous of his interrogators, seething with righteous indignation—it was Paul Robeson's last great public performance.

Like many a heavyweight fight, the Robeson–Robinson confrontation was a public battle between black men staged by and for whites, with a more than interested black audience looking on. Both men had become "representatives" of their race by virtue of their successes as performers, principally as performers for white audiences. But they differed radically in their interpretation of their duties as "representative" figures. The questions posed by the HUAC hearings—"Who speaks for black Americans?" and "Where do black Americans' loyalties lie?"—re-emerged in a fascinating exchange between Robinson and Malcolm X in 1963. In his syndicated column, Robinson had warned Adam Clayton Powell, Jr., "The Negro people are growing up, Adam, and I do not think they are sympathetic any longer to the business of supporting anything anyone does—wrong or right—simply because he belongs to the race." Robinson had singled out Powell's public dalliance with Malcolm and the Nation of Islam for criticism. In a letter to the *Amsterdam News*, Malcolm counter-attacked with glee, invoking Robeson to hit Robinson where it hurt:

> Shortly after the white man lifted you from poverty and obscurity to the Major Leagues, Paul Robeson was condemning America for her injustices against American Negroes. Mr. Robeson questioned the intelligence of Negroes fighting to defend a country that treated them with such open contempt and bestial brutality. Robeson's brilliant stand on behalf of our people left the guilty American whites speechless: they had no defence. They sought desperately to find another Negro who would be dumb enough to champion their bankrupt "white" cause against Paul Robeson. It was you who let yourself be used by whites even in those days against your own kind. You let them sic you on Paul Robeson.

Malcolm mocked Robinson's alleged subservience to white patrons—Nixon, Rockefeller, Branch Rickey, his employers in the instant coffee business—and warned that if he ever became "militant in behalf of your people . . . the same whites whom you now take to be your friends will be the first to put the bullet or the dagger in your back." Robinson replied at length, insisting he was "proud" of his associations with whites who had contributed to negro freedom. And he repeated that he believed negroes would reject Malcolm's "racism" because "our stake in America is worth fighting for." But it was when he pointed contemptuously to the gulf between Malcolm's aggressive rhetoric and his passive practice that he hit Malcolm's own sensitive spot:

> Whom do you think you are kidding, Malcolm, when you say that Negro leaders ought to be "thankful" that you were not personally present in Birmingham or Mississippi after racial atrocities had been committed there? . . . You would have done exactly what you did after your own Muslim brothers were shot and killed in Los Angeles. . . . You mouth a big and bitter battle, Malcolm, but it is noticeable that your militancy is mainly expressed in Harlem where it is safe.

In this exchange, Robinson had the last word. By this time, Malcolm had been silenced by Elijah Muhammad and was unable to reply. But Robinson's challenge had merely echoed Malcolm's own thoughts, and his answer, in the end, was his break with the Nation of Islam.

Robinson, who never wavered from his anti-communism or his conviction that America was fighting a just war in Vietnam, was frequently derided as an Uncle Tom by the young militants of the late sixties. But they were attacking the Jackie Robinson of American Cold War propaganda, not the real man, who was far more complex. In January 1964, he praised "the glorious, militant leadership" of the black youth pitting their bodies against Jim Crow, but he also warned of the obstacles they would face as the center of the struggle moved to the northern ghettos. "These formerly friendly white folk are becoming more and more leery. Prejudice is a sinful thing, in their eyes, so long as it exists in someone else's backyards. But let a negro protest against conditions in the backyard of the 'liberals,' the shoe begins to pinch." Still, he insisted, whatever the obstacles, "no matter what the liberals say—no matter how much they resent the new attitudes and sentiments and militancy of the negro, the Revolution will and must continue."

Robinson was a racial realist. He thought black people had to acquire economic and political power, and he tried to use the celebrity conferred on him by his sporting career to achieve it. But he was also acutely aware that this celebrity leverage worked two ways: it gave freedom and it took it away. Shortly after his attack on white liberals, he criticized Bayard Rustin for attending a cocktail party at the Soviet consulate in New York. He believed this "most foolish error" would be detrimental to the civil rights cause. In a weary reflection on the burdens of symbolic representation, he observed, "as unfair as it may seem to require a man to give up his personal prerogatives, the sacred mantle of leadership must be worn with great prudence."

In late 1964, Robinson left the coffee business to work for Nelson Rockefeller's presidential campaign. As a delegate to the San Francisco convention that nominated Barry Goldwater, he was an eyewitness to the birth of the New Right. "I had a better understanding of how it must have felt to be a Jew in Hitler's Germany," he observed bitterly. His autobiography, published shortly before his death in 1972, testifies to the sense of frustration that washed over Robinson in his last years. It's there in his comment on the HUAC hearings of 1949:

In those days I had more faith in the ultimate justice of the American white man than I have today. I would reject such an invitation if offered now. . . . I have grown wiser and closer to painful truths about America's destructiveness, and I do have increased respect for Paul Robeson who for over twenty years sacrificed himself, his career and the wealth and comfort he once enjoyed because, I believe, he was sincerely trying to help his people.

• • •

The fights between Johnson and Jeffries and Louis and Schmeling had been black against white. But in the sixties and seventies, the heavyweight division was dominated by blacks. This did not make the struggle for the title any less racially charged. On the contrary, the fights between Floyd Patterson, Sonny Liston and Muhammad Ali—and later between Ali and Ernie Terrell, Joe Frazier and George Foreman—all became valorized by the perceived relation of each fighter to white power. Like the Robeson–Robinson exchange, they became morality plays on the theme of black representation.

Like Mike Tyson, Floyd Patterson came out of the slums of Brooklyn and, like Tyson, he was raised from juvenile delinquency and trained in ringcraft by Cus D'Amato, a white Svengali who tried to keep both fighters out of the clutches of the crooks. Unlike Tyson, the studiously inoffensive, frugal and churchgoing Patterson became a hero to white America. Having become the youngest man ever to win the heavyweight title, he was invited to the White House, married a white woman, bought a house in a white neighborhood and became a symbol of the integrationist ideal. Norman Mailer called him "a liberal's liberal." In his 1962 autobiography, *Victory over Myself* (its cover graced with a photo of Patterson with JFK) he listed his role models as Joe Louis, Ralph Bunche and Jackie Robinson and made clear that his ambition was to live up to their example as "representatives of the race."

D'Amato lamented Patterson's lack of "viciousness." Yet it was D'Amato who for several years shielded Patterson from Sonny Liston, widely recognized as the number one contender and the toughest heavyweight on the circuit. D'Amato could get away with this because absolutely nobody wanted Sonny Liston to be the heavyweight champ. "Patterson draws the color line against his own race," Liston complained. "We have a hard enough time as it is in the white man's world." And it was true that until Liston, Patterson had agreed to meet only one black challenger.

Liston was the most disliked black sports star since Jack Johnson. He was introduced to boxing at the age of eighteen in the Missouri State Penitentiary and turned professional soon after his release. In between his early bouts, he provided debt-collecting muscle for local hoodlums. In 1956, he was arrested for assaulting a police officer, following a dispute outside his own home, and was sentenced to nine months in an Illinois workhouse. This conviction not only made it difficult for him to get fights (which, in turn, made him more dependent on the mob), it also made him a marked man for every white cop in the country. By 1962, he had a record of nineteen arrests. During his stay in Philadelphia, Liston, by now recognized as the leading heavyweight contender, was continually rousted by police, who charged him with a wide array of offenses, including impersonating a police officer. When he left the city for a new home in Denver, he told the press, "I'd rather be a lamppost in Denver than the mayor of Philadelphia."

Sonny was illiterate but quick-witted, and more than prepared to stand his ground against bullies in uniform. Despite his police record and his mob connections, used again and again to deny him a title shot, he was generous and sensitive, as well as prickly and wary. His biographer, Rob Steen, was right to observe, "All Sonny ever got were cheap shots." One of the most persistent concerned his date of birth, which was shrouded in mystery. For the press, Liston's inability to produce a birth certificate was evidence of criminality. In fact, Liston was born to a family of impoverished rural workers, with the aid of a midwife not a doctor, and he was his father's twenty-fourth child. Not surprisingly, his birth went unrecorded. Liston hailed from America's anonymous lower depths—and he was punished for it. Depicted as sullen, violent, ignorant and menacing, Liston was fair game for journalists, boxing authorities and politicians. Leroi Jones identified him as "the big black negro in every white man's hallway, waiting to do him in, deal him under, for all the hurt white men have been able to inflict on his world." But black leaders also froze him out, deeming him an unfit representative of the race. How could a mobbed-up street-brawler project the clean-cut, moderate, non-violent image by which they set such store? The NAACP urged Patterson not to give him a title shot. Back in 1932, W.E.B. Du Bois had decried the way "the emancipated and rising negro has tried desperately to disassociate himself from his own criminal class. He has been all too eager to class criminals as outcasts, and to condemn every negro who has the misfortune to be arrested or accused." Years later, Sonny Liston found himself at the mercy of the "combination of ignorance and Pharisaism" which Du Bois had railed against.

In the end, however, Liston got his chance, partly because Patterson was embarrassed by the allegations that he was dodging Sonny, but mainly because the promoters and authorities knew that excluding Liston would discredit the heavyweight title even more than giving it to him. The public backed Patterson, but it wanted his superiority proved in the ring.

Thus the scene was set for a fight with almost as many symbolic overtones as Louis–Schmeling. *Sports Illustrated* invoked the Cold War: "In this day and age we cannot afford an American heavyweight champion with Liston's unsavory record." The president of the National Boxing Association made no effort to disguise his bias: "In my opinion, Patterson is a fine representative of his race, and I believe the heavyweight champion of the world should be the kind of man our children could look up to." Patterson received messages of support from JFK, Ralph Bunche and Eleanor Roosevelt. Percy Sutton, then president of the Manhattan NAACP, later a millionaire power-broker in the Democratic party, declared: "I'm for Patterson because he represents us better than Liston ever could or would."

Not everyone in the black community subscribed to Sutton's view. "They painted Liston Black. They painted Patterson White. And that was the simple conflict," said Leroi Jones. "Which way would the black man go? This question traveled on all levels through society." Liston himself seemed resigned to his assigned role. "A prizefight is like a cowboy movie," he said. "There has to be a good guy and a bad guy. People pays their money to see me lose. Only in my cowboy movie, the bad guy always wins." Sure enough, Liston knocked out Patterson in the first round. In the rematch ten months later, he did it again. "Each time Patterson fell," Leroi Jones recalled, "a vision came to me of the whole colonial West crumbling in some sinister silence." The press now declared Liston "invincible"—but they still thought someone else should be champion. In December 1963, an *Esquire* fantasy feature pitted Liston against the champions of yesteryear. Sonny beat Louis and Rocky Marciano before succumbing to Dempsey.

It is hard to believe now, but at first Cassius Clay appeared to many Liston-haters as a "great white hope." Certainly he was happy enough in the beginning to join in the conventional role-play. At ringside for the Liston–Patterson fight, Thomas Hauser reports, "he shook Patterson's hand, looked towards Liston, threw his hands in the air in mock terror, and fled." In the build-up to the fight with the man he called "that big ugly bear," Clay dehumanized his opponent:

> Sonny Liston is nothing. The man can't talk. The man can't fight. The man needs talking lessons. The man needs boxing lessons. And since he's gonna fight me, he needs falling lessons. . . . After I whup Sonny Liston, I'm gonna whup those little green men from Jupiter and Mars. And looking at them won't scare me none because they can't be no uglier than Sonny Liston. . . . I'm gonna give him to the local zoo after I whup him. . . . I'm young, I'm handsome, I'm fast, I can't be beaten. . . . He's too ugly to be the world champ. The world champ should be pretty like me.

Here Clay echoed the racist stereotype of the black boxer as an uneducated animal, but he did so with a playful panache and impish vanity that neither the rigidly righteous Patterson nor the warily defensive Liston could hope to match. At a publicity stunt in Las Vegas, Clay so riled Liston that the usually taciturn champ called him a "nigger faggot." In evaluating the racial symbolism of the contest, it should be remembered that it was Liston, not Clay, who lent support to the civil rights movement by insisting on a contractual clause barring segregated movie theaters from showing the title bout on closed-circuit television. "Someday they're gonna write a blues song just for fighters," Sonny once said. "It will be for a slow guitar, soft trumpet and a bell." "He's lonely and he's been hurt," James Baldwin observed. "To me, Liston is sweet."

2

A Change Is Gonna Come

Engraved on the wall of the gymnasium at West Point are the words of General Douglas MacArthur, paraphrasing the Duke of Wellington: "Upon the fields of friendly strife are sown the seeds that, on other days in other fields, will bear the fruits of victory." In linking the benign pointlessness of sport to the death struggles of the battlefield, the public-school games ethic managed to debauch sport while lending warfare a spurious nobility. Early in their parallel evolution, a link was forged between modern sport and the destiny of the nation-state. Sport became both preparation and substitute for war, a theater of competition not merely between individuals and teams, but between nations and peoples.

During the Cold War, the sporting arena, notably the Olympic Games, became a field of battle by proxy, an arena in which competing social systems sought to demonstrate their superiority. Sporting success was viewed as a barometer of dynamism and modernity. In this context, the most significant moment of the 1960 Rome games was the victory of the barefoot Abebe Bikila of

Ethiopia in the marathon—the first black African to win a medal. But in America (and the Soviet Union) the spotlight fell on the Cold War medals table, which the Soviets topped. "The triumph of the Soviet athletes is a victory for the man of the new socialist society," crowed Khrushchev. Irritated American commentators urged the incoming Kennedy administration to take action. "The United States must take a new and hard look at its Olympic movement and efforts," declared the chairman of the US Olympic Development Program. "The Cold War and present international climate demand that we make the strongest possible showing to uphold the prestige of the United States." Here sports officials and politicians agreed. Both feared "the success, / Although particular, shall give a scantling / Of good or bad unto the general." It was simply assumed that the function of American athletes was to shoulder the burden of national representation on the global sporting stage. Not for the first time, the games ethic served to subordinate sports to nationalist propaganda. Curiously this did not seem to offend those officials and commentators who were later to object so volubly to Muhammad Ali "using sport to make propaganda" for the Nation of Islam.

Cassius Clay had been one of America's successes at the Rome Olympics. Asked by a Soviet reporter about the condition of blacks in the US, Clay fired back, "To me, the USA is still the best country in the world, counting yours." In those days he was proud of his Christian name: "Don't you think it's a beautiful name? Makes you think of the Colosseum and those Roman gladiators." On his return to Louisville he celebrated his Cold War triumph in his first published poem:

To make America the Greatest is my goal
So I beat the Russian and I beat the Pole
And for the USA won the Medal of Gold.

The good-looking eighteen year old turned professional and signed a sponsorship deal with a syndicate of white Louisville businessmen, who added the boxer to their interests in tobacco, bourbon, race-horses and baseball and football teams. Over the next three years, he fought and won nineteen bouts, culminating in his fifth-round knock-out of Henry Cooper in London (his first professional fight overseas). Keeping his hands low, moving backwards, he looked unorthodox but stylish. He made errors and was punished for them, but his opponents kept falling as he predicted and, amazingly, often in the round he predicted. In November 1963, after a barnstorming publicity campaign, he signed to fight Sonny Liston for the title.

Clay was already one of the most famous faces (and voices) in America. He had made the front pages of *Time* and *Life* and recorded an album of his verse. Hungry for publicity and always relishing an audience, he appeared at bowling alleys and coffee houses, nightclubs and television talk shows. He was well aware that progress in the boxing hierarchy—and with it a coveted world-title shot—depended on more than performance in the ring. Some boxers relied on connections, including mob connections; Cassius Clay relied on his mouth.

In the early sixties, boxing's popularity and prestige had taken a battering. Congressional hearings had given a high profile to its long-standing links with organized crime, and the image had been further sullied by the deaths of Davey Moore and Benny Paret from injuries inflicted in the ring. Television ratings had fallen, and network executives were losing interest in a pastime they regarded as depressingly down-market. In this context, the quick-talking, clean-cut Cassius Clay appeared as a godsend to the moguls of prizefighting.

Yet even before he became Muhammad Ali, Cassius Clay was beginning to change the way sports stars presented themselves. Hitherto, they were expected to be seen and not heard; modesty and deference had been the norm, for whites and especially for blacks. Of course, the swagger, the bragging, the manic competitive zeal had always been part of the subculture of big-time sports; but it was Cassius Clay who brought these qualities out of hiding and fashioned them into a saleable image. His egotism was bold and risky, but above all playful, and always softened by an undercurrent of self-mockery. The braggadocio which perplexed so many was a type of playground foolery orchestrated for the modern media circus. Ali later claimed to have copied his hyperbolic promotional style ("I'm the fastest thing on two feet") from a professional wrestler he encountered in a Las Vegas radio studio.

> They asked Gorgeous George about a wrestling match he was having in the same arena, and he started shouting, "I'll kill him; I'll tear his arm off. If this bum beats me, I'll crawl across the ring and cut off my hair, but it's not gonna happen because I'm the greatest wrestler in the world." And all the time, I was saying to myself, "Man, I want to see this fight. It don't matter if he wins or loses; I want to be there to see what happens." And the whole place was sold out when Gorgeous George

> wrestled. There was thousands of people including me. And that's when I decided I'd never been shy about talking, but if I talked even more, there was no telling how much money people would pay to see me.

It was typical of the young Clay to draw inspiration from that hardy survivor, professional wrestling, an ancient sport transformed into a post-modern entertainment. Clay relished, and learned from, its larger-than-life melodrama, its mix of comedy and violence, its inducements to spectator partisanship and vocal participation. Clay was a child of the popular audio-visual culture of the fifties. His monologues were studded with references to Hollywood movies, television and radio comedies, pop records, baseball as well as boxing and professional wrestling. In the early sixties, he seemed to share something of the apolitically irreverent spirit of *Mad* magazine. On TV his zany antics and mugging for the camera made him seem a cartoon-like figure, Bart Simpson in the flesh, immensely but somehow innocently pleased with his own mischief-making.

In the beginning, it was the dictates of the marketplace, and of boxing's peculiar place within it, that compelled Clay to dramatize his fights. He learned from the wrestlers how to rouse curiosity by making outlandish claims about himself and his opponents; and as he fought his way up the ladder, crisscrossing the country, he began to master the art of infusing a contest with significance for the casual spectator. As Muhammad Ali, he was to deploy these skills, this commercial instinct, to shape the meanings of his fights and to redefine the duties of the role model.

The voluble self-aggrandizing style was also an expression of the man's own gregarious spontaneity, which some have seen as over-compensation for a natural shyness. Even at the height of his fame, most people who enjoyed a one-to-one encounter with Ali found him subdued, thoughtful and focused. But in company he was never able to resist the urge to put on a show. He loved to act out and to play up, his mind and his mouth darting from topic to topic. And through boxing, above all through promoting boxing matches, he found an outlet for this quicksilver theatricality. In fact, at this time, among bona fide sports (as opposed to hybrid entertainments like wrestling and the Harlem Globetrotters) only boxing permitted this kind of vaudeville. Certainly it wouldn't have been tolerated by the baseball owners.

"I'm too beautiful to be a fighter," he boasted, casually breaking the taboo against exhibitions of male vanity. He was not only "the Greatest" but "the prettiest," a superlative usually associated with female attractiveness. For a black man to speak in this manner upturned so many assumptions—about both black and male physicality—that people just didn't know what to make of it. It was one of several exotic traits that made journalists wonder how seriously they were supposed to take this one-man circus. Yet the feminine side of this master pugilist was always an essential element of his popular chemistry. It fleshed out his humanity. It was an early and unthinking transgression, and it helped him undertake other, more jarring and perilous transgressions later on.

In fashioning his style, Cassius Clay drew heavily on black America's rich oral tradition, a tradition spanning North and South, pool hall and church. In the boasting, the doggerel, the predictions, it's easy to see traces of "the dozens," that playful competitive exercise in insult and hyperbole, verbal dexterity and metaphorical invention. Ali re-worked "the dozens," along with other features of black American oral culture, and projected them through the modern media to a new, mass audience. So it might be said that the young Cassius Clay was performing blackness for white spectators. In a curious comment in a 1963 profile of the young contender, Tom Wolfe claimed that "Cassius treats the fact of color—but not race—casually . . . he has a pronounced Negro accent of his own, which he makes no attempt to polish. He only turns it on heavier from time to time for comic effect." Clay faced his audience under the shadow of minstrelsy, the shadow that fell on so many innovative black entertainers, among them Louis Armstrong, Jack Johnson and even Paul Robeson. Yet often there were hidden messages in the minstrelsy, messages intelligible to black audiences, who thus shared a secret rapport with black entertainers, even as their "blackness" was commodified for white consumption. The young Clay was not afraid to make a fool of himself and quite reckless in courting the spotlight. No one in those days thought this crass comedian would become a worldwide symbol of black dignity. Indeed the very idea that he might do this without losing his sense of fun and his love of performing violated all the known stereotypes. A year before his title fight with Liston, he asked reporters:

> Where do you think I'd be next week, if I didn't know how to shout and holler and make the public take notice? I'd be poor and I'd probably be down in my home town, washing windows or running an elevator and saying "yes suh" and "no suh" and knowing my place. Instead, I'm one of the highest paid athletes

> in the world. Think about that. A southern coloured boy has made one million dollars.

In other words, the clowning, the minstrelsy, was a way of breaking out of the racist stranglehold. It was *Ebony*, in March 1963, which first reported the real significance of the emerging Clay story: "Cassius Marcellus Clay—and this fact has evaded the sports-writing fraternity—is a blast furnace of racial pride. His is a pride that would never mask itself with skin lighteners and processed hair, a pride scorched with memories of millions of little burns." But even *Ebony* could not have guessed that Cassius Clay, an ambitious, likeable young man beckoned by wealth and fame, had joined the Nation of Islam, the most vilified black organization in America.

• • •

Ali says he first heard about Elijah Muhammad during a Golden Gloves tournament in Chicago, the Nation's headquarters, in 1959, when he was seventeen. Two years later, while training in Miami, he ran into Captain Sam Saxon selling *Muhammad Speaks* on the street. Saxon, who ran a string of shoeshine concessions at Florida's racetracks, had converted to the Nation in 1955. As a boxing fan he recognized the young heavyweight and invited him to the nearby mosque. Clay was impressed by what he heard, and began reading *Muhammad Speaks* and listening to an LP called *A White Man's Heaven Is a Black Man's Hell*, recently released by the ex-calypso singer turned Muslim minister Louis X (later Louis Farrakhan). Saxon put Clay in touch with Jeremiah Shabazz, a prison convert who was now the Nation's Atlanta-based minister for the Deep South.

Initially, Elijah Muhammad took little interest in the new recruit, not least because the Nation of Islam disapproved of commercial spectator sports. Muhammad reprimanded Shabazz, reminding him he had been sent south "to make converts, not fool around with fighters." But Shabazz and Saxon persisted with Clay, and from late 1961 Saxon was traveling regularly with the young fighter. From 1962, Shabazz arranged for a Muslim cook to prepare all Clay's meals, in camp or on the road. As he moved around the country, building his career, he was able to take advantage of the Nation's far-flung network of restaurants and mosques. "He just sat there, wanting to learn," Saxon recalled. "He was a beautiful young man. All he wanted was what was right for our people."

Clay considered himself a member of the Nation from at least 1962, but he kept his link with the organization secret, and the Nation, for its part, was happy to guard that secret. A known Black Muslim had no chance of signing for a title fight. In the early sixties, Elijah Muhammad and Malcolm X were probably the two most hated men in America, feared and loathed by most whites and by nearly all the "respectable" members of their own community. In 1959, a television documentary, "The Hate that Hate Produced," had introduced white America to the Nation and its "reverse racism." The program-makers estimated the organization's membership at 250,000 (at least five times the real number) and used Elijah's lurid vision of America's impending Armageddon to stoke fears of a "race war." As a result of the television exposure, for several years the Nation became the focus for the media's salacious interest in "black racism." Civil rights leaders were asked to denounce the "hatemongers," and most complied. Thurgood Marshall told an NAACP conference that the Nation was "run by a bunch of thugs organized from prisons and jails and financed, I am sure, by Nasser or some Arab group." In reply, Muhammad dubbed Marshall "the Ugly American."

The organization that Clay joined in 1962 was at the time the largest, richest, most disciplined and longest-lived black nationalist formation in the country. Since its origins in Detroit in the early thirties, it had emerged as the principal custodian of the black nationalist tradition in America, but the form of black nationalism it promoted was idiosyncratic in the extreme. Elijah Muhammad assembled elements of the Qur'an, the Bible, Garveyism, the Moorish Science Temple of Noble Drew Ali, eugenics and popular science fiction, and attributed the exotic mix to the mysterious Wallace Fard, the incarnation of Allah who had anointed Elijah his Messenger. In many respects, the Nation was a typically American religious cult. With its homespun eschatology, emphasis on self-reliance and clean living, autocratic organization, pride in the fellowship of the elect and contentious engagement with the modern, secular world (and the nation-state), the Nation stands in a long line of hybrid millenarian American sects, including the Mormons and Jehovah's Witnesses.

What was distinctive about this characteristically American cultural product was that it demonized America. The descendants of African slaves were not "American negroes" but "*the Lost-Found Nation of Islam in the Wilderness of North America.*" The sect's imagery and rhetoric re-enforced the Manichean duality. On the one side were "Christianity, Slavery, Suffering, Death"—illustrated with the stars and stripes and the silhouette of a lynch victim hanging from a tree—and on the other, "Islam, Freedom, Justice, Equality"—

illustrated with the crescent. The Nation was a religious and social movement predicated on a political analysis, black nationalism, and a political program, separation. But its special appeal resided in its fusion of the personal and the political. Its promise of redemption linked the individual to the collective, self-discovery to nationhood. It was through the Nation of Islam that Cassius Clay first experienced that lived linkage, that social awakening of the self, and it was to transform him and his career inside and outside the ring. The Nation gave Cassius Clay more than a potted history and cosmology; it gave him a sense of his and his people's right to a place in the world.

In 1961 James Baldwin identified "the two most powerful movements in this country today" as the student integrationist movement whose goal was "nothing less than the liberation of an entire country from its crippling attitudes and habits," and "the Muslim movement" whose members "do not expect anything at all from the white people of this country." In this argument, Baldwin sided with the civil rights activists, though he conceded, "the Muslim movement has all the evidence on its side." Surveying the streets of Harlem, Baldwin concluded, "it is quite impossible to argue with a Muslim concerning the actual state of Negroes in this country—the truth, after all, is the truth. This is the great power a Muslim speaker has over his audience. His audience has not heard the truth of their daily lives honored by anyone else."

In joining the Nation of Islam, Clay was turning his back on the principal actors in the social drama of his day, the black youth whose challenge to Jim Crow was the first salvo in what was to become an international upsurge in youth protest, sprawling across the First, Second and Third Worlds. Clay made this rejection explicit when he told reporters after the Liston fight, "I know how to dodge boobytraps and dogs. I dodge them by staying in my own neighborhood. . . . I have never been to jail. I have never been in court. I don't join any integration marches. . . . I don't carry signs." Although he chose not to emulate them, Clay was only too aware of the efforts and sacrifices made by his contemporaries, and his choice was informed by that awareness. His negative reaction to their example did not deny their heroism but questioned, in Malcolm X's tart phraseology, their "intelligence."

As Baldwin observed, the activists risking life and limb in the freedom rides and sit-ins were trying to compel America to live up to its democratic credo. To the Nation of Islam, this strategy defied the logic of history. Malcolm told his audiences, "You're not an American, you're a victim of America." In keeping with its vision of white people as "devils" and America as an inferior civilization doomed to extinction, the Nation disapproved of all forms of political participation, not only voting, but also sit-ins, pickets and marches. Incompatible as these two strands of black thinking seemed, in practice they frequently intertwined. Paradoxically, the Nation benefited from the civil rights movement. The agitation in the South and the brutal white response seemed to confirm two of the Nation's central tenets: the beauty and strength of black people and the irredeemable racism of white America. Both the civil rights movement and the Nation of Islam were products of "the racial consciousness which has been so mercilessly injected into the negro" which, C.L.R. James noted in 1960, "is today a source of action and at the same time of discipline."

The particular form of racial solidarity preached by the Nation exercised an obvious appeal to the dispossessed and alienated. In the person of Malcolm X they saw a living example of the power of Elijah Muhammad, who had reached out to the thief and junkie in prison and redeemed him from the depths of self-hatred. But what accounts for the Nation's appeal to the law-abiding Cassius Clay, a talented young man with a bright future? The oft-told story of how, on returning from Rome, "with my gold medal round my neck I couldn't get a hamburger in my home town," can only be part of the answer. After all, there were other, highly publicized responses to racism available at the time.

Clay was far from an anomaly in the Nation. From the late fifties, Muhammad increasingly sought recruits among middle-class professionals. Garveyism had flourished in a time of despair and voicelessness. In contrast, the Nation's most dynamic period took place against a backdrop of comparative prosperity and apparent black progress. The genius of Elijah Muhammad was to play simultaneously on the hopes and the fears, the aspirations and the frustrations of a minority that was both insurgent and embattled. At the 1960 Savior's Day convention, the premier occasion in the Nation's annual calendar, the Messenger addressed a group of well-heeled blacks conspicuously seated directly in front of the rostrum. "Get behind me you professional people. Back me up. Why do you tremble when I ask you to join me? Join up with me and you won't have to open your mouth. I'll do all the talking and take all the chances."

It has to be remembered that by 1960 the Nation had become the largest black-owned business in America, with interests in a wide variety of commercial enterprises, including farming, publishing, banking and retail food and clothing outlets. For all his studied unworldliness, Muhammad himself was now a rich man (between 1955 and 1960, he purchased four new Cadillacs and a Lincoln). He disapproved of "the white man's greed," but subscribed to the capitalist system and frequently spoke of the benefits of black-owned enterprise. He lauded thrift and modesty, but also endorsed the pursuit of wealth and career advancement. "*You won't have to open your mouth. I'll do all the talking and take all the chances.*" To young, educated, ambitious blacks confronting the obstacles of racism at every turn, this was a tempting invitation. They were being offered a recipe for black dignity and personal success, and a means of reconciling the two. Though Clay came from a working-class background (his father was a sign-painter), he was very much one of the upwardly mobile new black elite to whom Muhammad was speaking. Ironically, in the end it was to be Muhammad Ali, and not Elijah Muhammad, who did most of the talking and certainly took all the chances.

The ritual and regimen of the Nation appealed to Clay for some of the same reasons he loved the discipline of training and the gym. Both demanded care and respect for the body and rewarded deferred gratification. More importantly, both offered a whole way of life, a shelter from the world outside and a means of prospering within it. Like many contemporary religious movements, the Nation of Islam was in part a protest against secular modernity. It offered personal purity, hierachical family values and race consciousness as a means of negotiating the rapids of social flux. Formally, it pitted the individual against the temptations of the modern world, while informally allowing him to come to an accommodation with it, even to exploit and master it. The Nation grew within and against the culture of the ghetto. It set itself up as a counter-attraction to all the temptations of ghetto life: drugs, gambling, prostitution, prizefighting. Yet for all Elijah Muhammad's contempt for "sporting life," his adherents knew the ropes. Long-standing Nation-member Booker Johnson worked for Archie Moore, and Wali Muhammad worked for Sugar Ray Robinson before becoming Ali's security man. Other members of the Nation worked in show business. Joining Elijah Muhammad's organization was a difficult choice for all these individuals, but it obviated other choices—between personal integrity and social participation, between acceptance of and opposition to racism—and that was no small part of its appeal.

Among the many paradoxes of the Nation's accommodation to the "America" it formally repudiated, none is as startling as its attempt to negotiate a pact with white supremacism. In a brief-lived common front of segregationists, George Lincoln Rockwell, the American Nazi leader, appeared at a Nation rally presided over by Elijah Muhammad himself. In January 1961, around the same time Clay first encountered Sam Saxon in Miami, Jeremiah Shabazz and Malcolm X were meeting secretly with the Ku Klux Klan in Atlanta. For several months, Shabazz attended Klan meetings as an official representative of Elijah Muhammad. For Shabazz, there was no contradiction between sitting with the Klan and the doctrine he was teaching Cassius Clay. In keeping with a persistent strand of conservative black nationalism, the Nation's aim was to survive, not transform America. In that context, a pact with the overtly racist Klan seemed less insidious than Martin Luther King's pact with the covertly racist liberal Democrats.

But creating a refuge from racism in the heart of a racist society proved a tortuous, contradictory business. It plunged the followers of Elijah Muhammad into conflict with the state and the stark reality of political engagement. Inexorably, Cassius Clay was drawn into that engagement, even as he sought to quickstep his way around it.

• • •

In 1961 the Nation of Islam was officially declared "un-American" by a committee of the California state legislature. In April 1962, an altercation on the streets led to an invasion of Mosque No. 27 by the Los Angeles Police Department. Ronald X Stokes, a twenty-eight-year-old Korea veteran and one of the first college-educated males to join the Nation, was shot through the heart from a distance of eight feet. He was unarmed and had raised his hands in the air. Six other Muslims were shot that day, and more beaten and arrested. Malcolm X flew in to take charge of the Nation's response. He conducted a vigorous investigation of the shootings and launched an uncompromising assault on the LAPD and Sam Yorty's city administration. In an unprecedented move for a Muslim, he sought out allies in southern California's Mexican and American Indian communities, and even among mainstream black churches and politicians. In May, an all-white coroner's jury declared the killing of Ronald Stokes "justifiable homicide." Malcolm wanted to press ahead with his campaign, but Elijah Muhammad was wary. He prohibited any retaliatory violence, or even any talk of armed self-defense, and sent a message to Los Angeles urging Malcolm "to cool his heels" and lay off the white politicians.

In June, an air crash in Europe took the lives of more than one hundred white citizens of Atlanta, Georgia. Malcolm seized on the tragedy as evidence of divine retribution for the Stokes murder. With an impish smile, he told a Los Angeles rally, "We hope that every day another plane falls from the sky." The remark precipitated the familiar avalanche of media hysteria and bolstered Malcolm's status as a national hate figure. Martin Luther King and other civil rights leaders rushed to assure America that their movement was built on goodwill and human brotherhood, but beyond the rhetorical battle between "love" and "hate" there lurked a more decisive strategic division. The message Malcolm had found himself compelled to preach in Los Angeles was one of trust in the will of Allah and patience here on earth. Nothing could be more at odds with the spirit of activism—of direct confrontation with the evil of white supremacy—that was fueling the civil rights movement, and Malcolm knew it.

For several years Malcolm had mocked the creed of non-violence and cast aspersions on the "manhood" of civil rights leaders who turned the other cheek while their flocks were clubbed and incarcerated. On his return to New York City, he confided to friends, "We spout our militant revolutionary rhetoric and we preach Armageddon . . . but when our own brothers are brutalized and killed, we do nothing. . . . We just sit tight on our hands."

During 1962, Cassius Clay, steadily building his reputation in the ring and his marketability outside it, fought three times in Los Angeles. He had knocked out George Logan in the fourth round only three days before the Stokes killing. He returned to Los Angeles in July, when he knocked out Alejandro Lavorante in the fifth. In November, he met the legendary Archie Moore, who was then in his late forties. It was Clay's first high-profile professional bout and his first big payday. By knocking out Moore in the fourth round, he established himself as a contender and set off on his madcap campaign for a title shot.

Clay had broken off training for the Moore fight to drive from Miami to Detroit to hear Elijah Muhammad speak in person for the first time. There he met Malcolm X, whose brother was a minister at the local mosque. It was the beginning of a sporadic but intense eighteen-month association which was to end abruptly with Malcolm's departure from the Nation in March 1964. Malcolm had never heard of the young boxer, but gave him his attention and treated him with respect. "Malcolm was very intelligent, with a good sense of humor, a wise man," Ali told Thomas Hauser three decades later. "When he talked, he held me spellbound for hours." In his autobiography, Malcolm recalled:

> I liked him. Some contagious quality about him made him one of the few people I ever invited to my home. Betty liked him. Our children were crazy about him. Cassius was simply a likeable, friendly, clean-cut, down-to-earth youngster. I noticed how alert he was even in little details. I suspected there was a plan in his public clowning.

Both Clay and Malcolm were performing bugbears for the white press. What outrageous thing would they say or do next? In Clay's case, it turned out to be nothing less than associating with Malcolm himself.

As he stripped back the layers of white hypocrisy and pried open his listeners' consciousness, Malcolm seemed to confront racism as no other black man had, and in an idiom intelligible to all. It's not hard to imagine the attraction of Malcolm's personality to the young Clay. He mixed deadly gravity with wry humor, didactic catechisms with folksy analogies. Indeed, in fusing the oral call-and-response traditions of the black church, the hard-headed realism of the streets and the rigors of the press conference and the television and radio studios, Malcolm forged a rhetoric Clay was to adopt and revise. Like others, Clay was also seduced by Malcolm's gentle, indulgent, intimate side; this hard, righteous teacher loved to tease and be teased. What made both Malcolm and Clay, future icons of black masculinity and patriarchy, so appealing was their humility and humor, their sense of play, indeed their "feminine" qualities. It was this side of both men that befuddled interviewers over the years and left observers muttering "enigma."

The crossing of Malcolm's and Ali's paths is the stuff of legend—though it is left out of both Spike Lee's *Malcolm X* and *When We Were Kings*. The problem is that the legend becomes merely an accoutrement of the icons; the living interplay of complex personalities in a rapidly changing environment is glossed over. Although many questions about Ali's relationship with Malcolm remain unanswered, what is undeniable is that these months witnessed both Malcolm's own transformation—a period of agony and uncertainty for him—and the gathering together within and around Cassius Clay of the threads he would later weave into the resplendent figure of Muhammad Ali.

Malcolm arranged for one of his followers, Osman Karriem, to act as Clay's road manager. He had done the same job for the Platters and, like other Muslims, understood the pressures of black life in the commercial fast-lane. Karriem disliked boxing and was initially skeptical about Clay, but agreed to keep an eye on him for Malcolm, and in particular to safeguard the young fighter from the predatory attentions of white businessmen. Karriem was well aware of the tensions within the Nation, as were many of the other Muslims Clay met as he traveled round the country.

By March 1963, the internal discord had grown so acute that the FBI's Chicago office advised J. Edgar Hoover to cease "disruption tactics" and leave the Nation to its own devices. Malcolm had become aware that Muhammad had conducted sexual affairs with young female members of the Nation in his employ and fathered several illegitimate children. This awareness distressed Malcolm and threatened Muhammad. But just as important in the making of the great schism was Malcolm's response to dramatic developments during a crucial phase of the civil rights movement.

• • •

"In three difficult years, the southern struggle had grown from a modest group of black students demonstrating peacefully at one lunch-counter to the largest mass movement for racial reform and civil rights in the twentieth century," wrote Manning Marable. "Between autumn 1961 and the spring of 1963, 20,000 men, women and children had been arrested. In 1963 alone another 15,000 were imprisoned; 1000 desegregation protests occurred across the region, in more than 100 cities." The epicenter of this social earthquake was Birmingham, Alabama. On 3 April 1963, the Southern Christian Leadership Council (SCLC) launched its assault on this citadel of segregation with sit-ins in restaurants and department stores.

Marches and vigils were broken up by police, and the jail cells began to fill. On Good Friday, Martin Luther King was arrested. In response to criticism from "moderate" local clergymen, King composed his "Letter from a Birmingham Jail," a classic formulation of the urgent righteousness of the sixties, issued from the belly of the beast:

> The Negro's greatest stumbling block in the stride toward freedom is . . . the white moderate who is more devoted to "order" than to justice . . . who paternalistically feels he can set the timetable for another man's freedom. . . . There comes a time when the cup of endurance runs over, and men are no longer willing to be plunged into the abyss of despair.

On 2 May, six thousand young blacks—aged from six to sixteen years—marched through the city. In front of national television, police dogs were set on children as they knelt to pray, and marchers were dispersed with firehoses and clubs. Nine hundred and fifty-nine children were jailed. The nationwide cry of protest, and not least America's global embarrassment, forced the hitherto inert Kennedy administration to act. On 10 May, under pressure from the federal government, Birmingham's white business and municipal leaders acceded to desegregation; black prisoners were released.

The bravery of the black youth of Birmingham posed a stern challenge to black celebrities, the symbolic representatives of their people. Shortly after the peace agreement, Floyd Patterson joined King to address a meeting at Birmingham's Sixth Avenue Baptist Church. Patterson had broken off his training for the second Liston fight to attend the meeting. "I felt very guilty . . . that here I was sitting in my camp watching you people, my people, go through this. . . . And I would like to thank you from the bottom of my heart." Jackie Robinson also spoke at the meeting: "I don't think you realize down here in Birmingham what you mean to us up there in New York." So while the two future icons of black militancy, Malcolm X and Cassius Clay, sat on the sidelines, those two "Uncle Toms," Robinson and Patterson, took themselves to the front.

The Birmingham agreement was one of the major victories of the civil rights movement, but in its wake racist violence and resistance to desegregation intensified. On 11 June, Medgar Evers, a local NAACP official, was assassinated on his doorstep in Jackson, Mississippi. The next day Kennedy announced his plan to introduce a civil rights bill; his hand had been forced by the insistence of the black upsurge in the South and the intransigence of white southern reaction to it. Reluctant as he was to jeopardize the southern white Democratic block, he was also driven by the demands of Cold War propaganda and competition with the Soviets in the newly independent African and Asian nations.

The March on Washington, on 28 August 1963, when 250,000 gathered in front of the Lincoln Memorial in Washington to hear an array of black leaders and white allies call for speedy passage of the president's civil rights bill, is usually considered the apogee of the movement. "We came here because we love our country," the SCLC's Fred Shuttleworth told the crowd, "because our country needs us and we need our country." But the more militant youth of the Student Non-Violent Co-ordinating Committee (SNCC)* took time

* For readers with no personal recollection of the sixties, it may be necessary to

off from the march to meet with Malcolm X, who poured scorn on what he called the "farce on Washington."

Two weeks later, Birmingham's white supremacists exacted revenge. On the morning of 15 September, dynamite ripped apart the Sixteenth Street Baptist Church, killing four black girls attending Sunday school. In the days that followed, hundreds of black youths battled with local police. Black communities across the country wept and raged, as did black artists like Langston Hughes:

It's not enough to mourn
And not enough to pray.
Sackcloth and ashes, anyhow,
Save for another day.

The Lord God himself
Would hardly desire
That men be burned to death—
And bless the fire.

Looking back at the Birmingham crusade from a distance of thirty years, Taylor Branch commented, "Never before was a country transformed, arguably redeemed, by the active moral witness of schoolchildren." This moral witness—in which the self was defined, even redeemed, through selfless political action—was the decade's

explain that this organization was commonly referred to simply by its acronym—SNCC—which was pronounced "snick."

most resonant exemplar. Later, in his stand against the Vietnam War, Muhammad Ali was to deploy this sixties motif in spheres of popular culture that had never before felt its power. But in 1963, he turned away from the challenge of direct confrontation with white racism. As he explained to the press eight months later in Miami, "I ain't no Christian. I can't be when I see all the colored people fighting for forced integration get blowed up. They get hit by stones and chewed by dogs and they blow up a Negro church and don't find the killers."

The cascade of events in 1963 was inspiring, bewildering, frustrating. "Every movement forward had been purchased at great cost. Bleeding ulcers, nervous breakdowns, mysterious ailments took their toll on young lives," wrote Vincent Harding, who knew the travails of the activists at first hand. "Every time they smashed away some obstacle to black freedom and equality, another larger, newly perceived hindrance loomed before them, challenging the last ounce of their strength and their spirit." The intermingling of victory and defeat, empowerment and disempowerment, the wild rhythm of advance and rebuff (the stuff of which the sixties were made) generated a new radicalism and broader sympathy for militant nationalism. Yet during this period the man most widely associated with that militancy, Malcolm X, sat silent at the command of Elijah Muhammad, a silence he bitterly regretted in his autobiography:

> When a high-powered rifle slug tore through the back of NAACP Field Secretary Medgar Evers in Mississippi, I wanted to say the blunt truths that needed to be said. When a bomb was exploded in a Negro Christian church in Birmingham,

> Alabama, snuffing out the lives of those four beautiful black girls, I made comments—but not what should have been said about the climate of hate the American white man was generating and nourishing.

Despite Elijah Muhammad's prohibition, Malcolm continued to flirt with civil rights activism, while retaining his skepticism about non-violence and his opposition to integration. Muhammad made Malcolm apologize for organizing a demonstration in Newark, New Jersey, but he went ahead with other discreet actions, visiting a picket line at a Brooklyn construction site that wouldn't hire blacks and making contacts with left-wing groups—a move which alarmed the FBI and Elijah Muhammad alike. Privately, Malcolm told Louis Lomax, "The Messenger has seen God. . . . He's willing to wait for Allah to deal with this devil. Well, sir, the rest of the black Muslims have not seen God. We don't have this gift of divine patience with the devil. The younger black Muslims want to see some action."

• • •

In September 1963, the *Philadelphia Daily News* reported that Cassius Clay had attended a Nation of Islam rally in the city. Clay told reporters he was not a Muslim, and the media seemed happy to write off the incident as another one of Cassius's bizarre stunts. On 5 November, the deal for the Liston fight was signed. For Malcolm, this was an obvious opportunity for the Nation, but Elijah urged Malcolm to keep his distance from the new challenger. He believed Clay would lose to Liston and that the Nation would be diminished by its association with him, a belief which betrayed his own creeping cynicism and lack of imagination. Unlike the rest of the black press, *Muhammad Speaks* failed to report the build-up to the fight and sent no reporters to cover it.

Malcolm did not keep his distance from Clay, nor did he respect a weightier injunction which issued from Chicago in the hours following the Kennedy assassination on 22 November. Elijah had decided that there was no milage to be had in bucking the tide of national grief. Accordingly, he ordered his ministers to refrain from any critical comments about the president whom they had routinely denounced as a "devil" for three years. In New York City on 1 December, in answer to questions from the press, Malcolm reminded Americans that the Kennedy administration had practiced political violence in Africa and Asia, and had sanctioned the assassinations of Lumumba in the Congo and Diem in Vietnam. The killing of JFK was, he said, a case of "chickens coming home to roost. . . . Being an old farm boy myself, chickens coming home to roost never did make me sad. They've always made me glad."

Press and politicians reacted to Malcolm's shock tactics with outrage. More significantly, so did Elijah Muhammad, who summoned Malcolm to Chicago to tell him, without a trace of irony, that "the president of the country is our president too." Malcolm's statement, Elijah said, was a major blunder for which his fellow Muslims would pay dearly. It was imperative that the Nation distance itself from his ill-judged comments, and therefore he would be suspended for ninety days, during which time he was not to make any public statements. *Muhammad Speaks* eulogized the slain president and gave prominence to the Messenger's decision to discipline his most famous apostle.

Elijah's response to the JFK assassination reflected both short- and long-term considerations. Bitter experience had taught him to fear the power of the federal government and the ire of the media. In particular, he wished to avoid another House Un-American Activities Committee investigation, not least because of the scrutiny his business empire would come under. His fear of repression was matched by his fear of schism. In the coming weeks, Elijah would come to see Malcolm X as the biggest threat to his carefully husbanded authority, his status in the movement and his personal wealth. He proceeded step by step to isolate Malcolm, undercutting his base in the organization, testing the loyalties of the membership.

The first death threat reached Malcolm's ears in late December. In his autobiography, he says that learning of Elijah Muhammad's order to eliminate him "was how, finally, I began to arrive at my psychological divorce from the Nation of Islam." In the first week of January 1964, Muhammad replaced Malcolm as minister at the Harlem mosque, and at their last private meeting he accused his disciple of plotting against him. Meanwhile, Muslim ministers whom Malcolm had trained were denouncing the Messenger's former favorite in mosques across the country.

On 15 January, under increasing pressure from both the Nation of Islam and the FBI, who dogged his every step, Malcolm phoned Clay in Miami, where he was training for the Liston fight, and told him he wanted to take up his offer to visit the challenger's camp with his family. According to the FBI report of the monitored phone call, Clay said, "That's the best news I've heard all day!" and offered to pick up Malcolm and his family at the airport. The next day Clay, Osman Karriem and Clarence X Gill, a Muslim bodyguard, met

Malcolm's party and, with an FBI tail in tow, drove them to the black hotel where the challenger's entourage was staying.

Clay told reporters he had given Malcolm and his wife Betty the round-trip all-expenses-paid vacation as a present for their sixth wedding anniversary. Later, Malcolm's daughters were to recall the Miami escapade as a rare interlude of family togetherness in the hectic and highly public life of their father. The day after their arrival, they helped Cassius celebrate his twenty-second birthday. Two days later Betty and the children flew back to New York, but Malcolm remained. Clay must have been aware that Malcolm was under suspension, that he had been barred from talking to the press and that the Messenger would frown on any association with him. Yet he kept Malcolm in his camp and made no secret of it.

On 21 January, Clay interrupted his training routine to fly to New York with Malcolm. There he addressed a rally at Rockland Palace, where Robeson had once breathed defiance to the white world. (Only a month before, Robeson had returned to the United States after six years abroad, ill and depressed, and promptly retreated into seclusion.) Malcolm helped Clay prepare his speech, but because he was under suspension, he was not allowed to attend the rally. Clay delivered a twenty-minute address to the 1600 Muslims packed into the hall. He asked for their support in his fight against Liston and read them some poetry. "I'm training on lamb chops and that big ugly bear is training on pork chops," he declared to loud applause. He also mentioned Malcolm X, perhaps the last time anyone was to say anything pleasant about the one-time national minister from an official Nation of Islam platform. Clay insisted he was "proud to walk the streets of Miami with Malcolm X." He noted, as he often did in the coming years, that Muslims refrained from smoking and drinking. "This is a miracle for the so-called Negroes, and this is why the white man is all shook up." An FBI informant was in the hall, noted Clay's presence and rushed outside to tip off the local media. Clay's apparent link to the Nation of Islam, a story which had been gestating for several months, was now out in the open and made front-page news the next day. In a revealing formulation, Clay was repeatedly asked by the press whether he was "a card-carrying member of the Black Muslims." "Card-carrying; what's does that mean?" he answered. "I'm a race man and every time I go to a Muslim meeting I get inspired." In a banner headline, the *Amsterdam News* reported the story, "Cassius Clay Almost Says He's a Muslim." The front pages of the black press were splashed with photos of the young fighter playing with Malcolm X's family. Elijah Muhammad must have been beside himself. The press hardly noticed when Clay took his military qualifying examination on 24 January. His results were so poor—he placed in the sixteenth percentile, way below the qualifying standard—that they roused suspicion, and Clay was asked to re-take the test after the Liston fight.

George Plimpton, who was to spend more than a decade covering Ali's career, was perplexed by Clay's connection with the Muslims and sought out Malcolm for an interview. Despite Elijah's proscription, Malcolm met Plimpton at the Hampton House Hotel in the heart of black Miami. A deep discomfort runs through the published version of the encounter, which appeared in *Harper's* in June 1964. "He often smiles broadly," Plimpton noted, "but not with humor." Behind the articulate exterior, Plimpton descried a "truly intractable" character. But, as the writer faithfully records, this "intractable," "caustic" man was also the first to detect the seriousness underlying Cassius Clay's antics, and to see in the loudmouth underdog the lineaments of the future Muhammad Ali. "Not many people know the quality of the mind he's got in there," Malcolm explained. "He fools them. One forgets that though a clown never imitates a wise man, the wise man can imitate the clown. He is sensitive, very humble, yet shrewd—with as much untapped mental energy as he has physical power." Noting that "our religion removes fear," he predicted Clay would topple Liston, then added, "We believe in exercise, physical fitness, but as for commercial sport, that's a racket. Commercial sport is the pleasure of the idle rich. The vice of gambling stems from it. . . . The Negro never comes out ahead—never one in the history of sport."

Malcolm liked to speak of himself as Clay's "older brother," a political mentor and spiritual guide. According to Malcolm's wife, Betty Shabazz, he spent hours talking with Cassius about the meaning of the title fight and the fighter's destiny in his people's future. As always, Malcolm's aim was to clear his disciple's mind of the disabling preconceptions bred by a racist society, to inculcate self-confidence through a deep, guiding sense of purpose. Like Frantz Fanon and C.L.R. James, Malcolm had studied the psychology of the oppressed, and much of his teaching was aimed at overcoming the psychological advantages that the rich and powerful always enjoy over the poor and weak. He believed that freedom demanded nothing less than a radical recreation of the self. What he was doing with Clay was what he had been doing in the Nation and what he was to continue to do in the last year of his life: preparing the actors of history for their role in it.

But for Malcolm himself, these days in Miami passed in a haze of anxiety and growing despair. "Whatever I was saying at any time was being handled by a small corner of my mind. The rest of my mind was filled with a parade of a thousand and one different scenes from the past," he reported to Alex Haley. "I told the various sportswriters repeatedly what I gradually had come to know within myself was a lie—that I would be reinstated within ninety days." Despite Malcolm's claims of reticence, it seems unlikely that he never discussed his worries with his host, the man with whom he was sharing the media spotlight. The depiction of Clay in these months as an innocent, unaware or unaffected by the struggle between Malcolm and Muhammad, is not credible. He was providing shelter and publicity to, and spending hours in private conversation with, a Muslim known to be at odds with the Messenger.

In early February Clay told the *Louisville Courier-Journal*, "I like the Muslims. I'm not going to get killed trying to force myself on people who don't want me. I like my life. Integration is wrong. The white people don't want integration. I don't believe in forcing it, and the Muslims don't believe in it. So what's wrong with the Muslims?" According to the paper, Clay's father, Cassius Sr., said both his sons had joined the organization, and accused the Nation of "ruining" his boys. As rumors circulated, panic gripped the fight promoters. Ticket sales had been slow, and it was feared that the challenger's association with the Muslims could generate a backlash against the fight. Clay was quick to spot the potential for a role reversal and told Liston: "I make you great. The fans love you because I'm the villain." Clay may have been amused, but his publicist, Harold Conrad, despaired: "The whole sales pitch for the fight had been Clay against

Liston, white hat against black hat, and now it looked like there'd be two black hats fighting."

It was a measure of Malcolm's symbolic power in the mind of white America that his mere presence by the side of the challenger could transform the values hitherto attached to the contest, and threaten its future. For Cassius Clay, this was a moment of truth, the first of many which he was to face in the coming years. It was made clear to him by friends, managers, promoters and journalists that it would be in his interest to renounce the Muslims. They told him he would be crazy to let this association jeopardize the chance of a lifetime, a chance he himself had worked so hard to secure. Quietly but firmly, the young fighter stood his ground. A compromise was agreed: there would be no statement, but Malcolm X would leave the camp, at least for the time being.

Meanwhile, the FBI was circulating details of the rift between Malcolm and Muhammad, reports of which began to appear in the mainstream press. Malcolm returned to Miami on 23 February, and was once again met by Clay at the airport, accompanied by Osman Karriem and Clarence X Gill. According to the FBI, Clay asked, "Any word from Chicago?" and Malcolm replied, "Nothing positive." Later, when the two men were approached by a *Miami Herald* reporter, Malcolm would make only one comment, "If you think Cassius Clay was loud, wait until I start talking on the first of March."

On the morning of the fight, 25 February, Malcolm phoned Elijah Muhammad. Muhammad accused Malcolm of attempting to blackmail him; Malcolm denied the charge. That night, in the dressing room before the fight, Malcolm prayed with Cassius and his brother Rudolph (later Rahaman Ali). Unlike almost everyone else, including

Elijah Muhammad, Malcolm X had always believed that Clay could win the fight. "It was Allah's intent for me to help Cassius prove Islam's superiority before the world—through proving that mind can win over brawn." He fortified Clay to face Liston by retelling the tale of David and Goliath. For Malcolm, Liston's whole life and career were proof that the struggle for integration was futile and debilitating. Clay, he felt, could represent something different. "Clay . . . is the finest Negro athlete I have ever known, the man who will mean more to his people than Jackie Robinson, because Robinson is the white man's hero." Malcolm saw Clay's symbolic power more clearly than anyone else at the time, and he helped Clay to realize that power in the ring:

> "This fight is the truth," I told Cassius. "It's the Cross and the Crescent fighting in a prize ring—for the first time. It's a modern crusades—a Christian and a Muslim facing each other with television to beam it off Telstar for the whole world to see what happens!" I told Cassius, "Do you think Allah has brought about all this, intending for you to leave the ring as anything but the champion?"

Malcolm sat prominently at the ringside, where he chatted to Clay's other star guest, Sam Cooke. Live attendance was disappointing but over one million people watched the fight on closed-circuit TV. A somewhat mystified *New York Times* reporter described the atmosphere at the screening in Harlem: "The general support for Clay seemed to transcend any betting considerations and even the normal empathy for an underdog."

In Miami, Clay danced his way around a lumbering Liston, his speed, footwork and amazing 360-degree ring-vision nullifying the champion's advantages in power and reach. When a bewildered and dejected Liston failed to come out for the seventh round, Clay was jubilant. "I want everyone to bear witness," he shouted. "I am the greatest! I shook up the world!" Many sportswriters, however, regarded the upset victory as a fluke. Malcolm was more perceptive: "The secret of one of fight history's greatest upsets was that, months before that night, Clay had out-thought Liston." Because of his rejection of the prevailing stereotypes of black sportsmen, Malcolm was able to see in Clay what the sportswriters refused to see: a supremely intelligent and inventive boxer inspired by more than just a lust for money. That night Clay received a telegram from Martin Luther King, the only black leader, besides Malcolm, to congratulate him on his victory.

Back in the Hampton House Hotel, in the euphoric hours after the fight, Malcolm phoned Alex Haley to share the good news. Haley recalled Malcolm's childlike delight that the new heavyweight champion was sitting next door. Perhaps at this juncture he entertained a flickering belief that this spectacular turn of events would sway the balance in his struggle with Elijah Muhammad. But even as Malcolm exulted on the telephone, Clay was telling Jim Brown that he would have to break with Malcolm and follow Elijah. Judging by his behavior in the next few days, however, Clay's mind was not entirely made up, and he may have hoped for some reconciliation between the two leaders.

On the day after Clay's public embrace of the Nation of Islam, both the FBI and the Department of Defense began inquiries into the new champion's Selective Service status. At a press conference, the Louisville draft board chairman said he expected Clay to be called up "within weeks." No one paid much attention because of the furore surrounding Clay's conversion to the Nation, which at that time seemed more likely to scupper his boxing career than the US military.

For the first time in a decade, Malcolm X was absent from the annual Savior's Day rally, held that evening in Chicago. In Malcolm's place, warming up the crowd for the Messenger, was Louis X of Boston. In front of an ecstatic crowd of five thousand, Muhammad confirmed to the world that Cassius Clay was his follower and claimed credit, with Allah, for his great victory. "I'm so glad that Cassius Clay was brave enough to say that he was a Muslim. . . . He was able, by confessing that Allah was his god and by following Muhammad, to whip a much tougher man. They wanted him to get his face torn up, but Allah and myself said 'No!' . . . Clay has confidence in Allah, and in me as his only messenger." Through his brother Rudolph, who had flown up from Miami, Clay sent a message to the faithful, thanking them for their prayers.

• • •

> Any upheaval in the universe is terrifying because it so profoundly attacks one's sense of one's own reality. Well, the black man has functioned in the white man's world as a fixed star, as an immovable pillar: and as he moves out of his place, heaven and earth are shaken to their foundations.
>
> *James Baldwin*

In his comments to the press in the days that followed the shock triumph over Liston, Clay groped towards a new self-definition, while making vain efforts to reassure the white press. "I'm no troublemaker. . . . I'm a good boy. I never have done anything wrong. I have never been in jail. I have never been in court. I don't join any integration marches. I don't pay any attention to all those white women who wink at me. I don't carry signs." In another context, these words would have been taken for the most slavish Uncle Tomism. But notice how Clay argued his case. In telling the press that he had never been in jail or court, he was saying, "I'm no Sonny Liston." In forswearing white women, he was saying, "I'm no Jack Johnson." In denouncing integration, he was saying, "I'm no Floyd Patterson." And most crucially, in saying he did not want to "carry a sign," he was repudiating the duties of representation. He seemed to be arguing that for all these reasons white people should not be threatened by him. But for all these reasons, many white people could not but regard him as a menace to their most precious assumptions. In this context, "*I don't have to be what you want me to be*" became nothing less than an outrageous provocation.

Clay undermined his own attempt to paint his conversion as purely religious and personal by his constant references to American racism, to dogs and firehoses and the four girls murdered in a Birmingham church. Perusing Clay's statements of the time, it is clear he saw the Nation of Islam as a means of black survival in a hostile racist world. "I don't believe Muhammad's conversion was a religious experience," said the born-again Christian George Foreman, years later. "I'll believe until the day I die that it was a social awakening. . . . It was something he needed at the time, something the whole country needed."

• • •

Malcolm flew back to New York City, where he told Captain Joseph, his former subordinate at the Harlem mosque, "The Nation is finished." Because of his fear of flying, Clay drove up from Miami and experienced the familiar roadside segregation as he passed through the South. On his arrival in New York he went straight to the Hotel Theresa in Harlem to meet with Malcolm. The two men then toured Times Square, where they were mobbed. "Malcolm X got more requests for autographs than I did," the new heavyweight champion told the press. "He's the greatest."

That was the evening of 29 February, four days after Clay's triumph over Liston. Malcolm's ninety-day suspension was to expire the next morning, but he received no word from Chicago. The next day, he and Clay toured the offices of the *Amsterdam News*. "Elijah Muhammad is the sweetest man in the world," Clay told the admiring staff. "Malcolm X? I fell in love with him on television discussing Islam with those educators—leaving them with their mouths right open. I will not be identified as an Uncle Tom. I will be known as Cassius X. The whole world recognizes me now that they know my religion is Islam. The religion is the truth and I am ready to die for the truth." He announced that he would be hiring a black lawyer to represent him in his future dealings with the Louisville syndicate.

On 4 March, he accompanied Malcolm on a two-hour tour of the United Nations. "I'm champion of the *whole* world," Clay explained, drawing out the adjective to emphasize his enlarging vision of his domain. "And I want to meet the people I am champion of." Malcolm introduced him to delegates from Mali, Liberia, Gambia, Congo—contacts he had been cultivating for several years. Indeed, Malcolm had become such a familiar figure at the UN that guards had standing instructions to admit him at will. The visit of this remarkable pair of African-Americans was reported to have set off the greatest tumult among UN delegates and officials since Khrushchev pounded his shoe on the table in 1960. Malcolm seized the opportunity to brief foreign journalists on the dire state of American race relations. Clay announced that he planned to tour Africa and Asia, and that "my companion on my world tour will be Minister Malcolm X."

Communication with UN and foreign diplomats was supposed to be conducted through official channels. Yet here were two black men taking themselves off to confer with the representatives of foreign powers without so much as a by-your-leave to the US government. Certainly no US sports star had ever contemplated such autonomous action. Like Robeson, Malcolm X and Cassius Clay met on an equal footing with foreign diplomats, as representatives not of "America" but of a people trapped within America. Their UN visit attracted the attention of both the CIA and the FBI, who began preparations to monitor the forthcoming foreign trip.

In the midst of personal and political crisis, Malcolm made spending time with Clay his priority. History was to prove that in doing so, he was at his most far-sighted. When he escorted the new heavyweight champion to the UN, Malcolm planted the seed of a great regeneration of popular pan-Africanism. Meanwhile, Elijah fumed at Malcolm's palpable defiance. He sent Louis X to replace Malcolm as

Minister at Mosque No. 7. The day after the UN visit, on 5 March, Malcolm received a letter from Muhammad informing him that his suspension would be "indefinite" because he had not "shown sufficient desire" to be "rehabilitated." That afternoon the government announced that Clay's Selective Service re-examination would be "expedited." Pressed by reporters about his poor performance in his first attempt, Clay insisted, "I tried my hardest to pass." Though it went largely unnoticed at the time, Clay was also asked if he would request exemption as a conscientious objector. "I don't like that name. It sounds ugly—like I wouldn't want to be called," he said, then added, "I'd need two hours on the radio—with a national hook-up—to explain my position."

Early the next morning, Malcolm and Clay met at the Theresa. Malcolm told Clay how he had evaded the draft in World War II, and insisted that it was possible for a clever man to beat the system. Together they returned to the UN at lunchtime. Here they met with the Nigerian delegate, who urged Clay to use the championship "in the name of world brotherhood." Outside the UN, Clay signed autographs. "My name is Cassius X Clay," he told a *New York Times* reporter. "X is what the slavemasters used to be called." Malcolm nudged Clay, who seemed to have realized he'd made a blunder, and fended off further questions.

After dropping off Clay at the Theresa, Malcolm returned home, where he was phoned by Leon 4X Ameer, who had been assigned to act as Clay's press secretary. Ameer had learned from Captain Joseph that Malcolm "had to be taken down." Clarence X Gill, Clay's bodyguard, had indicated there would be a reward for anyone who eliminated Malcolm. That night, in his regular radio broadcast, Elijah

Muhammad announced that he was renaming Cassius Clay. "Muhammad Ali is what I will give to him, as long as he believes in Allah and follows me." Listening to the speech on the radio in his car, Malcolm immediately saw the renaming as "a political move." That evening he told friends, "He did it to prevent him coming with me." Malcolm tried to phone Clay at the Theresa, but from this night on—only hours after their second tour of the UN—all communications between the two men were blocked by Nation loyalists who had quickly moved into place around the new champion.

The awarding of an "original name" was a rare honor in the Nation of Islam, one not bestowed even on Malcolm X. The latter's immediate assumption that it was a gesture to secure the loyalty of the new heavyweight champion was probably correct. Only days before, the FBI had tapped a conversation between Clay and Elijah Muhammad in which the ageing Messenger tried to convince a reluctant Clay to accept this special honor. Clay said he knew that many members waited ten years or more before being awarded an original name and he preferred the more modest Cassius X Clay. Muhammad persisted, arguing that an Arabic name would be more suitable for an international representative of the faith, a role which Clay would have to assume by virtue of his new title.

For the stunned white press the name change was yet another sinister transgression. As Ali himself was quick to point out, name changes were commonplace in American sports and entertainment: Joe Louis and Sugar Ray Robinson had done it; so had Edward G. Robinson and John Garfield. Professional wrestlers routinely adopted *noms de guerre*. But this was different. This was a black man signaling by his name change not a desire to ingratiate himself with mainstream

America, but a comprehensive rejection of it. By adopting the name Muhammad Ali at the command of Elijah Muhammad, Cassius Clay claimed a new heritage, a new nation, a new family. And in doing so, he exposed the American order as something other than a fact of nature. Ali may have accepted his new name reluctantly, but he was to prove tenacious in its defense. A week after the re-naming, he walked out of Madison Square Garden when the announcer insisted on introducing the new heavyweight champion, a ringside guest, as "Cassisus Clay." He had already seized on "Muhammad Ali" as a badge of pride and in battling to assert that pride, inside and outside the ring, he paved the way for millions. Today, it is commonplace for African-Americans to adopt Islamic or African names, and easy to forget what a bold step it was in 1964. Certainly it's not to be compared to the facile exercise in re-branding attempted by Mike Tyson during his time in prison. Johnson and Louis, Patterson and Liston had been endowed with their public identities by the white press; in assuming the name Muhammad Ali, the champion declared his intention to create his own, highly individual yet charged with social resonance.

He faced entrenched resistance. The *New York Times* insisted on calling him Cassius Clay throughout the 1960s. Ali could only have overcome such resistance with the wind of a great movement at his back. He tried to make a virtue of the Muslims' abstention from the civil rights movement, but, in the end, he would fight all the battles he sought to avoid, and on a grand scale. He would "carry a sign" by becoming a sign—a living symbol of African-American and ultimately global insurgency.

• • •

On 8 March, at a press conference in the Hotel Theresa (booked by Leon Ameer, who was still working for Ali), Malcolm announced his departure from the Nation of Islam and linked it to his quest for a new freedom of political action. "Internal differences within the Nation of Islam forced me out of it," he declared. "I did not leave of my own free will." He restated his commitment to black nationalism as a political, economic and cultural philosophy, but added that he would aim "to co-operate in local civil rights actions in the South and elsewhere . . . because every campaign for specific objectives can only heighten the political consciousness of Negroes and intensify their identification against white society." He pledged to "fight wherever Negroes ask for my help." He also noted—since he now found himself without an income of any kind—that he would once again make himself available to speak at colleges. "I find most white students are more attuned to the times than their parents and realize that something is fundamentally wrong in this country."

In Chicago, Elijah Muhammad wept before the white press. The *New York Times* reported Malcolm's resignation on its front page, alongside the opening of the Senate debate on the civil rights bill. Malcolm was called by an aide to Herbert Muhammad, who informed him that Herbert was now Ali's manager, and that Ali would not be traveling to Africa with him. Malcolm called Ali at his hotel eight times on 9 March, but was told each time that the champ wasn't there. On 10 March, Malcolm received a demand from the Nation of Islam for the return of the house he lived in with his wife and children. Two days later he held another press conference—to "clarify my position in the struggle." For the first time he publicly attacked officials of the Nation of Islam, while asking civil rights leaders to forgive the many bad things he'd said about them, as he would forgive the many bad things they had said about him. An editorial in the *New York Times* described him as an "embittered racist" and "irresponsible demagogue."

One week after their UN visit, Muhammad Ali broke with Malcolm X forever. "You just don't buck Mr. Muhammad and get away with it," he said. "I don't want to talk about him anymore." He reveled in his "original name, black man's name" and praised the Nation of Islam as "the most cleanest, most unified, most respected black people in America." On 13 March, he re-took the Selective Service examination, and failed again. A psychiatric report cleared him of malingering and two weeks later he was classified 1-Y, ineligible for service. Ali, who always had difficulty with the written word, was embarrassed. "I said I was the Greatest, not the smartest."

Cassius Clay was a ready-made young star, as macho and seductive as Malcolm X, but better known, richer and more pliable. His victory over Liston may well have hastened Muhammad's decision to finish with Malcolm. Muhammad's biographer, Claude Clegg, believes that his "willingness to jettison Malcolm X" owed much to "the upset victory of Cassius Clay." Yet initially, as Clegg points out, Clay was Malcolm's ace in the hole, his best bet to re-establish his eminence in the Nation of Islam, or at least to precipitate a major split in which he could take with him a substantial section of the organization. Malcolm's critics have claimed that he sought to use Ali politically, and that Elijah Muhammad intervened to stop him. Certainly, Malcolm devoted a great deal of time and thought to the young boxer, and he would not have stayed by his side during these most decisive, difficult months of his own life had he not seen Clay as a significant part of his evolving vision of the black freedom movement. Yet Malcolm also seems to have seen his main role as providing solidarity and disinterested guidance to a young man in extraordinary circumstances. He insisted to Alex Haley that he wished to avoid adding to the pressures on Ali. Haley himself believed "he simply wanted Ali to be free and strong."

Elijah Muhammad adopted a different tactic. Once he had established direct contact with the new champion, sometime during that week in New York, the last week of Cassius Clay, Muhammad applied himself to securing the loyalty of his new recruit, whose fame far exceded his own. Shortly after Malcolm's resignation, Ali visited the Muhammad mansion in Chicago and was photographed playing with Elijah's grandchildren, just as six weeks before he'd played with Malcolm's daughter. For Elijah Muhammad, Cassius Clay arrived propitiously, filling the public vacuum left by Malcolm X. But unlike Malcolm X, Cassius Clay was free of political ambitions and happy to be just another one of the Messenger's humble followers. Like many young, talented black men he succumbed to the old man's sweet sternness. Skeptics used to say that Elijah was just a picture on the temple wall, while Malcolm was a living man interacting with his congregations. But as Clegg explains, "more important than fiery oratory or a dynamic stage presence, he had the power to command the loyalty, services and resources of others." Elijah Muhammad never attended an Ali fight. He continued to deride boxing while freely taking his tithe of Ali's professional earnings. Yet Ali paid him public homage as the Messenger of Allah till the day of his death.

From the beginning, Ali was told by friends, family and business associates that the Nation of Islam was out to get his money. But giving away money, even being fleeced by friends, never bothered Ali. He was not unaware that he was a source of finance for the Nation, and for numerous individuals who flitted in and out of his entourage, but he believed that it was a small price to pay for what he got in return.

The bond between Malcolm and Ali was real and intense, for all that divided them. Malcolm was an ascetic, and Ali was definitely not. The gap between the puritanical code of the Nation and the actual practice of its leadership deeply distressed Malcolm, but Ali, who was later to flout his adulteries while spouting Muslim pieties, may have felt differently. After all, it was to some extent the institutionalized hypocrisy of the Nation, its complex accommodation to the modern world, that attracted him to it in the first place.

I suspect that at the core of Ali's decision to break with Malcolm and follow Elijah Muhammad was his suspicion that Malcolm would lead him deeper into political activism, expose him to greater danger. He kept saying he didn't want to face firehoses and dogs, and he meant it. Malcolm, on the other hand, was preparing to reach out to those facing the hoses and the dogs, and to join their struggle, on his own terms.

Later in 1964, Malcolm told BBC television that the reason Ali was hated by the white establishment was "they knew that if people begin to identify with Cassius and the type of image he was creating they'd have trouble out of these Negroes because they'd have Negroes walking around the streets saying 'I'm the Greatest' and also Negroes who were proud of being black." Unlike Malcolm, Elijah Muhammad was careful to defend his new convert not as a racial but a religious hero. "America is upset over his being a Muslim," Muhammad told his followers. The criticism of Ali was "an open manifestation of the hatred of Muslims and Islam in America." He declined even to treat Ali as a sporting hero. "He is giving up the world of the Christian, which is a world of sport and play, as being nothing. The hereafter is what he seeks." Like so many others in boxing's history, Muhammad wanted to cast his fighter in a role; he wanted Ali to represent something beyond and besides himself, just like the high priests of Americanism in the halls of Congress and the newspaper offices. But Muhammad wanted Ali to represent not "America," and not black people, but Islam or, more precisely, his version of it. "Islam will get the Negro recognition in the world," he argued, "and this is what America fears" in Muhammad Ali.

At a press conference on 26 March, Philbert X, reading a statement prepared by the Nation's Chicago headquarters, denounced his brother Malcolm as a Judas, a Brutas, a Benedict Arnold, and suggested that he was mentally ill. The next day Malcolm was in Washington, listening to the Senate debate on the civil rights bill. There he met Martin Luther King, for the first and only time, and the legendary photograph was snapped. Malcolm told the press, "I'm here to remind the white man of the alternative to Dr. King." King warned that if the bill was not passed, "our nation is in for a dark night of social disruption."

Another photograph of two charismatic black men—Elijah Muhammad and Muhammad Ali—appeared on the front page of the next week's *Muhammad Speaks*. Above it ran a bold injunction: "WALK THE WAY OF FREE MEN!" Inside, the paper noted that Ali was a "new type heavyweight champion" and praised him for staying in black hotels in black neighborhoods. "Too many of our actors, fighters and entertainers move to neighborhoods where their own people are not." Ali praised Elijah Muhammad for teaching "the truth about black people and the history of black people."

Why did Ali stay with Elijah Muhammad? He was a world-famous twenty-two year old who had just committed himself publicly to a highly controversial religious cult. This organization promised to protect and cherish him. Malcolm could offer him nothing but increasingly daunting challenges. Besides, if a strong-willed spirit like Malcolm X was only able to break with the Nation and Elijah Muhammad after years of tortured compromise, why should we expect more from the neophyte Ali, who was without Malcolm's intellectual resources or his political ambitions? And if Malcolm's own brother denounced him, why expect Ali to defend him?

Floyd Patterson thought Ali later found himself "trapped. . . . He could not get out of the Black Muslims even if he wanted to, I think, because he'd never know what might happen as a result." Certainly, as the split with Malcolm grew more bitter during the course of 1964, and as apostates were hunted down and punished, Ali must have been made aware that any attempt to follow Malcolm would be dangerous in the extreme. But I think Leroi Jones came closer to the truth about Ali in June 1964:

> His choice of Elijah Muhammad over Malcolm X means that he is still a "homeboy," embracing the folksy vector straight out of the hard spiritualism of poor negro aspiration. Cassius is right now just angry rather than (socio-politically) motivated.

Ali and Malcolm walked side by side for only a few months. They separated abruptly and decisively (though their paths were to cross one last time, in Africa). Yet I believe Malcolm exercised a long-term influence on Ali. Malcolm knew about self-invention; his autobiography is a long and stirring exercise in it. But he also knew that unless self-invention was shaped by higher loyalties, by an absorption of the self in a greater mission, it would degenerate into mere self-promotion. Malcolm was the first to intuit Ali's seriousness, to see the wisdom in the clowning. He taught Ali that it was only by cultivating an inner strength that he could hope to overcome the vast forces opposed to him in the world outside. He re-defined the arrogance of the ambitious young fighter as a deep pride, not merely in himself and his abilities, but in his people, and showed him how to honor and draw courage from their collective past and future.

• • •

> A great song arose, the loveliest thing born this side of the seas. It was a new song. It did not come from Africa, though the dark throb and beat of that Ancient of days was in it and through it. It did not come from white America—never from so pale and thin a thing, however deep these vulgar and surrounding tones had driven. . . . It was a new song and its deep and plaintive beauty, its great cadences and wild appeal wailed, throbbed and thundered on the world's ears with a message seldom voiced by man. . . . America's one gift to

> beauty; as slavery's one redemption, distilled from the dross of its dung.
>
> *W.E.B. Du Bois*

As a teenager, Cassius Clay was an R&B fan, and when singer Lloyd Price passed through Louisville in 1959, the seventeen-year-old Golden Gloves champion waited outside his motel for an autograph. Price had been one of the first R&B singers to cross over to the white charts, and that year he'd had a huge hit with his version of "Stagger Lee," the oft-told tale of the bold black criminal, rehearsed with a buoyant amorality. Price was also a bandleader, record producer and ambitious entrepreneur. He was charmed by the insouciance of the young Clay, who in the next few years would often stay with Price on his visits to New York City.

One of Price's early stablemates at Specialty Records, the country's most successful gospel label, was the young Sam Cooke, who by 1957 had established himself as the pre-eminent male star of the gospel circuit. That year he decided to make his own crossover bid for the white youth market. This was not only a shift from black to white, but also from religious to secular, and many of his long-standing fans felt betrayed, just as Dylan's folk acolytes did when their hero went electric. Cooke's first effort, "You Send Me," was a number-one chart success, and he followed it up with a string of hits, including million-sellers "Wonderful World," "Chain Gang," and "Twistin' the Night Away." R&B performers like Ray Charles and Fats Domino had already shown that white kids would pay money for black sounds. Cooke was more ambitious. His aim was to become nothing less than an all-American star on the scale of Crosby or

Sinatra. He recorded a series of middle-of-the-road albums stuffed with standards, played nightclubs and appeared on television. With his Ivy League sweater, smooth good looks and relaxed manner, he ingratiated himself with white audiences, while at the same time flirting discreetly with Malcolm and the Nation.

Cooke first met Cassius Clay in late 1963, when both men were staying at the Hotel Theresa in Harlem. The singer was in the middle of a week's stand at the nearby Apollo, where he treated black audiences to a sensuous, ecstatic and blues-soaked sound that was considered altogether too much for the white teen audience which had snapped up his carefully crafted pop records. Clay was an unabashed admirer of Cooke's music—all of it—as well as his style and success. The two men struck up a friendship, and both spent time that week with Malcolm X, whose office was at the Theresa. Two weeks after the Kennedy assassination, and days after Malcolm's notorious "chickens coming home to roost" remark, Cooke and Clay met up again in a television studio (appearing together on Jerry Lewis's short-lived national talk show); Clay invited Cooke to be his guest in Miami for the upcoming Liston fight.

Although neither Cooke nor Clay had taken any direct part in the civil rights movement, their ambitions for themselves, which would have been inconceivable in an earlier era, reflected the broader upsurge of black aspirations and black self-confidence that the movement both expressed and encouraged. Both also nurtured ambitions for their people which, at this stage, they were careful to conceal. Like Clay, Cooke married a strong race consciousness with an equally strong drive for personal success. Although he wanted to make it in the white world, he did not accept white values or white definitions of black people. He believed in black enterprise and put his belief into action by establishing a black-owned and -managed studio in Los Angeles.

Malcolm liked to think of himself as Clay's "older brother," but it was to men like Cooke and Lloyd Price that the young fighter turned for lessons in living. Both were sophisticated men about town who knew how to make money and how to spend it. They were attractive to the most attractive women. The youth from Louisville was impressed by their nonchalant sexual promiscuity, which he was to emulate in the years to come.

For all his easy-going hedonism Sam Cooke was a proud black man who took himself very seriously indeed. Like Clay, he was trying to work in a genre in which blacks performed for whites, and like Clay, he was trying to do so without sacrificing his personal dignity, without descending to minstrelsy. Cooke was determined to cross over, but he was also determined to retain his autonomy, both creative and financial. To some extent he succeeded, through pained efforts to cultivate a variety of audiences with a variety of sounds. Broadway show tunes, folk, calypso, rock and roll, Tin Pan Alley, sagas of teen romance, dance crazes, supper-club standards—Cooke recorded them all and enriched each with his supple voice and formidable musicianship. But in the long run, Cassius Clay was to achieve crossover appeal beyond even his old friend's most extravagant dreams. While retaining and even strengthening his home base in black America, he built a huge multi-racial and multi-national following, and did so without tailoring his act for anybody.

Like nearly all the early stars of R&B and soul, Cooke kept his distance from the demonstrations and pickets. Although the music, like the movement, had roots in the southern black church, it was also a creature of commercial realism. The received wisdom at the time was that politics and popular culture didn't mix. It was assumed that music buyers, like movie-goers, were seeking escape from the cares of the world, not a high-minded civics lesson. Like Hollywood, the music business had felt the cold hand of McCarthyism throughout the fifties, and it was considered wise to steer clear of sensitive issues in general, not to mention the explosive politics of racial justice.

The folk vogue of the early sixties precipitated a re-think. Peter, Paul and Mary had a hit with Dylan's "Blowin' in the Wind," a song which was soon covered in a bizarre array of styles by artists in several countries. One of them was Sam Cooke. More significantly, Dylan's song (and success) inspired Cooke to a bold leap forward in his own songwriting. Cooke remarked to friends that it was an embarrassment for black performers that it had been a white boy who first dared talk about race and politics in popular music. In January 1964, he wrote and recorded "A Change Is Gonna Come," perhaps the first masterpiece of socially conscious soul. Its long, sinuous, suspenseful melodic line is pregnant with the burdens of history and charged with the imminence of liberation. With its roots in the millennial longings of the southern black church, and its face turned boldly toward the modern world, the song trembles in the precarious balance between patience and impatience that characterized this phase of the movement, as pious yearning passed over into profound determination.

> I go to my brother and I say, brother, help me please
> but he winds up knockin me back down on my knees

it's been a long time coming but I know
a change is gonna come, oh yes it will.

In February, Cooke premiered the song to a national audience on the "Tonight Show." Two days later, the Beatles made their historic appearance on "The Ed Sullivan Show." Southern black R&B had crossed the Atlantic and found a following among British youth, who blended it with music hall and other elements, and re-exported it to America. Cooke liked the Beatles (he considered their music "emotional") and saw their advent as yet another opportunity to expand his market, but their impact on the fortunes of black American artists was ambivalent. Between 1955 and 1963, there had been a 50 percent increase in the number of top ten hits by black performers. By the end of 1964, however, one third of top ten hits were British. Despite the fertile crossover activity that marked the decade, it also entrenched the racial bifurcation of the American pop market, which persists to this day.

At the instigation of promoter Harold Conrad, the Beatles visited one of Clay's training sessions in Miami. There was a brief exchange of banter and a publicity shoot which, at the time, seemed nothing more than two novelty acts trying to cash in on each other. A few days later Cooke flew to Miami to join the Clay camp. At ringside, Cooke's new financial manager, Allen Klein (who was later to take a controversial hand in the Beatles' finances), sat between Cooke and Malcolm X. In the mayhem that followed Liston's defeat, an exuberant Clay interrupted a television interview to hug Cooke and proclaim him "the world's greatest rock n' roll singer!" Cooke, along with Malcolm, seems to have been one of the few observers unruffled by the evening's events. "Once he got by the first round, I just settled back and watched him work," the singer told the *Los Angeles Sentinel.* "Cassius Clay is one of the greatest entertainers and showmen I have ever seen. And he's a good example for our youth."

Cooke was one of the exclusive group of black men who spent that night with Clay in Malcolm X's rooms at the Hampton House. On his return to New York, he told his friend Rosko, the legendary DJ, about his growing interest in the Nation of Islam and his belief that black people in America were the victims of "colonial oppression." A few days later, the new champion, with Malcolm at his side, announced that he'd signed a recording deal and was going to work with his friend Sam Cooke—"He's the greatest too!" Cooke took Clay into the recording studios, where Cooke's band cut a rock and roll version of "Hail, Hail the Gang's All Here" as a tribute to the new champ. Within days, Malcolm had made his public break with the Nation and the newly christened Muhammad Ali had broken with Malcolm.

In April, Cooke appeared on "American Bandstand," where he was asked how he had managed to sustain his string of hit records over a seven-year period. "I think the secret is really observation," Cooke replied. "If you observe what's going on—try to figure out how people are thinking and determine the times of your day—I think you can always write something that people understand." Here Cooke was speaking both as an astute observer of commercial trends and as an artist responding to the changing political climate.

In June he headlined at New York's Copacabana Club, where he was visited backstage by Ali. Besides his own hits, Cooke treated his well-heeled audience to standards like "Bill Bailey," "Tennessee Waltz," "If I Had a Hammer" and "Blowin' in the Wind." The show was a success (the album, *Sam Cooke at the Copa*, stayed in the charts for a year); the next month, this musical chameleon played an equally successful (if less remunerative) week in the Harlem Club in Atlantic City, where his 95 percent black audience reveled in a blazing string of gospel, R&B and throaty soul classics. In July, Cooke donated a version of "A Change Is Gonna Come" to an SCLC fund-raising LP. In August, he stopped by Gary, Indiana, to congratulate Ali on his recent marriage. Cooke's next target was a headline gig in Las Vegas, the seal of crossover legitimacy.

In December 1964, he was shot dead in a cheap hotel in Watts, Los Angeles, following a dispute over an alleged theft by a prostitute. A copy of *Muhammad Speaks* and a bottle of whiskey were found in his car. Cooke's murder was front-page news in the black press, but little noted in the white, for all his efforts to cross over. Among Cooke's legions of black fans, there was dismay. How could this urbane, wealthy young man have come to such a brutal, squalid end? Many doubted the police version and questioned the decision not to prosecute the hotel manageress for murder, among them Muhammad Ali, who was one of the thousands attending Cooke's Chicago funeral. "I don't like the way he was shot. I don't like the way it was investigated," he told a local radio reporter. "If Cooke had been Frank Sinatra, the Beatles, or Ricky Nelson, the FBI would be investigating yet and that woman would have been sent to prison."

Three days after the funeral, "A Change Is Gonna Come" was released as a single. However, with Cooke's permission, one verse had been excised:

> I go to the movies and I go downtown
> somebody keeps telling me don't hang around
> it's been a long time coming but I know
> a change is gonna come, oh yes it will.

As late as 1964, it seems, even such an oblique reference to the battles being waged in the streets of southern cities could be considered controversial. Comparing these mild-mannered, color-blind lyrics to the kind of upfront declamations which were to become commonplace in black popular music within the decade, I am struck once again by both the scale of the change in popular culture wrought by pioneers like Cooke and Ali, and its sheer rapidity.

3

Bringing It All Back Home

One three centuries removed
From the scenes his fathers loved,
Spicy grove, cinnamon tree,
What is Africa to me?

Countee Cullen

"Leading American Negroes are today widely ignorant of the history and present situation in Africa and indifferent to the fate of African Negroes," W.E.B. Du Bois complained in 1955. "This represents a great change from the past." He was referring to a rich history of transatlantic interchange, in which ideas and aspirations circulated between Africa, North America, Europe and the Caribbean, a history always marginalized, but over which a veil had now been drawn by the Cold War, with its two great opposing blocks, both dominated by white people.

Du Bois's own efforts to build a pan-African organization—and pan-African consciousness on both sides of the Atlantic—were no small part of this history. He helped organize the first Pan-African Conference in London in 1900 and the second in Paris in 1919. Through two world wars, the Bolshevik Revolution and the rise of fascism, Du Bois struggled to keep alive the idea of a common interest and a common future of freedom for Africans and people of African descent.

Du Bois's great cadences invoked and echoed across what Paul Gilroy has called the Black Atlantic world. With its origins in the horrors of the middle passage, the Black Atlantic evolved, rarely noticed by the white world, through an interchange of political and religious ideas, music, literature, dance and sport. Although for most of its existence only tiny minorities on either side of the ocean were conscious of it, the Black Atlantic nonetheless produced what Gilroy has called "structures of feeling, producing, communicating and remembering" on which many millions have drawn—among them Muhammad Ali. Indeed, it is impossible to understand Ali fully unless he is placed within the Black Atlantic, which shaped him and which he helped to shape and ultimately to project into popular consciousness as never before.

Among the early trailblazers of the Black Atlantic were intellectuals and agitators like Frederick Douglass, Alexander Crummell and Martin Delany, as well as a steady stream of black American boxers, from Bill Richmond, Tom Molineaux and Massa Sutton to Bobby Dobbs and Jack Johnson himself. In London and Paris, traveling black Americans—seamen, musicians, fighters, clergy—encountered small concentrations of African students. In 1873, the Fisk Jubilee Singers brought Europe (and Africans living in Europe) their first taste of the gospel sound, the "sorrow songs" which Du Bois praised as the only authentically American art form, even as he celebrated its African source. In Europe, black Americans came to see more clearly the anomaly of their position in the United States, as well as their link to an Africa then under near total colonial domination. In other words, they acquired a world picture of themselves. In *Dusk of Dawn*, published in 1940, Du Bois contemplated both the mystery and the potency of this emerging vision:

> As I face Africa I ask myself: what is it between us that constitutes a tie that I can feel better than I can explain? Africa is, of course, my fatherland. Yet neither my father nor my father's father ever saw Africa or knew its meaning or cared overmuch for it. . . . The badge of color [is] relatively unimportant save as a badge; the real essence of this kinship is its social heritage of slavery, the discrimination and insult; and this heritage binds together not simply the children of Africa, but extends through yellow Asia and into the South Seas. It is this unity that draws me to Africa.

However, it was not through the reasoned appeals of the erudite Du Bois, but the charismatic populism of the Jamaican Marcus Garvey, that pan-African ideas burst into the mainstream of African-American life. Founded in 1917, his United Negro Improvement Association (UNIA) demanded "Africa for the Africans, at home and abroad," spread rapidly across the African diaspora in North America and the Caribbean, and found adherents in West and Southern Africa. Garvey's speeches made their way even into the African bush, where the young Jomo Kenyatta was stirred by them. Garvey declared himself "provisional president of Africa." By 1920 the UNIA claimed two million members and had become the first mass organization of black Americans and of the African diaspora. However, in the early twenties, faced with the rise of the Klan and harassment from the federal government, Garvey began to downplay his political challenge to colonialism and Jim Crow, and emphasized instead racial purity and "repatriation" to Africa as the answers to black misery. Like Elijah Muhammad in 1961, he even made overtures to white supremacists, including the Klan.

Initially, Du Bois had welcomed Garveyism's assertive racial spirit and its commitment to pan-Africanism. But Garvey's mercurial egotism alarmed him, and he was outraged by the "unholy alliance" with the Klan. "He is either a lunatic or a traitor," Du Bois declared. Garvey replied by calling Du Bois "a lazy dependent mulatto." Du Bois attacked Garvey as a corrupt autocrat, and Garvey labeled Du Bois a white man's negro. The feud between these two great champions of pan-Africa was dubbed by A. Philip Randolph (himself a recent apostate from Garvey's "magic romanticism of color") the "Heavyweight Championship Bout for the Afro-American–West Indian Belt, Between Battling Du Bois and Kid Garvey."

The boxing analogy was not accidental. Boxing—more than politics, the performing arts or other sports—was at this time black America's dominant public arena, the place where black heroes met in battle, either with each other or with representatives of the white majority. What's more, in the twenties it was becoming one of the major features of the Black Atlantic, a common interest binding together blacks in the US, the Caribbean, western Europe and West

Africa. After serving in the French Army in World War I, the Senegalese known as Battling Siki had made a name for himself as a pugilist. In 1922, he fought Georges Carpentier for the light heavyweight title in Paris (becoming the first black to fight for a title in any division since Jack Johnson's defeat). It has been alleged that the fight was fixed for Carpentier, but after a few desultory rounds something in Siki snapped and he thrashed Carpentier from one corner to another. Carpentier fell, but the referee ruled he had been fouled by Siki. The Frenchman was declared the winner. The crowd reacted angrily, the boxing commissioner stepped into the ring, reversed the referee's decision and awarded the fight and title to Siki.

Siki basked in his sudden wealth and fame, and in doing so earned the enmity of the Parisian press. The next year he lost his title in Dublin and departed for America. There, he gained a popular following among the black populations of the northern cities, and his extravagant lifestyle and frequent brushes with the police were extensively covered by the black press. He was found shot dead in Harlem in December 1925. In *The Greatest*, Muhammad Ali recalled: "I used to hang around the gym and hear the pros talk about famous old fighters and their feats, and it sounded more exciting and daring to me than any tales of the Wild West: stories about Black Deacon, Tiger Flowers, Boston Tar Baby, Kid Chocolate, Joe Gans, Battling Siki, and others just as good who fought all across the country, almost always in places where the audience wanted to see them stomped."

As Gerald Early has pointed out, though Siki was embraced by black America, he was often seen as a wild primitive, an impression strengthened by his style in the ring and his adventures outside it.

Black Americans might view Africans and Africa with sympathy, but by and large they also viewed them as uncivilized, wanting in the refinements and restraint introduced by Christianity and industrialization. As Du Bois sadly observed, black Americans had been taught that "Africa has no history and no culture and they became ashamed of any connection with it."

But it was difficult even for those who were proud of the connection to grasp the reality of the continent, and even the most worldly black Americans still tended to see Africa through a veil of exoticism. The obstacles to building a pan-African consciousness and an authentic African presence in modern popular culture can be gauged by a glance at Paul Robeson's career in the cinema. Initially, Robeson's interest in Africa was primarily cultural. His musicological and linguistic studies were part of a search for "an art that was purely Negro." In London in the late twenties, Robeson, relishing his freedom from Jim Crow America and in search of his roots, began a study of African languages at the University of London. Over the next decade he met and worked with African and Caribbean students and future leaders, among them Nnamdi Azikiwe, Kenyatta and C.L.R. James. As he grew more deeply involved with the anti-colonial activists, Robeson's cultural curiosity became increasingly tied to political commitment. In the mid thirties, he starred in C.L.R. James's dramatic adaptation of the life of Toussaint L'Ouverture in London's West End. The Black Atlantic had found a niche in British culture, but it was still a remote and largely unimagined reality to the masses of black people.

When the Korda brothers offered Robeson a leading role as an African prince in their epic, *Sanders of the River*, the actor-activist was delighted. At last, a popular film promised to treat the African reality with a degree of integrity. Jomo Kenyatta was among the African students in London who earned much-needed cash as an extra on the film, and Robeson hoped their presence would enhance the film's authenticity. He was to be bitterly disappointed. Despite Robeson's efforts, his character—Bosambo—remains a caricature, and the film as a whole takes for granted the benevolence of the white man's rule over the grinning and fearful natives. Robeson was embarrassed, but the experience did not deter him from trying repeatedly in the coming years to inject the African presence into popular cinema. In *Song of Freedom*, he plays a London dockworker whom fate (and a convoluted plot) transforms first into a famous concert singer and then into an African king. In *King Solomon's Mines*, his character reclaims an ancient royal right—though still under the aegis of imperialism. In *Jericho*, Robeson portrays a medical student in the army who, unjustly court-martialed, escapes to Africa, where he becomes the leader of a tribe and a benefactor of the people. In all of these, the African landscape is merely an exotic background for crude melodrama and African peoples are depicted as childlike and in need of guidance from a higher authority. Watching Robeson struggle with a series of improbable characters drawn largely from the stock supply of stereotypes is a chastening experience, an object lesson in the limitations imposed on even the most extraordinary individual talents by the hierarchies which shape popular culture.

It was impossible, even for the rich white men who made the movies, to see Paul Robeson as other than a free man, graceful, intelligent, proud, composed, authoritative. But there was simply no place in the popular cinema for this type of black man at this time.

So it became necessary to encase his undeniable qualities in a framework of subordination. It is this dilemma (one for the filmmakers as much as for Robeson) that accounts for the magical transformations, in social status and even ethnic identity, which his characters of the thirties repeatedly undergo. Where qualities of leadership or intellect are discovered, unexpectedly, among the lowly, they must be explained away, either—as in Shakespeare—by hidden royal lineage or—in a more modern twist—by the virtues of (white) western education. Robeson remained profoundly dissatisfied with his film roles. As the thirties progressed, he came to believe that there could be no freedom for himself as an artist as long as there was no freedom for his people.

Just as Robeson believed that "in every black man flows the rhythm of Africa," so many commentators believed they intuited this rhythm, this germ of Africa, in Robeson's performances. This had the effect of turning an exquisite and cultivated artist into a pure force of nature. Far from being immune to this racist reductionism, the left shared and even celebrated it. Neruda sang Robeson's praises in precisely those terms: "You have been the voice of man, / the story of the germinating earth, / the river and the movement of nature."

While Robeson was in Europe exploring and trying to give artistic expression to his African heritage, Kwame Nkrumah crossed the Atlantic and immersed himself in black America. At the age of twenty-five, he left the British colony of the Gold Coast in West Africa to live for a decade in the United States, studying at Lincoln University and later at the University of Pennsylvania, and founding the African Students' Organization, the first organization of Africans in North America. Nkrumah was only one of several future African and Caribbean leaders to study at black American institutions in the thirties and forties, among them Azikiwe and George Padmore. Nkrumah's colleague and critic, C.L.R. James—Trinidadian Marxist, pioneer student of popular culture and embodiment of the Black Atlantic—believed these years in the US were crucial in the development of the man who was to lead Africa's first successful anti-colonial revolution:

> This African lived an intensely active life among all classes of the coloured people in the United States, and that life is the life of a very advanced and highly civilised community, sharpened and broadened by its incessant conflict against the domination and persecution of official society. Not only in books but in his contact with people and his very active intellectual and political life, he was the inheritor of the centuries of material struggle and intellectual thought which the Negro people in the United States had developed from all sources in order to help them in their effort to emancipate themselves.

Nkrumah studied black American music, investigated the churches and social institutions, and dabbled in black nationalism. He was briefly an adherent of the messianic cult of Father Divine, encountered proselytizers from the Nation of Islam while working as a fish seller in Harlem in 1936 and became an admirer of Garvey. Some twenty years later he arranged for the new Ghanaian government to purchase the UNIA's Black Star Liner.

In 1945, he moved to London and worked with George Padmore, James and Du Bois in organizing the historic Pan-African Conference, held in Manchester that year. In 1947, he returned to the Gold Coast. Declaring that "freedom is not something one people can bestow on another as a gift," he launched the decade-long political insurgency that would make Ghana Africa's first independent, post-colonial state.

In 1951, the eighty-two-year-old Du Bois was indicted for "failure to register as an agent of a foreign principal." With anti-Communist hysteria at its height, even the ACLU refused to defend him. Although the case against him was dismissed, his passport was withdrawn for five years. As the Cold War intensified, the State Department and the CIA grew ever more hostile to adverse comments by traveling black Americans on the state of race relations back home. The boundaries delineated in the Robeson affair remained in force. Only black American leaders who subscribed to those boundaries—Randolph, Walter White and Roy Wilkins—were licensed to speak for and about America abroad.

Stripped of their passports, neither Du Bois nor Robeson was able to attend the historic Bandung conference of non-aligned, emergent nations, organized by Nasser, Nehru and Sukarno in 1955. Alarmed at the very idea of an autonomous block of African and Asian nations, American officials boycotted the conference and dissuaded mainstream black leaders from participating. As a result, the only American voice heard at Bandung belonged to Adam Clayton Powell, Jr., the maverick congressman from Harlem and pastor of the Abyssinan Baptist Church. A close ally of the Communist party during the thirties and forties, Powell had swum with the anti-Communist tide, but in the eyes of the establishment he remained unpredictable and untrustworthy. They viewed with unease his solid black political base, his independently cultivated ties to African and Asian leaders, as well as his non-puritanical attitudes towards alcohol, sex and money. Like Jack Johnson, Powell was a victim of double standards; like Johnson, he infuriated whites and unsettled mainstream black leaders while winning the affection of millions of poor and working-class blacks. But at Bandung, Powell chose to play the loyal American. In his speech to the conference, he lauded US progress in race relations, illustrated by his own family's rise from slavery to a seat in Congress in just two generations. The American media were delighted by Powell's patriotic performance. He was congratulated by southern congressmen, but his judgement was questioned in the black press.

In May 1956, Louis Armstrong undertook a State Department-sponsored tour, with a CBS crew in tow, of what was then still the Gold Coast colony. Thanks to his recordings and radio and movie appearances, Armstrong was probably at this time the best known black American outside the United States, and he received a rapturous welcome in Accra, where he told the crowds, "I still have African blood in me." Armstrong's genius was well known to Nkrumah, who received the American jazz master as an honored guest not of the dying colonial regime (whose officials urged Armstrong not to stir up the natives by playing too fast), but of the emergent free people of Ghana. Thus Nkrumah, with the help of the American State Department, brought jazz back to its roots and opened yet another channel for the currents of the Black Atlantic. At the same time, Armstrong's visit was part of the official repackaging of jazz as "America's music," a means of selling the American dream to the emergent Third World.

The tour was regarded as a diplomatic success for the US and a personal triumph for "Ambassador Satchmo," then at the height of his fame. Nothing could better illustrate the tragic contradictions facing the African-American performer in the first half of this century than Armstrong's remarkable career, combining modernism and minstrelsy, genius and buffoonery, an elliptical, knowing, consciously black style with a shameless pandering to white assumptions. Yet even the eternally wary and ever-pragmatic Armstrong was not immune to the stirrings of black revolt. In September 1957, Armstrong watched scenes from Little Rock on television. "The way they are treating my people in the South," he told a reporter, "the government can go to hell." Then he added, unknowingly echoing the remark that had brought Paul Robeson down only ten years before, "It's getting so bad, a colored man hasn't got any country." He canceled a second overseas "goodwill tour," explaining, "The people over there ask me what's wrong with my country, what am I supposed to say?"

Armstrong's remarks provoked an outcry from right-wing columnists, a short-lived radio boycott of his recordings and a spate of concert cancellations. He was denounced by Powell and Sammy Davis, Jr. Initially, at least, the adverse reaction only fueled his anger. He declared he'd rather play in the Soviet Union than in Arkansas and that he wouldn't play at all in New Orleans, the cradle of his art, because of a Louisiana state law banning inter-racial performances. "I don't care if I ever see that city again. They treat me better all over the world than they do in my hometown." The FBI opened a file on Armstrong and his managers feared he would suffer Robeson's fate. But Armstrong was too popular with white audiences, and ultimately too accommodating, to linger long outside the circle of official approval. In 1959, he was formally designated an American Goodwill Ambassador. In 1960, he and his band returned to Ghana, then proceeded, at the State Department's urging, to the Congo, where Patrice Lumumba awaited martyrdom.

• • •

The independence of Ghana in 1957 inaugurated a major shift in the balance of the Black Atlantic. In the West Indies, the calypsonian Lord Kitchener celebrated the epoch-marking event:

> This day will never be forgotten,
> The sixth of March 1957,
> When the Gold Coast successfully
> Got their independence officially.
> Ghana, Ghana is the name
> Ghana, we wish to proclaim
> We will be jolly, merry and gay,
> The sixth of March, independence day.

Among Nkrumah's American guests were not only Vice-President Nixon, but A. Phillip Randolph, Ralph Bunche, Adam Clayon Powell and the young Martin Luther King, whom Nkrumah invited for a private luncheon. On his return to America, King spoke of the lessons he'd learned, principally that "privileged classes never give up their privileges without strong resistance . . . freedom comes only through persistent revolt." Nkrumah had invited Du Bois and Robeson to the ceremonies, but both were still barred from foreign travel by the US government. Du Bois wrote to Nkrumah expressing his hope that independent Africa would "teach mankind what non-violence and courtesy, literature and art, music and dancing can do for this greedy, selfish and war-stricken world." But much to Du Bois's disappointment, Nkrumah (strongly influenced by Padmore's virulent anti-Sovietism) initially pursued pro-American policies. In March 1958, seeking aid from the Eisenhower administration, he visited the United States. In an attempt to appease the government he argued—contrary to his own experience and commitment—that "the racial question in the United States" had been "exaggerated deliberately." Such statements did not deter Harlemites from staging a grand reception for their adopted son, attended by both Powell and Malcolm X, who met with Nkrumah again later that year when the Ghanaian returned for another visit to the United Nations. Their communication aroused the suspicions of the CIA, which asked for and received the FBI dossier on the Nation of Islam.

In 1960, Martin Luther King published an essay called "The Rising Tide of Racial Consciousness," in which he attributed "the new sense of dignity and self-respect on the part of the Negro" in part to "the awareness that his struggle is a part of a world-wide struggle. He has watched developments in Asia and Africa with rapt attention. [His] drama is being played out on the stage of the world with spectators and supporters from every continent." Although King here placed himself in the internationalist tradition of Du Bois, his concern remained the liberation of black Americans as Americans, and he made no mention of the role black Americans might play in the liberation of Africa or Asia. Yet with the emergence of new nations in Africa, an increasingly vocal black American minority began re-conceiving the ancient link. Africa was no longer merely a collection of mysterious images, vague folk memories or messianic aspirations; and Africa was no longer looking to the diaspora to articulate itself. The new Africa came to Harlem, to black America, living and breathing fire—in the persons of Nkrumah and above all of Patrice Lumumba, who was to have a huge impact on Malcolm X, and therefore an indirect impact on Muhammad Ali.

In June 1960, Lumumba, a former civil servant, trade unionist, pan-Africanist and founder of the Mouvement National Congolais (MNC), became the first (and last) democratically elected prime minister of the newly independent Democratic Republic of the Congo. He was immediately faced with a challenge to his rule from a breakaway Katanga republic, headed by Moise Tshombe, defended by Belgian mercenaries and funded by western interests. On 24 July, after conferring with Nkrumah in Accra, Lumumba flew to New York City, where he was besieged by reporters demanding to know if he was a Communist. He replied that he was a nationalist and that his new nation would pursue a policy of "positive neutralism."

> For the Congo there are no blocs, because we are an African people. . . . We desire no political programs from the US or USSR; we seek only technical assistance.

But he was also seeking, more controversially—and ultimately unsuccessfully—the withdrawal from the region of all foreign forces, including Belgian mercenaries. He expounded his case in speeches at Howard University and to a gathering in Harlem, after which he met with Malcolm X, who was deeply affected by Lumumba's vision of an autonomous, cohesive Africa charting its own course of modern development. Personally, Malcolm was overwhelmed by Lumumba, whom he called "the greatest black man who ever walked the African continent." It was not an accident that he referred to Lumumba in his response to the JFK assassination, nor that he would invoke his name again and again during his own final months.

Joseph Mobutu had joined Lumumba's MNC in 1958 and was appointed a defense minister—effectively the army's paymaster—in Lumumba's first cabinet. Acting with CIA encouragement, Mobutu staged a coup on 5 September, and placed Lumumba under house arrest in the capital, Léopoldville. At the State Department's request, Louis Armstrong, then completing an eight-week African tour, made an unscheduled visit to the city. He was received enthusiastically, hoisted on a chair and paraded through the streets. Armstrong's visit provided a timely diversion from the political crisis and Lumumba's plight. It may also have helped camouflage the presence in the country of other Americans, some of whom were involved, at that moment, in plotting the liquidation of both Lumumba and the democratic experiment in the Congo. Armstrong himself struck up a friendship with Tshombe. "The cat was so nice to me," Armstrong later recalled. "Kept me in his big palace and all, fed me good, stayed up all night gassing. I had this little tape recorder that cost me several big bills and Tshombe dug it so much I laid it on him."

In October, Nkrumah attended the UN General Assembly session and met with Nasser, Nehru and Sukarno. All had been pressing Lumumba's case, and all were disturbed by big power machinations in Africa. In Harlem, Nkrumah addressed a crowd of one thousand in front of the Theresa. "The twenty million Americans of African ancestry constitute the strongest link between the people of North

America and the people of Africa," he told them. Malcolm X also addressed the rally, praised the imprisoned Lumumba and warned that black Americans would not accept US meddling in the Congo.

In November, Lumumba escaped house arrest, only to be re-arrested by Mobutu's troops on 2 December. In collusion with CIA operatives and Belgian and British mercenaries, he was delivered into Tshombe's hands on 17 January, tortured and murdered. Under the new western-backed regime in Léopoldville, Mobutu became commander in chief of the armed forces. The conflict in the Congo reverberated around the Black Atlantic. In Trinidad, people danced to the new global politics recounted in Lord Briner's ska hit, "Congo War," which wryly recites the names of the contestants for power, Kasavubu, Mobutu, Tshombe, Lumumba.

> My father made me to know
> that my great great grandfather
> came from the Congo
> in the western province of Katanga
> but I can't remember his name
> because it was so long
> and if I call the name
> I might have to bite me tongue.

News of Lumumba's execution was concealed for some weeks, but the people he'd touched in Harlem had not forgotten him. On 14 February 1961, they demonstrated in front of the UN and had the effrontery to disrupt US ambassador Adlai Stevenson's speech to the General Assembly. Although this was only one—and by no means the largest or most violent—of the pro-Lumumba demonstrations staged across the world in these weeks, it alarmed and appalled the American establishment. These weren't the usual "anti-American elements" burning US flags in foreign streets. These were "American negroes." And they were protesting against their government's policy on a world stage, before the United Nations. The UN demonstration was denounced by Roy Wilkins, who declared, "Belgian colonizers should not be replaced by Soviet colonizers." The next week Ralph Bunche used his speech to the NAACP conference to berate the "misguided misfits" who had demonstrated at the UN and to apologize for their behavior. Questioning Bunche's "mandate from his people," Lorraine Hansberry caustically replied, "I hasten to publicly apologize to Mme. Pauline Lumumba and the Congolese people for our Dr. Bunche."

Reflecting on the events at the UN, James Baldwin reported that "the impact of this political assassination on Negroes in Harlem had—has—captured the popular imagination there." There was no use blaming "outside agitators," Baldwin argued, because "the Negroes who rioted at the UN are but a very small echo of the black discontent now abroad in the world." He still believed that "the American Negro deludes himself if he imagines himself capable of any loyalty other than to the United States. He is an American, too, and he will survive or perish in this country." But he also now insisted that the old terms of black adaptation to America were changing irrevocably: "The American Negro can no longer, nor will he ever again, be controlled by white America's image of him. This fact has everything to do with the rise of Africa in world affairs." Young blacks, Baldwin wrote, are no longer "merely the descendants of slaves," but are "also related to kings and princes in an ancestral homeland, far away. And this has proved to be a great antidote to the poison of self-hatred."

The UN demonstration had been the initiative of three talented young black women, the singer Abbey Lincoln and the future writers Rosa Guy and Maya Angelou. They had been inspired by Malcolm's speeches on Africa and African-Americans and sought him out in his office at the Theresa. To their surprise, Malcolm told them they were wasting their time. "The people of Harlem are angry. And they have reason to be angry. But going to the United Nations, shouting and carrying placards, will not win freedom for anyone." Although he disguised it from the young women, Malcolm's enforced inaction in response to Lumumba's murder was one of several gut-wrenching abstentions which were to help turn him away from Elijah Muhammad over the next three years.

Kwame Nkrumah was also affected by Lumumba's fate. From 1960, his government turned away from America in order to chart an explicitly neutralist course. In 1960, a plebiscite made Ghana a republic; the government adopted a policy of "Africanization" and prioritized infrastructure development in city and countryside. Nkrumah invited Du Bois to live as his personal guest in Accra and to edit an authoritative *Encyclopedia Africana*, a project Du Bois had been promoting for half a century. Nkrumah also invited Paul Robeson to assume the chair of music and drama at Accra University, but his health was poor and he was never able to set foot in independent Africa.

In October 1961, the ninety-three-year-old Du Bois applied for membership of the US Communist party. A month later he moved to Ghana. Shortly before his death in Accra two years later, on the eve of the great March on Washington, he renounced his US citizenship. It had been a long, tortuous road from his articulation of black America's "double consciousness" at the turn of the century to this unequivocal rejection—transcendence—of American national identity. In America itself he was nearly a forgotten man. Nonetheless, a young black vanguard was even then beginning to re-examine his work in the light of their own traumatic experiences in the struggle for civil rights. As Lorraine Hansberry observed, "His ideas have influenced a multitude who do not even know his name." And one of those was surely Muhammad Ali.

• • •

In establishing the Organization of African Unity in 1963, Nkrumah fulfilled an old pan-Africanist dream. But even as his stature in the Third World grew (accompanied by escalating American displeasure), his regime at home came under severe economic and political stress, fed in part by external, Cold War pressures. Nkrumah assumed ever greater presidential powers. C.L.R. James observed that "in 1957 over a large part of Ghana Nkrumah could have walked for days without a single attendant." Now he moved nowhere without an armed guard. In 1962, in response to an assassination attempt, draconian security legislation was introduced. In 1963, Nkrumah dismissed the hitherto independent chief justice. "Africa had crossed a Rubicon," James remarked presciently. "By this single act, Nkrumah prepared the population of Ghana for the morals of the Mafia." Early in 1964, shortly before the visits of Ali and Malcolm, Ghana was officially designated a one-party state, with Nkrumah as life president and *Osgeyafo* (Messiah). Two years later, he was overthrown by the army while on a visit to China. "Like Cromwell and Lenin, he initiated the destruction of a regime in decay—a tremendous achievement," James said in his final assessment of the man, "but like them, he failed to create a new society."

In 1962, James noted that among black Americans "there is a greater knowledge of the real history of the development of Africa than exists proportionately in any other sector of the world." But, he lamented, "they too have been contaminated by the prevailing myth and, try as they may, cannot rid themselves of it." Among the "contaminated" were not only the white-god-worshipping black American Christians, but also the black-god-worshipping non-American Muslim Elijah Muhammad, who derided Africans' "bushy hair" as "the style of savages" and who in the heyday of American pan-Africanism in the late sixties prohibited the wearing of dashikis, beards and Afro hairstyles. In Muhammad's mythology, black Americans were not merely ex-slaves, nor the descendants of heathen African tribes, but members of "the Lost-Found Nation of Islam," an extension of the prelapsarian Arab-Islamic culture which had once been shared by all dark peoples, before the disastrous rise of the uncivilized whites. It was precisely because Elijah put such emphasis on the "civilized" character of the "original people" that he made a point of distinguishing them from the black Africans his followers had seen in Hollywood films.

The Nation itself was a distinctive product of the Black Atlantic: it is self-consciously a belief system of, by and for the diaspora. And it celebrated the emergence of independent black Africa and urged black Americans to emulate their brothers by claiming part of the United States as their own independent territory. But it remained aloof from the highly politicized version of pan-Africanism promoted by Du Bois, Padmore, James and Nkrumah.

From the days of the early black American missionaries, and even in the works of the founding prophets of black nationalism, Crummell and Delany, Africa was perceived as a backward land in need of western values and skills, ranging from Christianity to technology. "Deep down in the soul of many American Negroes," Harold Cruse observed in 1967, "is ingrained the conviction that the African has just barely emerged out of his primitive-tribal past!" This deep ambivalence about Africa remains strong among African-Americans, and indeed among Afro-Caribbeans in Britain, to this day. Ali shared it. Black Americans, as creatures of the modern world, wrestled with the reality of modern Africa. Here was a source of redemption that itself required redemption.

• • •

In its celebration of the glorious triumph of Ali's second trip to Africa in 1974, *When We Were Kings* makes no mention of his first trip, undertaken only weeks after his victory over Liston and public conversion. During the course of this trip Ali fought no title fights, and was for the most part ignored in the United States, but the journey remains one of the formative events of his career.

Malcolm X planted the seed of Ali's first trip to Africa, but others gathered the fruit. Arrangements were made by Malcolm's friend Osman Karriem, who had remained with the Nation and who hoped that the time away from America would give the young champion a chance to relax. On the eve of their departure, Ali told a Boston crowd that "many negro celebrities take State Department goodwill tours of Africa or Asia, but few have received personal invitations from so many world leaders." For Elijah Muhammad, Ali's tour was principally a promotional exercise for the Nation of Islam. In the pages of *Muhammad Speaks*, Ali was presented as Elijah's emissary, and his enthusiastic reception as evidence of the stature of Elijah Muhammad in the Islamic world. But something much deeper was happening, to both Ali and the world's vision of Ali.

Ali and his companions—Karriem; Ali's brother Rudolph; his friend, photographer Howard Bingham; and his new advisor, Herbert Muhammad, Elijah's son—first touched African soil in Accra, where they were welcomed by a high-level delegation of ministers and businessmen, and garlanded by the Ghana Young Pioneers. "I am anxious to get around and see Africa and meet my brothers and sisters," Ali told the local press. "I haven't been home for four hundred years." The foreign minister informed Ali that since he had arrived on a Saturday, he would be given the additional name Kwame, in honor of the founder of the nation, who had been born on a Saturday.

Ali and his friends then proceeded into the city in an open-top convertible, cheered by thousands along the way. They took note of the placards reading, "Welcome Home, King of the World" and "Ghana is your motherland, Cassius Clay." Later, at an elite reception at the Ambassador Hotel, Ali spoke quietly to Ghanaian journalists. "We are glad to be back home to see things for ourselves, meet pretty Ghanaian girls, take pictures and then go back to the States and tell our people that there are more things to be seen in Africa than lions, tigers and elephants." Like Malcolm, Ali made much of the presence in Africa of familiar American technology—

cars, airplanes, television—and especially of the sight of black people working at technical or professional jobs that were still the preserve of white people in America. "I'm surprised to find the beautiful cities with their tall buildings and other modern features," he said, pleased that the motherland was also a modern land.

The next day the front page of the *Ghanaian Times* featured a photo of Ali in his car, under the headline " 'King' Clay Waves Back." The caption read: "Muhammad Kwame Ali feels completely at home as he makes his triumphal entry into his motherland—Africa." The local *Daily Graphic* celebrated the occasion with a simple banner headline, " 'King' Clay in Ghana." The champion was granted an instant audience with Nkrumah, who presented him with copies of his books on colonialism and the African future. Ali was dressed in traditional Ghanaian kente cloth. His brother wore a suit and tie. Nkrumah wore his trademark open-necked shirt, traditional yet modern, casual yet formal. Ali told the president he hoped to buy a home in Ghana and spend time there each year. Nkrumah, the newspapers reported, welcomed this news as "an indication of the ties of friendship between black Americans and Africa." Nkrumah, of course, was not a Muslim, and for the Nation of Islam his meeting with Ali was of significance only in so far as it re-enforced the world standing of Ali's master, the Honorable Elijah Muhammad. But Nkrumah was at this time the acknowledged leader of the pan-African movement and an arch foe of the US State Department. Ali's visit with him was viewed with suspicion by the CIA. Nkrumah was the first head of state, in fact the first major politician anywhere, to embrace Ali. Over the next decade he would be embraced by many more, but it was not until late 1974, after his triumph in Kinshasa, that an American president would shake his hand.

The *Ghanaian Times* diarist noted the simultaneous presence in town of Malcolm X. This "complex, intriguing figure," the diarist reported, had mesmerized a group of young Ghanaian intellectuals for two hours. The American had donned African dress and was pictured eating African-style—with his hands—a meal of yams, plantains and rice.

Malcolm had been traveling in the Middle East and Africa for more than a month. In Mecca, he had completed the hajj and discovered, in the words of poet Robert Hayden, "Allah the raceless one in whose blazing Oneness all / were one." The hajj has loomed large in the mythology of Malcolm X, the final act in his drama of self-discovery, a reconciliation with the white race and repudiation of the most unpalatable elements of the Nation of Islam. Religious faith was central to Malcolm (as it was to Martin Luther King) and his conversion to orthodox Islam was a genuine one. But he had already visited the Middle East in 1959, as Elijah's emissary, and he had long been aware of the multi-racial character of the Muslim world and the theological gulf between its beliefs and practices and those advocated by Elijah Muhammad. Malcolm was able to use his hajj to rise above the parochialism of the Nation, to reinvent himself as a member of a world religion; paradoxically, the hajj was also the prelude for a move away from obscurantist religion and toward a secular, political agenda. In the end, the hajj was only one of the epiphanies Malcolm was to experience during the foreign peregrinations that were to consume half the life remaining to him when he left the Nation of Islam on 8 March 1964. It was part of a broader outward evolution, an evolution that owed more to pan-Africanism than pan-Islamism.

After the hajj, Malcolm visited Egypt, Nigeria and Ghana; he met with students, journalists and government leaders. In Accra, he was warmly welcomed by the small but lively colony of black American expatriates. In her memoir of her time in Ghana, Maya Angelou recalls a light-hearted, talkative Malcolm, immensely excited by his travels, somehow breathing more freely now that he had escaped from the constrictions of the Nation. He was already building support for the project that was to preoccupy him for the rest of his life, a petition that would place the grievances of black Americans before the United Nations. By re-forging the link between Africa and African-Americans, American blacks, Malcolm believed, would gain a new global leverage against their domestic oppressors. Instead of appealing to American whites, they would appeal to the vast, non-white, non-American majority, a majority in revolt against American economic and military power.

In Accra, Malcolm talked to editors and educators, students and ministers, and diplomats from Africa, Europe, Cuba and China. He charmed everyone. The Ghana Press Club threw him a party (where he refused to dance). "I don't consider myself American," he told his hosts. "I am a black Muslim man of African heritage." Thanks to Shirley Du Bois, whose husband had died in Ghana less than a year before, he was granted an audience with Nkrumah (who had already received Ali) on the morning of his last day in Accra. Malcolm considered the meeting one of the high points of his pilgrimage, as inspirational politically as the visit to Mecca was spiritually. After leaving Nkrumah, he met his American friends at the Ambassador, where a convoy of limousines waited to escort him to the airport. Among their passengers were Nigerian, Chinese, Cuban, Algerian and Egyptian diplomats. To the expatriate Americans, it was an extraordinary sight—a black man isolated and vilified at home honored as a leader and teacher abroad. Maya Angelou remembered the moment, and the even more extraordinary encounter that followed.

> We were all laughing with pleasure when we heard the familiar sounds of black American speech. We turned around and saw Muhammad Ali coming out of the hotel with a large retinue of black men. They were all talking and joking among themselves. One minute after we saw them, they saw Malcolm.
>
> The moment froze, as if caught on a daguerreotype, and the next minutes moved as a slow montage. Muhammad stopped, then turned and spoke to a companion. His friends looked at him. Then they looked back at Malcolm. Malcolm also stopped, but he didn't speak to us, nor did any of us have the presence of mind to say anything to him.
>
> Malcolm had told us that after he severed ties to the Nation of Islam, many of his former friends had become hostile. Muhammad and his group were the first to turn away. They started walking toward a row of parked cars. Malcolm, with a rush, left us and headed toward the departing men. We followed Malcolm. He shouted, "Brother Muhammad. Brother Muhammad."
>
> Muhammad and his companions stopped and turned to face Malcolm.

"Brother, I still love you, and you are still the greatest." Malcolm smiled a sad little smile. Muhammad looked hard at Malcolm, and shook his head.

"You left the Honorable Elijah Muhammad. That was the wrong thing to do, Brother Malcolm." His face and voice were also sad. Malcolm had been his supporter and hero. Disappointment and hurt lay on Muhammad's face like dust. Abruptly, he turned and walked away. His coterie followed. After a few steps they began talking again, loudly.

Malcolm's shoulders sagged and his face was suddenly gloomy. "I've lost a lot. A lot. Almost too much." He led us back to my car. . . . Julian asked him if Muhammad's actions at the hotel came as a surprise, and Malcolm did not answer directly. "He is young. The Honorable Elijah Muhammad is his prophet and his father, I understand. Be kind to him for his sake, and mine. He has a place in my heart."

In Ghana, Ali's training sessions attracted huge crowds. He traveled up country to fight an exhibition in Kumasi, where five thousand people greeted him at the makeshift local airport, and a mile-long convoy of horn-blowing vehicles escorted him into town. The local Harlem School of Boxing made him an honorary member and presented him with a copy of the Qur'an. As always, he played with the children—vast crowds of them laughing and leaping in excitement—and told the press, "I want them to learn how beautiful and great they are."

The warmth of the spontaneous welcome he received from the poor in Africa had a huge impact on the young champion. It was one thing to meet diplomats at the UN; it was another to be confronted with the African masses, without protocol and without a common language. Ali learned for the first time that he could overcome the barriers and clown and tease and mime his way into people's hearts. His constituency was broader than the ghettos and television studios of America, and the more he came to realize that, the more he felt responsible to this broader constituency. The African crowds helped deepen his sense of mission.

After Ghana, Ali visited Nigeria and Egypt, where he toured the pyramids and was welcomed by Nasser, another stalwart of the non-aligned movement and American bogeyman. Ali later claimed that Nasser had offered him a palace on the Nile and one of his daughters to marry—a typical example of his flip fusion of Hollywood exoticism and international politics. The reception in Egypt was more subdued than in Ghana. This was an Islamic country. Elijah Muhammad had cultivated clerical and business contacts there for some time, and the official itinerary took precedence over unscripted interaction with people in the streets. What's more, Egypt, unlike Ghana, had no boxing culture, and Ali was more admired there as a hero of the faith than of the ring. But wherever he went, Ali noted the contrast between the respect he was accorded abroad and the insults heaped on him at home. Years later, Osman Karriem, who was removed from Ali's camp shortly after the African trip because of his suspected links with Malcolm, told Hauser: "I'll remember that trip to Africa as long as I live, because that was where I saw Cassius Clay become Muhammad Ali. . . . It was in Africa that he became something he hadn't been before."

One of the few American journalists to cover Ali's African journey was Charles P. Howard, a veteran pan-Africanist who had been among Paul Robeson's most vocal defenders, and who was now working as an international correspondent for *Muhammad Speaks* and other black newspapers. Noting that the new heavyweight champ already boasted "the strongest international following of any American fighter in history," Howard praised him as "basically a democratic, grassroots type of Afro-American, although he wears at all times the unseen mantle and the dignified demeanor befitting his rank." Ali may be an "assertive, cocksure, determined and don't-fence-me-in type, but isn't the new African-American all of this? Isn't this the pattern of thousands of black youth who are being beaten, kicked, arrested, mistreated all across the United States? They are making it plain to white America that they have had enough and that they are not asking the white man for a thing—they are going to take what is rightfully theirs come hell or high water." All of which sounded a lot more like Malcolm's vision of insurgent black America than Elijah Muhammad's "Lost-Found Nation of Islam."

The irony of Ali's curt and bitter meeting with Malcolm in Accra was that both men were, in their different ways, heading towards the same destiny, a fusion of black pride with universal humanism. Malcolm confessed to Alex Haley that he had been deeply wounded by the encounter and by Ali's later comment to the press about it: "No one listens to Malcolm any more." But Ali was wrong about Malcolm. The renegade was not alone. From Accra he had flown to Liberia, Senegal, Morocco and Algeria. On his return to New York in late May, he announced his plans to take the plight of American blacks before the UN. In June, he founded his Organization of Afro-American Unity, inspired by Nkrumah's Organization of African

Unity, which in turn had been inspired by Du Bois's pan-African conferences. Just as black American song had been exported to Britain, repackaged and sold back to America, so a black American political project had been relocated to Africa, and from there returned to America in an invigorated form. In both music and politics, these cycles of the Black Atlantic interchange catalyzed artistic and political vanguards and, ultimately, changes in popular consciousness.

• • •

In July 1964, Wallace Muhammad publicly denounced his father and the Nation of Islam as "ruthless and fanatic." His studies of the Qur'an had led him to reject Elijah's heterodox version of Islam, and he disapproved of his father's adulteries and the luxurious lifestyle of his intimate circle. After his statement, Wallace was left without an income or a job, without friends or family, and subject to a steady stream of menaces. His brother Herbert, a more easy-going personality, had by now assumed charge of Ali's financial affairs. According to Jeremiah Shabazz, Herbert liked "the boxing business and the money that was involved." He ran a photography studio and introduced Ali to one of his models, Sonji. Forty-one days later she became Ali's first wife.

Meanwhile, Elijah Muhammad's attorney, Chauncey Eskridge, had become Ali's legal representative and was trying to organize a replacement for the Louisville syndicate. Eskridge was not a member of the Nation of Islam. He was a former IRS agent and accountant who was now a partner in a prestigious Chicago law firm, a worldly and wealthy black professional. He had already represented both Malcolm X and Martin Luther King, and had formed a close friendship with the latter (four years later, when King was assassinated in a Memphis hotel, Eskridge was at his side). In September, while visiting Ali in his Miami training camp, Eskridge called King to discuss business matters, then put Ali on the phone. Thanks to the FBI, we have an agent's summary of the conversation:

> MLK spoke to Cassius, they exchanged greetings, MLK wished him well on his recent marriage, C invited MLK to be his guest at his next championship fight, MLK said he would like to attend. C said he is keeping up with MLK, that MLK is his brother, and he's with him 100% but can't take any chances, and that MLK should take care of himself, that MLK is known worldwide and should watch out for them whities, said that people in Nigeria, Egypt and Ghana asked about MLK.

Ali spoke to King at the end of one of the civil rights movement's most bruising summers. In May 1964, outside Philadelphia, Mississippi, civil rights workers Chaney, Goodman and Schwerner had been murdered by the Klan in collusion with local police. The killings were meant to serve as a warning to outside agitators and their local black allies, but failed to deter hundreds of volunteers, black and white, flooding into the state to play their part in "Freedom Summer"—a mass campaign of voter education and registration. The volunteers faced mob violence, arrests and arson. By the summer's end there were 6 dead, 1000 jailed, 30 buildings bombed and 36 black churches burned. Yet for all their pains the activists had succeeded in registering only 1600 blacks, while 16,000 more had been turned away by obdurate local authorities.

In the course of that summer, however, 80,000 blacks did join the Mississippi Freedom Democratic party (MFDP), which challenged the official, whites-only Mississippi state delegation at that year's Democratic convention in Atlantic City. The refusal of Johnson and the official party machine to seat the MFDP was a traumatic setback for the movement. Significantly, the blow was delivered by the movement's own white liberal allies: Hubert Humphrey, Walter Mondale and Walter Reuther. It seemed that Humphrey's vice-presidential nomination, LBJ's determination to hold the South in the coming presidential election and the moderate civil rights leaders' desire to placate Johnson would supersede the MFDP's unanswerable case for enfranchisement. It was a bitter defeat for the workers of the Student Non-Violent Co-ordinating Committee (SNCC), which had emerged from the sit-ins of 1960 and whose grass-roots organizing efforts were at the heart of the MFDP. Their mood was summed up by Charles Sherrod: "We are a country of racists with a racist heritage, a racist economy, a racist language, a racist religion, a racist philosophy of living and we need a naked confrontation with ourselves." Harry Belafonte, the black celebrity who most consistently supported the freedom movement, arranged for the activists to take a much-needed break in Ghana, where they were received as heroes of the African-American struggle. Two of the SNCC tourists, John Lewis and Don Harris, proceeded further into Africa. In Nairobi, they ran into Malcolm X, who was staying at the same hotel, and spent several hours in discussion with him.

Malcolm had returned to Africa in July to attend the second meeting of the Organization of African Unity in Cairo. The invitation to this gathering, issued by Nkrumah and Nasser, was the chief fruit of Malcolm's visit earlier in the year and had been issued in defiance of State Department pressure. Like both Garvey and Du Bois, Malcolm had decided that "the time has come to internationalize the American Negro problem. This can only be done by linking the fate of the new African states with that of American Negroes." He found African leaders sympathetic, but reluctant to take on the United States, especially given the chain of events in the Congo.

Malcolm had remained in Egypt until the end of the summer. He then moved on to Saudi Arabia and Kuwait. In Ethiopia, he was spurned by Haile Selassie, a State Department ally, but in Tanzania he enjoyed a three-hour audience with Nyerere. He was in Kenya to meet Kenyatta when he ran into Lewis and Harris. "The man who sat with us in that hotel room was enthusiastic and excited—not angry, not brooding," Lewis recalled. "He seemed very hopeful." Malcolm spoke of the need to shift the movement's focus "from race to class." "He said that was the root of our problems, not just in America but all over the world." Lewis also observed that "beyond his excitement and blossoming optimism, there was fear in the man, a nervousness that was written all over him." Throughout his travels, he had been under CIA surveillance. A State Department memorandum noted that Malcolm X "has for all practical purposes, renounced his US citizenship." From Kenya, Malcolm proceeded to Nigeria, Ghana, Liberia and Guinea, where he was Sekou Turé's house guest. After stops in North Africa and Europe, he returned to New York City on 24 November.

The day before, Johnson had ordered air strikes in the Congo, allegedly to protect American citizens caught in the civil war. Malcolm was quick to denounce the US intervention, which, he said, was designed to assist "Moise Tshombe's hired killers," who had now assumed control in Léopoldville. En route to receive his Nobel Prize, Martin Luther King called for the withdrawal of all "foreign elements" from the region. Randolph, Young and Wilkins also expressed concern. Malcolm threw himself into a whirlwind of public and private meetings with African and Asian diplomats, who were mounting an attack on US "neo-colonialism" in the United Nations. At the end of December, he shared a platform with MFDP leader Fannie Lou Hamer in Harlem. Hamer asked why the US could intervene to protect white settlers in the Congo but not negro citizens in Mississippi. Malcolm measured American claims against American realities and concluded that the US was "the most hypocritical government since the world began."

Ali was in Boston training for his rematch with Liston when he suffered a hernia. The match was postponed. In a Boston hotel on Christmas Day 1964, Leon 4X Ameer, Ali's "press secretary," was beaten up by members of the Nation of Islam posing as newsmen. Among the assailants was Ali's bodyguard, Clarence X Gill. Ameer was treated in hospital, but assaulted again on his return to the hotel.

Although Ameer had been a confidant of Malcolm X, he had remained in Ali's employ. On 9 January 1965, he called a press conference in the Theresa to publicize his ordeal, including his fractured skull, broken ribs and ruptured eardrum. He claimed the champion was "beginning to have grave doubts about" powerful figures in the Nation of Islam and said he feared Ali might be injured or killed in "Black Muslim in-fighting." "I joined the movement in 1956 and was a member of the inner circle. I taught the Muslims karate from Miami to Buffalo," Ameer told the press. "Clay is being used to woo young men and women into the Muslim fold. He is a dedicated young man who believes in the spiritual movement of the Muslims, but the truth is that the spiritual sense of the organization is just about dead and a strong ruthless structure has taken over." In another room in the hotel, Ali held a press conference of his own. "Ameer's nothing to me," he said. "He was welcomed as a friend so long as he was a registered Muslim, but not anymore. And he was never my press secretary. I do my own press work and publicity." A few days later, at a Fruit of Islam dinner-dance at the Audubon Ballroom, Ali told the faithful, "Malcolm believed the white press which referred to him as the number two man, and became disillusioned."

In February, *Muhammad Speaks* claimed Ameer was plotting to kill Elijah Muhammad and ran the headline "WANTED" over his photograph. According to Ameer, the Nation was out to get him for two reasons. First, because they knew he had broken his oath of secrecy by informing Malcolm of the plans to kill him. Second, because he had told Muhammad Ali that the Nation was "milking him," and as a result Ali had complained to the Chicago office. Around the same time, Betty Shabazz ran into Ali at the Theresa. She recalled to Hauser how she had reproached the former family friend. "You see what they're doing to my husband, don't you?" "And he said to me with his hands in the air, 'I haven't done anything. I'm not doing anything to him.'"

On 4 February, Malcolm made his first visit to the frontlines of the civil rights battle in the South. In the previous week, hundreds of Selma schoolchildren had been attacked by George Wallace's Alabama state troopers. King himself had been arrested. Malcolm met with King's wife and warned the media that if the moderate Dr. King wasn't listened to, the white man would have to deal with "other factions" who would "try to do it another way." Malcolm then flew to Britain, where he addressed the Council of African Organizations and a meeting at the London School of Economics. He proceeded to Paris, where he was denied entry as an "undesirable." He returned to New York on 13 February; the next day, his home was firebombed.

In one of his last press conferences he tried to explain his evolving philosophy:

> We are living in an era of revolution, and the revolt of the American Negro is part of the rebellion against the oppression and colonialism which has characterized this era. . . . It is incorrect to classify the revolt of the Negro as simply a racial conflict of black against white, or as a purely American problem. Rather, we are today seeing a global rebellion of the oppressed against the oppressor, the exploited against the exploiter."

In the end, Robert Hayden wrote, Malcolm X "became / much more than there was time for him to be." On 21 February, he was gunned down in front of his own supporters, the Organization of Afro-American Unity, on his own turf, the Audubon Ballroom in Harlem, in the presence of agents of the New York Police Department and the FBI. Elijah Muhammad called the act "divine chastisement." That night, a fire of unknown origin blazed in Ali's apartment. Asked if he feared an act of vengeance by Malcolm's people, Ali sneered, "Malcolm ain't got no people." If this was so, it raised the question of just who staged the arson attack that same night on the Nation's Mosque No. 7, Malcolm's old Harlem pulpit. In Africa, the US

Information Agency did its best to play down Malcolm's significance, reminding foreign editors that he had enjoyed no sizeable following in the US. But his assassination was front-page news in the countries he had visited. The *Ghanaian Times* praised him as a man in the tradition of John Brown and Patrice Lumumba.

A week later, at the annual Savior's Day rally in Chicago, Elijah Muhammad told his followers, "We didn't want to kill Malcolm and didn't try to kill Malcolm. They know I didn't harm Malcolm. They know I loved him. His foolish teaching brought him to his own end." Ali sat behind the Messenger on the platform and cheered with the rest. What must he have thought as the repentant Wallace was paraded before his father's followers to confess his "great mistake" and declare his acceptance of all his father's views?

On 10 March, Leon 4X Ameer called the FBI to discuss Malcolm's death and to offer help in identifying the assassins. A meeting was arranged for 12 March. On 11 March, a maid found him dead in his hotel room. It was later ruled that the thirty-two year old had died from unspecified natural causes.

The Autobiography of Malcolm X was rushed into print. It sold 250,000 copies in paperback and laid the basis for his posthumous legend. "It was a pity and a disgrace he died like that," Ali told Thomas Hauser, twenty-five years on, "because what Malcolm saw was right, and after he left us, we went his way anyway. Color didn't make a man a devil. It's the heart, soul and mind that counts."

• • •

Ali did not fight for fifteen months after winning the title, which gave the press plenty of opportunity to snipe at his private life. Although

Ali had met Sonji through Herbert Muhammad, she bridled at the Nation's strict rules about women's dress and demeanor. As she tells the story, she was also beginning to ask awkward questions about Elijah Muhammad and his lieutenants, and found herself "frozen out" of her husband's life. The couple separated and filed for divorce.

On 25 May, in Lewiston, Maine, Ali at last defended his title, knocking out Liston in the first round. The famous "phantom punch" that put Liston on the mat did little, however, to enhance Ali's fighting reputation or his standing with the press. He signed to fight the long-time white favorite, Floyd Patterson, in Las Vegas.

Shortly after Ali's first victory over Liston, Patterson had declared that, "as a Catholic," it was his duty to "reclaim the title for America"—as if a foreigner had won it. Three weeks later, the earnest advocate of integration was forced to sell his $140,000 house in Yonkers, New York, for a $20,000 loss after white neighbors subjected his family to racist abuse. In October 1965, Patterson wrote in *Sports Illustrated*, "Cassius Clay is disgracing himself and the Negro race. . . . The image of a Black Muslim as the world heavyweight champion disgraces the sport and the nation. Cassius Clay must be beaten and the Black Muslim scourge removed from boxing." Patterson initiated the battle of the role models, but Ali met the challenge head-on, subjecting Patterson to weeks of verbal abuse.

> Patterson says he's gonna bring the title back to America. If you don't believe the title already is in America, just see who I pay taxes to. I'm American. But he's a deaf dumb so-called Negro who needs a spanking. I plan to punish him for the

> things he said; cause him pain. . . . The little old pork-chop eater don't have a chance.

According to Arthur Ashe, "No black athlete had ever publicly spoken so disparagingly to another black athlete." Ali's doggerel was cruel:

> I'm gonna put him flat on his back,
> So that he will start acting black,
> Because when he was champ he didn't do as he should,
> He tried to force himself into an all-white neighborhood.

At the fight itself, Patterson was outclassed. Heedless of the mounting outrage of ringside commentators, Ali dragged the fight out to the twelfth round, punishing Patterson with his fists, then stepping back and allowing him time to recover while taunting him, "Come on America! Come on white America!" The white press denounced it as a cruel and malicious performance. At the other extreme, Eldridge Cleaver called the fight "ideologically, a pivotal event, reflecting the consolidation of certain psychic gains of the Negro revolution. . . . Symbolic proof of the victory of the autonomous over the subordinate Negro . . . the victory of a new world over an old world, of life and light over Lazarus and the darkness of the grave." Patterson's partisans could have accepted that last, Manichean view of the forces in conflict in this fight, only they would have reversed the polarity. Discounting the trademark Cleaver hyperbole, this passage in *Soul on Ice* does reveal how symbolically charged Ali's fights had become, even at this early stage of his career. He had re-configured all the values previously associated with black men in the ring, and had done so with not a little assistance from Floyd Patterson.

In retrospect, Gerald Early believes that Patterson was "the most disturbed and disturbing black presence in the history of American popular culture." Certainly, he embraced the duties of the role model with ardor, and lived out its contradictions in pain. Patterson himself commented later: "There is so much hate among people, so much contempt inside people who'd like to think they're moral, that they have to hire prizefighters to do their hating for them. And we do. We get into a ring and act out other people's hates. We are happy to do it. How else can Negroes like Clay and myself, born in the South, poor, and with little education, make so much money?"

Despite the avalanche of press criticism, Ali remained unrepentant. "People are always telling me what a good example I could be if I just wasn't a Muslim," he said. "I've heard it over and over, how come I couldn't be like Joe Louis and Sugar Ray. Well, they're gone now, and the black man's condition is just the same, ain't it? We're still catching hell."

In the Congo, three days after the Patterson fight, Joseph Mobutu staged a coup d'etat with American support. The former army paymaster announced he was assuming the presidency for five years. Moving quickly to consolidate power, he employed Belgian, South African and British mercenaries to crush rivals and rebels. Moise Tshombe, who had backed Mobutu, was forced into exile in Europe, where he confessed his role in Lumumba's execution.

• • •

In early July 1963, the twenty-one-year-old Bob Dylan flew from New York to Greenwood, Mississippi, where SNCC activists were conducting a voter registration drive. For decades, the black population in the delta country around Greenwood had been terrorized by one of the most tyrannical Jim Crow regimes anywhere in the South. In the six months before Dylan's visit, civil rights workers had faced beatings, shootings, arson and imprisonment. They needed outside support and media attention, and Dylan's visit, which had been organized by Pete Seeger, promised both.

It was Dylan's first close-up look at Jim Crow and at the people who had risen to challenge it. Like others, his evolution was to be profoundly affected by his brief encounter with the era's premier agents of social change. But distressed as he was by his first sight of a whites-only water fountain, Dylan did not come unprepared. For at least two years he had been writing songs inspired by the freedom struggle ("Death of Emmett Till," "Oxford Town") and by the emergent new left critique of the Cold War ("Talkin' John Birch Paranoid Blues," "Let Me Die in My Footsteps"). In the early sixties, the folk revival and the civil rights movement had become intimately linked, not only because the folk singers were more prepared than other entertainers to put their time at the disposal of the activists, but also because they shared a self-consciously American idealism ("This land is our land . . ."), sharply counterposed to the fast-buck America epitomized by the cynical pop music industry.

Dylan's early topical protest songs are sometimes dismissed as derivative and didactic, but the best of them have proved remarkably durable. They are rarely without flashes of acid originality and are less sentimental than other products of the folk revival. What's more, the issues they deal with have remained topical, thanks to the radical edge of Dylan's political perspective. This is most strikingly revealed in his narratives of racial and class oppression, "Hollis Brown" and "Hattie Carroll," and in his indictment of the hidden profiteers of the Cold War; his "Masters of War" was written five years before students across the country rose up against university collusion with the military-industrial complex: "You that build the death planes / you that build the big bombs / you that hide behind walls / you that hide behind desks." In "With God on Our Side" Dylan subjected the whole of American history and national identity to an iconoclastic revision worthy of Malcolm X. Even before his break with the liberals, he was no liberal.

Dylan spent two and a half days with the spartan SNCC workers and their poverty-stricken local allies, and by all accounts was awed by their courage and commitment, suffering and directness. He exchanged ideas with Jim Foreman, Julian Bond and Berenice Johnson Reagon of the SNCC Freedom Singers (and later of Sweet Honey in the Rock), whom he'd already met at the Newport Folk Festival. Along with Seeger and others, he performed on the back of a truck at the edge of a cotton field to a crowd of three hundred, mostly local blacks, plus a TV crew from New York, which captured Dylan's raw performance of a new protest classic, "Only a Pawn in Their Game," a song composed just weeks before in response to the assassination of Medgar Evers. In contrast to the moralistic and utopian rhetoric favored by the movement at this time, Dylan's song argued that racist violence was the product of political manipulation and an unjust social system. As it happened, the killer of Medgar Evers, the wealthy and well-connected Byron de la Beckwith, was not "only a pawn in their game." Nonetheless, Dylan's exposé of the white elite's divide-and-rule strategy and his insistence on the link between poverty and racism struck powerful chords among the SNCC activists, whose thinking about the nature of the challenge they faced was undergoing rapid evolution.

After his brief stay in one of America's poorest and most oppressed communities, Dylan was whisked off to a Columbia Records sales conference in Puerto Rico. *Freewheelin'*, his second album, just released, was on its way to selling more than 200,000 copies—unprecedented for a folk singer. Peter, Paul and Mary's cover of "Blowin' in the Wind" had become the first "protest song" to achieve chart success. Dylan was a hot commercial property. But he was clearly, also, not just another studio-manufactured pop star. His audiences were young but serious, and they came not just for the music but for the message. To the media, Dylan quickly became "the voice of a generation," one of the earliest of a succession of youth cult heroes, a social phenomenon requiring interpretation and interrogation. This status was re-enforced in August, seven weeks after his visit to Greenwood, at the March on Washington, where Peter, Paul and Mary sang "Blowin' in the Wind" and Dylan himself performed "Only a Pawn in Their Game," a song more in tune with the bitter and impatient mood of John Lewis's partially censored speech than with King's dream of racial reconciliation.

Dylan's class-based approach was welcomed by the veterans of the old left, the torch-bearers of the Popular Front through years of repression. Many saw in Dylan the people's artist they'd been seeking since Robeson was silenced, someone who could speak to the masses in an accessible idiom while at the same time placing his art at the service of the crusade for social justice. In recognition of his achievement, Dylan was awarded the 1963 Tom Paine Award by the Emergency Civil Liberties Committee (ECLC), an organization that had battled McCarthyism at its height. On 13 December, three weeks after the Kennedy assassination, Dylan attended the ECLC's annual Bill of Rights dinner in New York to receive the award. He drank heavily during the course of the evening, and his rambling acceptance speech managed to offend just about everyone in the house. "It's took me a long time to get young and now I consider myself young and I'm proud of it," he told this conclave of ageing left-wingers. He wanted "to see faces with hair on their head" because "old people when their hair grows out they should go out."

> I've never seen one history book that tells me how anybody feels. . . . And it don't help me one little bit to look back . . . there's no black and white, left and right to me anymore. . . . I was at the March on Washington up on the platform and I looked around at all the negroes there and I didn't see any negroes that looked like none of my friends. My friends don't wear suits. My friends don't have to wear any kind of thing to prove they're respectable negroes.

Dylan claimed he was accepting the award on behalf of SNCC, James Foreman and a socialist youth group that had gone to Cuba, all of which enhanced his left-wing, grass-roots credentials. He also declared himself in favor of free travel to Cuba, a sentiment which must have pleased most of those present, though it would have terrified his record executives. Still, Dylan had not said all he had to say:

> I'll stand up and to get uncompromiseable about it, which I have to be to be honest, I just got to be, as I got to admit that the man who shot President Kennedy, Lee Oswald, I don't know exactly where, what he thought he was doing, but I got to admit that I too—I saw something of myself in him.

The young singer was vigorously booed by his elders. At that moment, to speak ill of the dead president—worse yet, to identify with his killer—was to breach the most daunting taboo in America, a taboo which neither the old left nor the liberals were prepared to violate. Interestingly, it was the same taboo that Malcolm had breached two weeks earlier, thereby precipitating his final split with Elijah Muhammad.

Dylan's impromptu speech outraged many of his admirers, and at this distance it seems fair to describe it as the drunken, spiteful outburst of an immature young man. But there was method in it, and even in the identification with Oswald there was more than just the desire to shock. Six months later, commenting on the incident to Nat Hentoff, Dylan repudiated his role as political spokesperson and insisted, "I just can't make it with any organization." As for his behavior at the Bill of Rights dinner, he blamed it on a negative reaction to finding himself in a room full of well-heeled whites salving their social consciences. "Here were these people who'd been all involved with the left in the thirties and now they're supporting civil rights drives. That's groovy, but they also had minks and jewels, and it was like they were giving their money out of guilt. . . . These people at that dinner were the same as everybody else. They're doing their time. They're chained to what they're doing."

Clearly, even as he was lauded as the voice of an awakening social conscience, something was being born inside Dylan which could not be squeezed into the identities fixed for him either by the record execs or the political missionaries. The tangled themes of Dylan's rant at the Bill of Rights dinner, which reappear in his master songs of the mid sixties, tell us much about this central figure of the decade at a critical moment in his development. The contempt for liberalism, which informs Dylan's writing from the earliest days, seems driven here by hip anti-intellectualism as much as by impatient radicalism. His assertion of the pre-eminence of youth might be taken as a declaration of independence, echoing the messianic generational challenge of "The Times They Are A-Changin'" (released a month after the dinner). But there is also something despairing and embittered in this repudiation of history and all existing political categories, and not surprisingly Dylan was to be repeatedly accused of nihilism in the years to come. The concern with class guilt is intertwined with a search for personal authenticity, an authenticity embodied for Dylan in Foreman and the SNCC activists, whose immediate involvement in the struggle exposed the comfortable detachment of middle-class do-gooders. The example of black youth in the South and America's violent response to their challenge posed probing questions for Dylan, as they did for Ali. Strangely, for different reasons and in different ways, in both cases the example served as a pretext for withdrawing from active political struggle. In "11 Outlined Epitaphs," the liner notes for *The Times They Are A Changin'*, Dylan addresses Foreman:

> Jim, Jim
> where is our party?

where is the party that's one
where all members're held equal
an' vow t'infiltrate that thought
among the people it hopes t'serve
an' sets a respected road
for all of those like me

For Dylan, the incandescent purity of SNCC's face-to-face struggle in the South had exposed the emptiness not only of traditional politics, but of the entire discourse of American democracy. Dylan criticized the ECLC patrons because "they're doing their time," making an accommodation with American materialism, whose grasp he had come to see (under the influence of Allen Ginsberg) reaching into the deepest recesses of the soul. His identification with Oswald was a powerful means of registering an alienation from American norms that had gone way beyond disquiet over racism and nuclear arms. It was also in keeping with Dylan's fondness for the outlaw conceit ("I may look like Robert Ford but I feel just like Jesse James"), a conceit that crops up throughout the history of popular culture, not least in the blues and country traditions which Dylan had studied so well. Above all, in declaring his independence from the movement, and disdaining the "protest singer" appellation, Dylan was spurning his symbolic and representative role, the role both the media and the movement had assigned to him.

In early February 1964, Dylan embarked on a long, wayward, drug-fueled road trip. He visited coal miners in Harlan County, Carl Sandburg in Asheville, Berenice Johnson Reagon in Atlanta, Bob Moses and Tom Hayden in Mississippi. He was in New Orleans for

Mardi Gras and in Dallas he haunted Dealey Plaza. On the night Cassius Clay deposed Sonny Liston in Miami, Dylan performed his first major West Coast gig, at the University of California at Berkeley, which was to be convulsed by the Free Speech Movement later that year. In May, he traveled to London, Paris and Greece. Shortly after his return in June, he recorded in two nights the eleven songs that make up *Another Side of Bob Dylan.*

When the album was released later that year it distressed many of his most passionate defenders, confirming rumors of Dylan's apostasy from the political and aesthetic creed of the folk revival. Not only did much of it seem excessively personal ("It Ain't Me Babe," "Ballad in Plain D"), and some of it expressly anti-intellectual ("All I Really Want to Do") and anti-political ("My Back Pages"); worse yet, much of it was obscure—an unforgivable sin for a people's artist. Even "Chimes of Freedom," conceived as Dylan drove through a stormy Mississippi night, was damned for its profuse imagery and metaphysical conundrums. Here, as the thunder and lightning of contemporary history clash and flash in the background, Dylan invokes the SNCC workers he'd met in Greenwood ("the warriors whose strength is not to fight"), but links their fate to an epic cast of the dispossessed, ranging from "the mistreated mateless mother, the mistitled prostitute" to "each unharmful gentle soul misplaced inside a jail," and ultimately embracing "the countless confused, accused, misused, strung-out ones an' worse." It was Dylan's most sweeping vision of solidarity with the oppressed, and one of the most moving expressions of the broadening of sympathies that was an underlying (but by no means uncontested) trend of the

Top. Paul Robeson as "Bosambo" in *Sanders on the River, The Museum of Modern Art Film Stills Archive,* New York. *Bottom.* Tommy Smith and John Carlos make their protest at the 1968 Olympics in Mexico City. *Schomburg Center for Research in Black Culture,* New York

Top. The Hotel Theresa in the heart of Harlem, where Ali, Malcolm X and Sam Cooke met in 1963. *Photograph by Austin Hansen, used by permission of Joyce Hansen and the Schomburg Center for Research in Black Culture. Bottom.* Olympic gold medallist Cassius Clay, on his return to America, 1960. *Pan American World Airways Systems*

Top. One side of Sam Cooke: performing for a black audience, 1963. *The Chicago Defender. Bottom.* Escorted by police, Ali leaves Arsenal stadium in London after defeating Henry Cooper, 1966. *AP Worldwide Photos*

Top. Jackie Robinson testifies at a Senate hearing, 1963. *Baseball Hall of Fame Library, Cooperstown, New York.* *Bottom.* Ali appeals against his I-A draft classification, March 1966. *AP Worldwide Photos*

Ali with Martin Luther King, Louisville, March 1967. *AP Worldwide Photos*

The new heavyweight champion tours Harlem with Malcolm X. *Robert L. Haggins*

Ali promoting *Muhammad Speaks*, the paper of the Nation of Islam, 1964. *Robert L. Haggins*

Don King and Ali confer in Kinshasa, 1974, under a portrait of dictator Mobutu Sese Seko. *Corbis/Bettmann-UPI*

era. Yet it appears on the same album as "My Back Pages," in which Dylan transmuted the rude incoherence of his Bill of Rights rant into the organized density of art. Here, he recants his own political past, those days (not long before) when, "proud neath heated brow," his time was consumed by "memorizing politics of ancient history," before he discovered, "I'd become my enemy in the instant that I preach."

> A self-ordained professor's tongue
> Too serious to fool
> Spouted out that liberty
> Is just equality in school
> Equality I spoke the word
> As if a wedding vow
> Oh but I was so much older then,
> I'm younger than that now.

Like Malcolm (and Ali), Dylan had come to see the integrationist struggle ("equality in school") as an irrelevance. He had discovered that "liberty" was more elusive than he had assumed. But, unlike the black radicals, he turned this political crisis into an existential one: "Good and bad I define these terms, quite clear, no doubt, somehow." Was anyone ever as quickly, or as tenderly, disillusioned as the young Dylan? And was anyone ever more arrogant?

One of the lesser songs on *Another Side* is "I Shall Be Free No. 10," a light-hearted exercise in doggerel in which Dylan takes sideswipes at liberals, conservatives and just about anyone who takes themselves too seriously. I have to admit I had totally forgotten it until, in the course of researching this book, I listened to the album for the first time in years and its second verse leapt out at me:

> I was shadow-boxing earlier in the day
> I figured I was ready for Cassius Clay
> I said fee, fie, fo, fum, Cassius Clay, here I come
> 26, 27, 28, 29, I'm gonna make your face look just like mine
> 5, 4, 3, 2, 1, Cassius Clay you'd better run
> 99, 100, 101, 102, your ma won't even recognize you
> 14, 15, 16, 17, 18, 19, gonna knock him clean right out of his spleen

The topical reference to the new heavyweight champion was in keeping with the folk tradition, but in his efforts to match the Louisville Lip rhyme for rhyme, boast for boast, Dylan strayed into new territory. This serious young man was on a quest to transcend seriousness; it's not surprising that the wise fool Cassius Clay should enter his fantasies.

The dour elements of the folk set resented Dylan's love of nonsense, his manic humor, his compulsive need to puncture the solemnity of public ritual—traits he shared with Ali, and which were to become as much the hallmarks of the sixties (and not only in America) as po-faced political protest. In the face of violence and disorder at home and abroad, and the corruption of official discourse, absurdist humor flourished; in context, it appeared a form of radical honesty, promising even at times an alternative rationality. Dylan and Ali shared a love of the shaggy dog story, but it is important to note that even as the embittered Dylan elaborated his persecution fantasies ("Look out kid / It's something you did / God knows when but you're doin' it again"), it was the more accommodating Ali who was actually being persecuted.

The saga of Dylan's going electric, and the response of his erstwhile fans, is an oft-told tale, but it was his earlier repudiation of "the movement" that really broke his ties with the folk revival and the older generation, and unleashed his innovative genius. Dylan's turn away from politics was to become a recurring motif in the years to come, as wave after wave of young people engaged in and were scarred by political activity. Strange as it may sound when speaking of such a politically polarized era, Dylan's shift from the political to the personal was one of the defining moments of the American sixties, as surely as Ali's embrace of the Nation of Islam. "*I don't have to be what you want me to be.*" It could almost be a line from a Dylan song:

Well I try my best
To be just like I am
But everybody wants you
To be just like them

Dylan's rejection of political involvement and his conversion to rock and roll put him beyond the comprehension of the traditional left as surely as Cassius Clay's embrace of the Nation of Islam. Yet ultimately both proved more in tune with an evolving mass audience than their critics could even begin to imagine. All the clout, the social reach, that the "people's artists" of yesteryear had sought in vain, all the cultural ambitions of the Popular Front, these kids seemed to achieve without solemnity, without humility, without ideology.

Dylan and Ali were born within eight months of each other. In the early sixties, they emerged simultaneously into a remarkable historical conjuncture in which economic growth, demographic change (the emergence of youth as a market for consumer goods) and technological innovation (in broadcasting and recording) collided with an insurgent mass politics founded in resistance to racism and war. Sports and popular music were both entering into a more intimate relationship with the newly dominant medium, television, which was then taking its first tentative transcontinental steps. It is impossible to imagine either the careers or the mystiques of these two "sixties icons" unfolding outside this conjuncture. In their very early twenties they found themselves enmeshed in a formative phase of today's global celebrity culture. Even as fame of unprecedented dimensions enveloped them, they were just embarking on their individual journeys of self-discovery.

Like Ali, Dylan had changed his name; unlike Ali, he did so quietly and covertly, in the old show-business tradition. Later, the press delighted in exposing the exotic Bob Dylan as the ordinary Robert Zimmerman. Both Dylan and Ali were avid for self-definition and dissatisfied with the available models of pop celebrity. Both struggled to control their own careers and to retain their personal integrity amid the demands of commerce and the media. Swept up in the vortex of the American success machinery, and intensely aware of its perils, Dylan and Ali remained determined to set their own goals and speak in their own voices. Both felt themselves part of a separate culture, wedded to values at odds with America's mainstream; and both were aware, often uncomfortably, that they were expected to speak for a separate, silent constituency. But here their ways parted, as they seized upon radically divergent strategies to deal with fame and the burdens of representation.

Dylan had sought celebrity, as determinedly as Ali, but he found its impositions and intrusions painfully disorientating. This twenty-two year old wanted the freedom to experiment with life—not easy under the klieg lights. In an effort to recapture and protect his identity—and not least his capacity to change and grow—Dylan retreated behind a mask of truculent enigma ("Don't ask me nothin' 'bout nothin'—I just might tell you the truth"). The opening scene of that magnificently mordant sneer, "Ballad of a Thin Man," sums up Dylan's mid-sixties view of the media:

You walk into the room
With your pencil in your hand
You see somebody naked
And you say, who is that man?
You try so hard
But you don't understand
Just what you'll say when you get home
Because something is happening here
But you don't know what it is,
Do you, Mr. Jones?

Confronted with Dylan and Ali, bewildered older journalists asked how seriously they were supposed to take these pop-poet clowns? How seriously did they take themselves? Even George Plimpton wondered if the whole Ali show was no more than a "gigantic put-on." However, while Dylan could be obnoxious toward interviewers (and members of his own entourage), Ali, who was probably more goaded and provoked, preferred to extend the benefit of the doubt. Where Dylan was suspicious, withdrawn and hostile, Ali was expansive, accessible and usually good-humored. As Dylan came to speak less and less, and in ever more gnostic riddles, Ali came to speak more and more, and ever more plainly. Dylan's response to misrepresentation by the media was to abandon all attempts to communicate outside his music, to satirize and fracture the very idea of a shared public discourse that could say anything meaningful about individual lives. Ali's response was to seize and master the tools of the trade—the press conference, the photo opportunity, the television lens and the radio microphone—in an attempt to construct his own image and reach out to his own public. Ali loved to bait and tease the journalists, but if they played along with him they were in for the ride of their lives. This rapport was to stand him in good stead during his long battle with the government and boxing officialdom, when Lipsyte, Cosell, the BBC's Harry Carpenter, McIlvanney, Plimpton, Mailer, Wolf and others ensured his case was heard. For anyone with eyes to see it, there was always self-doubt beneath Ali's bravado, and it was a measure of his trusting humanity that he was able to preserve and even share this trait under the glare of the limelight, just as it was a measure of Dylan's very different nature that he was not.

Ali and Dylan were first-generation children of the burgeoning electronic audio-visual culture, which was still at that time largely unrecognized as anything other than an inferior and distant cousin to the mature forms of western "high culture." Their public achievements and the controversies that surrounded them helped compel the intelligentsia to take pop culture seriously. By their boldness, their ambitions and, paradoxically, their playfulness, they made their disciplines—sport and popular music—worthy of study. Dylan himself liked to toy with this theme of high and low, elite and popular culture, reminding us that "Mona Lisa must've had the highway blues, you can tell by the way she smiles."

> And Ezra Pound and T.S. Eliot,
> Fighting in the captain's tower,
> While calypso singers laugh at them
> And fishermen hold flowers.

In 1965, Dylan told an interviewer, "Music is the only thing that's in tune with what's happening. It's not in book form, it's not on the stage. . . . It's not the bomb that has to go, man, it's the museums."

Out of this spirit of wise-guy iconoclasm and lofty superiority (and the loneliness and vulnerability they concealed) Dylan fashioned his three great albums of the mid sixties, *Bringing It All Back Home*, *Highway 61* and *Blonde on Blonde*. In these works, Dylan wears his bewilderment as a badge of truth-telling. Even as Dylan's earlier style was at its peak of popularity—adapted by Sonny and Cher, the Byrds, Buffy Sainte Marie, the Turtles, Barry McGuire and Donovan—he was heading off into the musical unknown, spewing out an astonishing flow of unique and powerful songs. Like Ali, he derived from the era an extraordinary self-confidence that enabled him to go his own way. His restlessness was a reflection of the age and became a stimulus to it. Even as he repudiated his representative function, his retreat into enigmatic silence induced his fans to scrutinize his every utterance and gesture for representative significance. Figuring out what Dylan was saying or thinking, where he was really at, became a preoccupation of the era.

From its ersatz hillbilly and Greenwich Village hipster origins, Dylan's voice evolved into a distinctively expressive instrument, soaring among the rock and roll clatter. Mixing magisterial put-downs and an aching sense of loss, delirious self-pity and ecstatic glee, Dylan really did become the voice of a generation. He mapped the inchoate emotional confusion of young people growing up amid the mayhem of a violent era marked by clashes over fundamental values. It is striking how often political events and concerns surface in these avowedly non-political songs. Dylan's critique of American society had broadened and deepened, so much so that it had gone beyond the merely political, but the targets can still be clearly identified: phone taps and paranoid DAs, lying media ("propaganda all is phoney"), omnipresent commercialism ("money doesn't talk, it swears"), affluent liberals with their "tax deductible charity organizations." In "Maggie's Farm"—inspired by "Penny's Farm," a protest song of the twenties—Dylan produced a masterpiece of anti-authoritarian venom, laced with class and generational contempt. Throughout this innovatory and demanding period, he was propelled (like Malcolm X) by the conviction that "he not busy being born / is busy dying."

Like Ali, Dylan took his fans on a journey. At times they traversed common terrain, but in the end reached different destinations. Dylan never spoke out against the Vietnam War. There's a brief reference in the liner notes for *Bringing It All Back Home*, where Dylan imagines a "middle-aged druggist up for district attorney" who "starts screaming at me, you're the one, you're the one that's been causin' all them riots over in Vietnam." But he wrote this in early 1965, and through the remaining eight years of direct American participation in the war, and more than a hundred published songs, he avoided the subject. The poet Michael McClure recalled discussing Vietnam with Dylan in 1966 and characterized the singer's beliefs at that time as Pentagon-style "first strike capability." For years Dylan ignored appeals from Allen Ginsberg and Joan Baez to appear at anti-war events. In the summer of 1968, he snapped at a presumptuous interviewer, "How do you know that I'm not, as you say, *for* the war?"

Even as the flags and draft cards were burned, Dylan sought a deeper engagement with American culture. In his flight from the escalating social conflict of the second half of the sixties, he abandoned the exotic and baroque elaboration of *Blonde on Blonde* for the conservatism of *The Basement Tapes* and *John Wesley Harding*. Here, he invoked a vanished, pre-commercial America of eccentrics and wastrels, thwarted hopes and buried suffering, an America assembled, as Greil Marcus has explained, from the fragments of a dark-tinged folk tradition neglected by the propagandists of the folk revival. Vietnam remains unmentioned, yet it's impossible to listen to Dylan's music of this period without feeling the war and the disorder it engendered hovering somehow in the background; and it's hard to see *The Basement Tapes* as other than a cry of loss from a secluded bunker. Dylan made art out of the chaos of the era, but for him that chaos was painful. Increasingly, he yearned for simplicity and permanence, and sought escape in an imagined America from the fires of fame and the demands of a social movement. History, not least the history of blackness in America, was to deny Ali that option.

Much as he may have disliked it, Dylan's music continued to provide the inescapable soundtrack to the student-based anti-war movement. In early 1964, "The Times They Are A Changin'" was fanciful hyperbole; by 1970, as the select band of earnest and idealistic students swelled into a youth army comprising millions, the lyrics seemed no more than an account of the salient facts of the era. It was no accident that toward the end of the decade one of his anti-authoritarian aphorisms—"You don't need a weatherman to know which way the wind blows"—provided a name for America's most notorious band of youth guerillas. Dylan once said the sixties were "like a flying saucer landed. . . . Everybody heard about it, but only a few really saw it." But thanks in part to Dylan himself, and Ali, and the mass market they served, many in fact did see it and felt themselves part of it.

In the mid seventies, Dylan returned briefly to protest. In "Hurricane," his ballad about the black boxer Rubin "Hurricane" Carter, imprisoned for a crime he did not commit, Dylan stressed the endurance of racism as the American norm:

> All of Rubin's cards were marked in advance
> The trial was a pig-circus, he never had a chance,
> The judge made Rubin's witnesses drunkards from the slums
> To the white folks who watched he was a revolutionary bum
> And to the black folks he was just a crazy nigger.
> No one doubted that he pulled the trigger.
> And though they could not produce the gun,

The DA said he was the one who did the deed
And the all-white jury agreed.

Ali and Dylan made their only joint public appearance at a mid-seventies benefit for the "Hurricane" at Madison Square Garden. "I know you all came here to see me," Ali declared buoyantly, "because Bob Dylan just ain't that big." Surveying the wealthy audience, whose diamonds and furs would have put the ECLC Bill of Rights gathering to shame, he reminded them: "You've got the connections and the complexion to get the protection." Despite his friends in high places, Carter was to spend another decade in jail before finally being freed following a judge's ruling that his earlier trial had been compromised by "appeals to racism."

4

Beyond the Confines of America

As the Vietnam War intensified, the draft call-up was expanded. In early 1966, the passing percentile in the intelligence test was lowered from 30 to 15, making Ali eligible for service. On 14 February, his lawyer asked the Louisville draft board either to postpone his reclassification or grant him a deferral. Three days later the request was denied and at the age of twenty-four—the top of the eligible range—Ali was reclassified 1-A, fit for combat.

Ali was training in Miami when he heard the news. His first reaction was bafflement. "Why me?" he kept asking. "I can't understand it." Robert Lipsyte, the *New York Times* sportswriter who spent much of that day with him, has described how, inundated by press queries, the disoriented champion finally blurted out the fateful riposte: "*Man, I ain't got no quarrel with them Vietcong.*"

This sentence would prove to be one of the most resonant of the sixties, but unlike Ali's exultant declaration after first winning the heavyweight championship—"*I don't have to be what you want me to be*"—it was an off-the-cuff remark, a cry of defensiveness and uncertainty. No one, least of all Ali himself, could foresee the huge impact it was to have on his future, the future of boxing and the global opposition to the war in Vietnam. Today there are many, even among his admirers, who see Ali's outburst as an accident, dismiss his heroism and question his motives. They note that Ali didn't know where Vietnam was and that he kept calling the people there "Viet-manese." The conservative commentator Stanley Crouch hails Ali as a great sports stylist, but regards his stand on the war as the action of "a dupe . . . not to be taken seriously." From a different political perspective, Gerald Early believes that "Ali's reasons for not wanting to join the army were never terribly convincing." The man "hadn't a single idea in his head" and relied instead on the "shallow simplistic sincerity that protected him like amulet or juju." Yet the closer one looks at Ali's actions and reactions in 1966 and 1967 and their historical context, the clearer it becomes that this man had many ideas in his head, and that it was his choice to act on them, come what may.

• • •

Ali's outburst came eighteen months after the United States Congress had approved the Tonkin Gulf resolution licensing direct US attacks on North Vietnam. Johnson assured the electorate that "we will seek no wider war," but as the Pentagon Papers make clear, with congressional endorsement of this "retaliatory action" (in preparation for at least five months before the alleged North Vietnamese aggression), "an important threshold in the war" had been breached with "virtually no domestic opposition."

Six months later, in February 1965, the US launched its Rolling

Thunder air war against North Vietnam. By the time the cease-fire was signed in January 1973, US planes and pilots had dropped on Vietnam three times the total tonnage of bombs unloaded on all of Europe, Africa and Asia in World War II. On 8 March 1965, the marines landed at Da Nang to become the first (officially acknowledged) US combat troops. They began offensive action against the insurgents on 1 April, initiating a ground war that was to last more than seven years. By July, 100,000 US soldiers had arrived in the country. Six months later, their numbers had doubled.

In early 1966, the United States was waging ferocious war against the Vietnamese population. Among the tactics deployed—and extensively documented—were crop destruction, rice denial, saturation bombings, forced evacuations, torture and mutilation of prisoners, immolation of homes and whole villages. The weapons used included napalm and anti-personnel cluster bombs. US pilots were flying 1500 sorties a week against the North, opposed only by anti-aircraft fire from below.

Although the reality of mass destruction was largely concealed from Americans by a compliant media, protests against the government's policy grew steadily as the war escalated. The first signs of domestic dissent became visible in the spring of 1965, when anti-war teach-ins were held at more than one hundred universities across the country. The teach-in was a variation on the sit-in, the tactic popularized by black students in the South; in its early days, many of the activists in the nascent anti-war movement were veterans of the civil rights struggle, and they infused the gathering anti-war protests with its language and methods.

On 17 April 1965, in the first major national protest, 25,000 marched against the war in Washington, DC. The march was called by the Students for a Democratic Society (SDS), and helped launch the organization's meteoric career as the vanguard of the country's radical white youth. In the call for the march, SDS had drawn explicitly on the experiences of the black freedom movement. The leaflet asked: "WHAT KIND OF AMERICA IS IT WHOSE RESPONSE TO POVERTY AND OPPRESSION IN VIETNAM IS NAPALM AND DEFOLIATION? WHOSE RESPONSE TO POVERTY AND OPPRESSION IN MISSISSIPPI IS SILENCE?"

At the demonstration itself, Paul Potter, the SDS president, delivered an impassioned indictment not only of the conduct of the war in Vietnam, but of the very premises of US foreign policy. It was necessary, he declared, to "build a movement that understands Vietnam in all its horror as but a symptom of a deeper malaise." At the next major national action, held in Washington in October, Carl Oglesby, Potter's successor as SDS president, took the analysis further. He lambasted the American liberal establishment—the tradition of Roosevelt, Truman, Kennedy and Johnson—whose aim in Vietnam was "to safeguard what they take to be American interests around the world against revolution or revolutionary change, which they always call communism." Invoking Jefferson and Paine, he lamented that America had lost "that mysterious social desire for human equity that from time to time has given us genuine moral drive." Many people would "make of it that I sound mighty anti-American," Oglesby concluded, "to them I say, don't blame *me* for *that*! Blame those who mouthed my liberal values and broke my American heart." In the coming years, this disenchantment, not only with the policies of the American government, but with the promises and premises of

America itself, was to grow rapidly, affecting huge numbers of white youth, and incidentally creating a new constituency of support for Muhammad Ali, whose religious-political break with America had shocked so many only a few years before.

• • •

> I agree with Paul Robeson absolutely that Negroes should never willingly fight in an unjust war. I do not share his honest hope that all will not. A certain sheep-like disposition, inevitably, born of slavery, will, I am afraid, lead many of them to join America in any enterprise, provided the whites will grant them equal rights to do wrong.
>
> *W.E.B. Du Bois*

In the early years of the anti-war movement, organizers were much concerned by the absence of black faces from the protests. Yet opinion polls showed that blacks were always more likely than whites to question the government's war polices, more likely to support complete withdrawal from Vietnam and less likely to support escalation. In 1965, 25 percent of blacks favored withdrawal; 50 percent a cease-fire; and 25 percent escalation. In the same year, white opinion divided 15 percent for withdrawal, 36 percent for a cease-fire, and 49 percent for escalation. Indeed, until 1970, blacks, low-income families and the over-sixties were the only sections of the population in which greater numbers favored withdrawal than escalation. Yet the notion that anti-war sentiment was largely a white middle-class student phenomenon remains widespread, among both critics and some (white, middle-class) veterans of the movement.

Vietnam was to become the first American war in which the dominant attitude among blacks was oppositional. Previously, participation in America's war efforts was seen as a way of pressing claims for full citizenship and unfettered inclusion in American society. By serving his country in time of war, it was argued, the negro would re-enforce his claims for equality in time of peace. In 1918, Du Bois penned a famous editorial in *The Crisis*, the NAACP magazine, urging black people to "Close Ranks" with white Americans in the "fight for democracy."

> This is our country: We have worked for it, we have suffered for it, we have fought for it . . . then this is our war.

Du Bois later regretted this statement, especially as it was followed by the infamous "Red Summer" of 1919, when American whites lynched seventy blacks, including ten soldiers in uniform. But it remained the conventional wisdom up to and during World War II, which both the NAACP and the Communist party regarded as a great opportunity for the black struggle. According to an optimistic Langston Hughes, "Pearl Harbor put Jim Crow on the run." But as Roosevelt, widely viewed as the best friend the negro had ever had in the White House, refused to desegregate the American armed forces, a note of bitterness crept into the Popular Front celebrations of the anti-Fascist effort. "Will V-Day Be Me Day Too?" asked Hughes in more forlorn mood. In Chicago, young blacks took this spirit further by forming a group called Conscientious Objectors Against Jim Crow and refusing military service.

During World War II, conscientious objection was mainly the preserve of the established pacifist sects. Like the Jehovah's Witnesses, the Nation of Islam was in principle opposed to secular power, but its attitude to military service was also shaped by its rejection of American national identity in favor of a diasporic identity that was by definition extra-territorial. Accordingly, Elijah Muhammad and his followers refused to register for Selective Service. The FBI, which saw black nationalists as potential saboteurs, secured Elijah Muhammad's indictment for draft evasion and sedition. The latter charge was dismissed, but in December 1942 Muhammad was convicted of violating Selective Service regulations and sentenced to one to five years in prison. Parole was denied in June 1945. Physically weakened but more determined than ever to build his Nation, Muhammad was finally released in August 1946.

The Nation's ideologically motivated defiance was only one expression of a more widespread, informal black resistance to the draft in World War II. There was, as so often in black history, a gap between official and unofficial black perspectives on the war, between the gung ho commitment of recognized black leaders and the often cynical and pragmatic approach adopted by anonymous black youth. In 1943, during his street-hustler phase, the young Malcolm Little was called up for induction in Manhattan. He had no intention of subjecting himself to military discipline and acted crazy and drunk. "Daddy-o, now you and me, we're from up north here," he told a startled psychiatrist, "so don't you tell nobody . . . I want to get sent down south. Organize them nigger soldiers, you dig? Steal us some guns and kill up some crackers." Malcolm was declared psychologically unfit and exempt from service. In 1946, he was jailed on burglary charges. While in prison he underwent his famous conversion to the cult of Elijah Muhammad. He was released on parole in August 1952, in the midst of the Korean War. Malcolm was twenty-seven and therefore unlikely to serve (the age limit at the time was twenty-six) but refused to register on principle. Threatened with a return to jail, he acquiesced and applied for conscientious objector (CO) status. Once again, he was examined by an army psychiatrist. This time he was declared an "asocial personality with paranoid trends" and classified 4-F, unfit for duty.

In 1953, the Messenger's son Wallace was classified 1-A but applied for CO status, which he was granted in 1957. Chauncey Eskridge, the Muhammad family attorney, used his political connections to arrange two years of alternative service for Wallace, but Elijah wouldn't allow his son to take up the offer. In 1958, after Wallace refused to report to a state hospital for his work assignment, he was indicted, tried and convicted. Because of a technical error in the government's handling of his service orders, a new trial was held in April 1960. The judge ruled that there was no factual basis to Wallace's claim to be a minister of the Muslim faith and sentenced him to three years' imprisonment, which commenced following the failure of his appeals in October 1961. The twenty-eight year old then spent fourteen months in a federal prison, where he studied the Bible and the Qur'an and concluded that his father's teachings could not be reconciled with Islamic sources.

Ali was aware of the Nation's history of draft resistance and of the black community's informal tradition of draft evasion. He knew that his friend Howard Bingham had escaped conscription in early 1963 by feigning illness and a speech impediment. But it is telling that in his early responses to his draft reclassification, Ali made few references to the Nation's policies. From the beginning, he tried to place his dilemma in a larger political context, however incompletely understood.

• • •

Black opposition to Vietnam was initially a product of the brutal cost of the war to black communities, coupled with the new expectations and intensified frustrations issuing from the civil rights struggle. During the entire course of the 1960s, 30 percent of black but only 18 percent of white males of eligible age were drafted. In 1966, black soldiers comprised 22 percent of all US casualties in Vietnam but only 11 percent of all US troops. In addition, blacks made up 13.5 percent of army enlisted personnel but only 3.4 percent of officers.

In Vietnam, integration on the battlefield came to seem cruel and hypocritical, not an advance for blacks but a further injury. A *Newsweek* poll showed 35 percent of blacks opposing the war abroad specifically because of the lack of freedom at home. As early as January 1964, this link was made explicit in a letter from a Harlem resident to the *Amsterdam News*. Responding to the dispute between Malcolm and Jackie Robinson, the correspondent argued:

> As for Jackie Robinson I have one point to make. I will not fight for this country in war. . . . The most forceful thing that black men could have done after the Birmingham bombings

> would have been to send all draft notices back to the Defense Department until the bombers were found and punished. As long as I am treated as a second-class citizen I will act as a second-class patriot.

The mainstream of the civil rights movement had invested heavily in the rhetoric of American exceptionalism and at this stage endorsed uncritically the ideology of the Cold War. Malcolm, who had long since dispensed with the baggage of "Americanism," was among the first major black voices to oppose the war. As early as 1963, he had condemned America's meddling in Southeast Asia and its support for the corrupt dictatorship in Saigon. In the course of his last year, he had become increasingly preoccupied with US foreign policy, and his critique of the intervention in the Congo was often accompanied by references to American hypocrisy in Vietnam. In January 1965, reflecting on events of the previous year in Vietnam, the Congo and the Caribbean, he observed acidly:

> The government should feel lucky that our people aren't anti-American. They should get down on their hands and knees every morning and thank god that 22 million black people have not become anti-American. You've given us every right to. The whole world would side with us if we became anti-American. You know, that's something to think about.

Three weeks later, in Alabama, Vietnam was one of the major themes in Malcolm's addresses to black students and civil rights activists. It was taken up by SNCC chairman John Lewis. After Lewis was assaulted by police in Selma, he complained, "I don't see how President Johnson can send troops to Vietnam . . . to the Congo . . . to Africa and can't send troops to Selma, Alabama." In April, Lewis's SNCC co-worker Bob Moses addressed the SDS rally in Washington. In July, activists in McComb, Mississippi (some of whom had spoken with Malcolm about Vietnam on a visit north in late 1964), issued a leaflet headed "Our Fight Is Here At Home!" It was the first formal protest against the war by an active civil rights group. The leaflet urged mothers to encourage their sons to evade the draft and not to risk their lives "fighting in Vietnam for 'freedom' not enjoyed by the Negro community of McComb." A few weeks later, SNCC issued its first official statement on the war, arguing that blacks should not "fight in Vietnam, until all the Negro people are free in Mississippi." Later in the year, the MFDP held a prayer meeting on the war, and Fannie Lou Hamer sent a telegram to Johnson demanding that US troops be withdrawn from Vietnam and sent to enforce black voting rights in the South.

In January 1966, SNCC strengthened its anti-war stand: "We maintain that our country's cry of 'preserve freedom in the world' is a hypocritical mask behind which it squashed liberation movements which are not bound and refuse to be bound by the expedience of the United States' Cold War policy." The organization offered support to all young men "unwilling to respond to the military draft which would compel them to contribute their lives to US aggression in the name of the 'freedom' we find so false in this country." As a result of this statement and others, Julian Bond, SNCC's communications director, was barred by the Georgia House of Representatives from taking the Atlanta assembly seat he had won in November. Roy Wilkins and the

NAACP castigated Bond and SNCC for giving the enemies of the civil rights movement a chance to attack it as "disloyal" and "un-American." In contrast, Martin Luther King backed Bond's right to free speech, but was careful, at this stage, not to condone draft evasion. Meanwhile, in a speech at Morgan State University, SNCC's Stokely Carmichael issued an unequivocal and emotionally charged declaration: "Either you go to Leavenworth Federal Penitentiary in Kansas or you become a killer. I will choose to suffer. I will go to jail." Then, in a flourish that appalled both older civil rights leaders and editorial writers, he added, "To hell with this country."

Clearly, "*I ain't got no quarrel with them Vietcong*" did not come from nowhere. In February 1966, Muhammad Ali was by no means alone in his reaction to the war, and his outburst in Miami should be seen as one manifestation among many of insurgent opposition in the black community, opposition that the community's designated representatives were failing to articulate. Ali was part of a gathering wave of dissent that would ultimately wash across the whole of America and much of the rest of the world. But the full flood of anti-war protest was still several years away, and in February 1966 the heavyweight champion found himself part of a beleaguered and derided minority. At this stage, no significant figure in the Democratic party had come out against the war. No major newspaper or television network had questioned its premises, though some were becoming disturbed about its costs and conduct. And apart from a handful of actors and singers with long-standing connections to the left, no American celebrity performer—whether from movies, music or sports—had spoken out. Protesters (whom the media initially dubbed "Vietniks") were routinely disparaged as unwashed idlers, psychiatric cases, spoiled adolescents or Communist dupes. Public dissent against American foreign policy was widely regarded as unpatriotic, even treasonous, and an affront to the brave boys on the battlefields. Even as Ali declared that he had no quarrel with the Vietcong, Barry Sadler's belligerent "Ballad of the Green Berets" was climbing the charts and would hold the number one spot for several weeks in March. In a special issue entitled "Vietnam: The War Is Worth Winning", *Life* magazine's editorial staff cited "our massive build-up" and "the new mobility of our strike force" in confidently predicting a US victory within the year.

All of which makes Ali's outburst against the war that much more remarkable. At a time when most educated people in the United States supported their government's policy in Vietnam, and indeed when some of the most able minds in American academia were preoccupied with devising more efficient means of prosecuting it, Ali—the barely literate pugilist, the erratic loudmouth and one-man media circus—knew that something was deeply wrong, and that this wrong somehow affected himself and all people of color, well beyond America's shores.

Ali's response to the draft was a major boost to the anti-war movement. This was not an academic or a clergyman, not a beatnik or a bohemian, not someone whose style and image were alien to American working-class people. This was a heavyweight boxer, a figure from the mainstream of popular culture and one who could not be dismissed as "unmanly" or "cowardly," as much an icon of masculine dominance as Miss America was of feminine subservience. Ali was, and remained, by far the most famous of the growing pantheon of anti-war heroes. What's more, he was black, and his association with anti-war feeling gave that feeling legitimacy in the black communities and helped erode the lily-white image of the movement.

• • •

In his response to the draft threat, Ali was initially confused, uncertain, inconsistent. At first, his grievance seemed largely personal. "I buy a lot of bullets, at least three jet bombers a year, and pay the salary of fifty thousand fighting men with the money they take from me after my fights." This was an argument he abandoned in the weeks to come. Nonetheless, it has been cited by historians (as it was by the Justice Department) as evidence that Ali's claim of conscientious objection was bogus, an expedient concocted late in the day to justify his aversion to military service. But Robert Lipsyte's contemporary report from the champ's camp hints at the real background to Ali's momentous utterance. Between phone calls from the press and banter with his entourage, Ali sang "Blowin' in the Wind" to himself. Sam Saxon, a Korean War veteran, reminded Ali and anyone else in earshot, "I was dressed in the uniform of the United States Army and they still called me nigger." Ali himself told Lipsyte:

> Boxing is nothing, just satisfying to some bloodthirsty people. I'm no longer a Cassius Clay, a Negro from Kentucky. I belong to the world, the black world. I'll always have a home in Pakistan, in Algeria, in Ethiopia. This is more than money.

This comment attracted little attention from the American media, who were preoccupied with the sensational "I ain't got no quarrel" crack, but it shows that even at this early stage in his struggle against the draft, Ali defined himself and his social responsibilities in internationalist terms.

This is not to deny that among Ali's immediate reactions to the draft threat were fear and personal resentment. The day after his reclassification, he vented his bewilderment to a television interviewer: "For two years the army told everyone I was a nut and I was ashamed. And now they decide I am a wise man. Now, without ever testing me to see if I am wiser or worser than before, they decide I can go into the army. . . . I can't understand it, out of all the baseball players, all of the football players, all of the basketball players—why seek out me, the world's only heavyweight champion?" Ali had reason to believe the government was out to get him. At this time, local draft boards across the South were calling up black civil rights activists. SNCC leaders John Lewis and Bob Moses had already been reclassified, apparently as punishment for their militancy. At the age of twenty-four, Ali must have assumed he'd slipped through the net. Had he refrained from criticism of the war, he could have quietly arranged an alternative to combat, as did so many others, including the future president Bill Clinton.

"*I ain't got no quarrel with them Vietcong.*" Was any declaration from the mouth of a sports star ever to prove so contentious, so audacious, so inspiring? The reaction was immediate, hostile and ferocious. Jimmy Cannon saw in Ali everything he detested in the era:

> He fits in with the famous singers no one can hear and the punks riding motorcycles with iron crosses pinned to their leather jackets and Batman and the boys with their long dirty hair and the girls with the unwashed look and the college kids dancing naked at secret proms held in apartments and the revolt of students who get a check from dad every first of the month and the painters who copy the labels off soup cans and the surf bums who refuse to work and the whole pampered style-making cult of the bored young.

The Kentucky state legislature, which had honored Ali when he won an Olympic gold medal, now condemned him for bringing discredit to "all loyal Kentuckians." In Congress, politicians called for a boycott of his upcoming fight with Ernie Terrell, scheduled for 29 March in Chicago. Congressman Frank Clark of Pennsylvania was among the most outspoken:

> The heavyweight champion has been a complete and total disgrace. I urge the citizens of the nation as a whole to boycott any of his performances. To leave these theater seats empty would be the finest tribute possible to that boy whose hearse may pass by the open doors of the theater on Main Street, USA.

Terrell, who held the WBA version of the heavyweight crown, called his opponent "an irresponsible kid" whose "statement was unbecoming." At 6 foot 6 inches Terrell was considered too tall for military service and was classified 1-Y, but that didn't stop him declaring "when you're called you have to go." The *Chicago Tribune* demanded a ban on the fight; Governor Otto Kerner and Mayor Richard Daley echoed the call. Under pressure from the promoters, Ali agreed to appear before the Illinois State Commission to clarify his position. On 22 February, a *New York Times* headline claimed, "Clay Plans to Apologize for Remarks about Draft Classification." This proved to be wishful thinking on the part of the boxing establishment. In Chicago, Ali told the commissioners: "I'm not here to make a showdown plea or apologize the way the press said. I came here because certain people would be hurt financially over what I said." The commissioners asked again and again if he was apologizing for his remarks, but "I'm apologizing for making them to sportswriters and newspapers" was all Ali would offer. That day, the Illinois attorney general ruled the Terrell fight illegal, ostensibly because Ali had failed to sign his correct name on the contract. The promoters searched desperately for an alternative venue, but political pressure ruled out New York, Las Vegas, Miami, Louisville and Pittsburgh. They were forced to look beyond the borders of the US and agreed on Toronto. But with closed-circuit theaters being drawn into the boycott, Terrell himself withdrew from the fight. Canadian George Chuvalo stepped in. Ali's promoter, Bob Arum, declared his client "a dead piece of merchandise. He's through as far as big-money closed-circuit is concerned."

On 28 February Ali made his first formal application for deferment as a conscientious objector. It was one of a sequence of steps he was to take in the coming year which diminished his room for retreat or maneuver, and which increasingly sharpened and politicized his conflict with the draft laws. On 17 March, he appeared before the Louisville draft board to request exemption, citing both his financial responsibilities and his conscientious objection. The board denied his request, and the long and circuitous process of appeal began.

Even at this stage, Ali could have apologized for his remark, or merely refrained from repeating it, while his attorneys negotiated a deal with the government. He chose another course:

> Keep asking me, no matter how long
> On the war in Vietnam, I sing this song
> I ain't got no quarrel with the Vietcong.

Ali's hardening determination not to lend support to the American effort in Vietnam infuriated many, whose long-standing reservations about the champion now burst into the open. "Cassius Clay has been the world's heavyweight champion for two years," said Milton Gross in the *New York Post*, "Nobody has ever done less with the time and the title, and destroyed his image more." Red Smith declared, "Cassius makes himself as sorry a spectacle as those unwashed punks who picket and demonstrate against the war." In the *Los Angeles Times*, Jim Murray derided the champ as "the white man's burden."

However, there was also sympathy, if not support, from unexpected quarters, including from two prominent black sportsmen who strongly backed Johnson's war policy. "During my own career in sports I came to learn that there are many writers who like tame Negroes who 'stay in their place,' " wrote Jackie Robinson. "Of course, by backing up his words with deeds, Clay or Ali has clearly demonstrated where his 'place' is." Floyd Patterson was another unlikely but powerful ally. "What bothers me about Cassius Clay's situation is that he is being made to pay too stiff a penalty for saying and doing what he thinks is right," said the man who had been humiliated by Ali only a few months earlier. "The prizefighter in America is not supposed to shoot off his mouth about politics, particularly if his views oppose the government's and might influence many among the working classes who follow boxing." When he wasn't promoting himself as an all-American hero, Patterson was among the most thoughtful analysts of the realities of the ring. In his defense of Ali, he noted that boxers were expected to play roles in order to sell fights to the public. "Maybe he has overplayed the part, made it bigger than it was supposed to be, and the public is not sure that it likes its fighters, its hired haters, to go beyond the role it expects them to play, which does not include joining the Black Muslims or denouncing the draft or criticizing America's policy in the Vietnamese War."

• • •

On 5 June 1966, James Meredith, who four years before had braved racist mobs to enroll as the University of Mississippi's first black student, set out on his "walk against fear" from Memphis to Jackson. The next day he was shot from ambush. The movement was appalled. If black civil rights workers couldn't walk in safety on the public highway in broad daylight, what had been won in the South during these last years of sacrifice and suffering? SNCC, the Congress of Racial Equality (CORE) and the SCLC rallied to complete Meredith's march (after clashes with SNCC, the NAACP and the

Urban League withdrew). Within days four hundred volunteers were edging their way towards Jackson in the face of vigilante provocation and police harassment. They watched as Byron de la Beckwith, the killer of Medgar Evers, drove slowly up and down the length of their column. In Greenwood, where voter registration had made little headway since Dylan's visit three years earlier, Stokely Carmichael was arrested for trespassing after he tried to set up a camp for the marchers in the playground of a black school. On his release, he addressed a crowd of supporters:

> This is the twenty-seventh time I have been arrested. I ain't going to jail no more. What we gonna start saying now is Black Power.

The slogan was picked up by the marchers and within days became a national cause célèbre. Carmichael's fellow marcher Martin Luther King regretted "the term black power . . . because it tends to give the impression of black nationalism." As the Meredith march continued, it came under repeated physical attack. The tear gas, clubs and shootings drove an ever-deepening wedge between older moderates and younger militants. At the final rally in Jackson, King told a reporter, "The government has got to give me some victories if I'm going to keep people non-violent."

The Black Power slogan provoked outrage across the spectrum of white opinion. The *New York Times* described it as "a hopeless, futile, destructive course expressive merely of a sense of black impotence." Vice-President Humphrey warned the NAACP, "There is no room in America for racism of any color." And on behalf of the

NAACP, Roy Wilkins rejected Black Power as "reverse Ku Klux Klan." Rustin dismissed the new militancy as "utopian and reactionary." Randolph called it "a menace to racial peace and prosperity." Politicians up and down the country lambasted the "racist demagogues" and their message of "violence and hate."

For the media, Black Power was principally a rejection of nonviolence. And it was always the statements about violence, or anything that could be construed as a threat of violence, that received the most high-profile attention. One of the tragedies of the period was the falsely polarized debate that ensued, a debate in which tactics, strategies and principles were thrown together in a bewildering muddle. However, it must be remembered that in the face of racist violence and the abject failure of the state to protect black lives, self-defense was an urgent issue for activists. Physical attacks on blacks by white supremacists had increased fivefold between 1961 and 1966. In 1966, it seemed that racists could assault any black person any time, anywhere, and get away with it. It was not only that most whites thought blacks should turn the other cheek, but also that they somehow discounted racial violence as an unfortunate anomaly; whereas for many black people it was a defining and unavoidable American reality, and had long been recognized as such. The Meredith march, the last great assembly of the civil rights phase of the black freedom movement, was a "march against fear"—a public refusal to be cowed by white terror. From the beginning, the conquest, through collective action, of black fear of white power had been one of the driving motives of the southern activists. The Black Power slogan was initially raised in pursuit of that motive. Though it often took the form of a repudiation, Black Power was a logical outgrowth of the civil rights movement, a response to its mix of success and failure.

Twelve years after the Supreme Court's order to desegregate public schools "with all deliberate speed," integrated schools remained a rarity, both North and South. Many doubted whether the federal government would or could enforce the movement's two great legislative victories, the Civil Rights Act of 1964 and the Voting Rights Act of 1965, or whether either act would affect the core of racial inequality. Activists felt they had paid a terrible price for such uncertain advances: scores of murders, tens of thousands of beatings and arrests. Throughout, the federal government and the white establishment had stood aloof, and were even now catering to a "white backlash" against the nominal gains of the movement. Real equality seemed as distant as ever. It became commonplace to ask, what use was the right to eat in an integrated restaurant if you couldn't afford the price of a hamburger? Here blacks North and South shared common ground.

The nationally televised struggles in the South had already made a powerful impact on the ghettos of the North and West, stoking a new, impatient and uncompromising race consciousness. The summers of 1964 through 1968 witnessed black rebellions in every major city of the country. Among the casualties were 250 dead (nearly all of them black) and 10,000 seriously injured; there were 60,000 arrests. After touring riot-stricken Watts in 1965, Martin Luther King told reporters, "it was a class revolt of under-privileged against privileged." A year later, King was forced to concede that "these legislative and judicial victories did very little to improve the lot of millions of Negroes in the teeming ghettos of the north."

The drive for legal equality had brought the movement face to face with economic inequality, a much more intractable obstacle. Black Power was a response to this impasse, but it was not a consistent one. While there was a general consensus on the desire to empower black communities, there was profound disagreement on the measures needed to achieve this. To the surprise of some, the slogan was quickly adopted by black businessmen and professionals. "Much of the black militant talk these days is actually in terms far closer to the doctrines of free enterprise than to those of the welfarist thirties," Nixon noted during his 1968 presidential campaign. He called for "more black ownership, for from this can flow the rest—black pride, black jobs, black opportunity and yes, black power."

In contrast, another strand of Black Power argued that blacks could not secure economic equality unless there was a general assault on economic privilege. This was the position held by both Malcolm X and Martin Luther King in the last years of their lives. Others went further, arguing that black freedom could not be won inside the capitalist system—because that system created and perpetuated racism. Thus a new generation arrived, by a new route, at the position held by Du Bois at the end of his long journey through "double consciousness." Black Power engendered a revived black Marxism, as well as a new black working-class vanguard organized into groups such as Detroit's League of Revolutionary Black Workers.

It is easy in retrospect to separate the individualist and collectivist, elitist and democratic strands of Black Power, but the distinctions were not so clear at the time. King always insisted Black Power was "a slogan without a program." In 1967, Harold Cruse dismissed it as "nothing but the economic and political philosophy of Booker T.

Washington given a 1960s shot in the arm." The ambiguities and incompleteness of Black Power, its hybrid character, are what the movement, or rather the historical moment, is all about.

Black Power is often blamed, along with other sixties "excesses," for the rise of the New Right and the political stranglehold it gained in the eighties and nineties. But the fact is that the New Right was on the march long before any of the alleged excesses gave it an excuse. The "white backlash" rolled across the country from 1964, when George Wallace took his presidential primary campaign to the North and secured 34 percent of the Democratic vote in Wisconsin. Seeking to capitalize on the sentiments uncovered by the Wallace campaign, George Bush, running for the Senate in Texas, told voters later that year, "The new civil rights act was passed to protect 14 percent of the people; I'm also worried about the other 86 percent." In November 1966, Republicans rode the backlash to a stunning mid-term congressional victory. "The roots of racism are very deep in America," Martin Luther King reflected sadly. From then on, through Nixon, Reagan, Bush and Gingrich, there remained at the core of the Republican political appeal a rejection of the claims of blacks and resentment of their partial advances. To many militants, the backlash confirmed that the civil rights movement's strategy of appealing to white conscience was doomed. Black Power was thus as much a response to the nascent backlash as it was a source of it. It was one of the most characteristic products of the dialectic of rising expectations and deepening frustrations that shaped the interlocking social movements associated with the sixties.

In his rejection of integrationism, Ali had preceded Black Power by two years. Black separatism was always a sore point with the media, which was itself almost totally white. Malcolm, of course, was the bridge between the Nation of Islam and the new, secular advocates of Black Power, and it was his vision of autonomous black political and economic power, rooted in black solidarity, that stirred the militants. Black Power was a declaration of independence from white power, notably white political power in the form of the liberal wing of the Democratic party. "We don't need white liberals," said Carmichael, and those who remembered the Mississippi Freedom Democratic party and the sell-out of Atlantic City were quick to agree. SNCC and CORE converted themselves into black-only organizations, and in the coming years black-only caucuses were founded in a wide variety of occupations and institutions. Many white allies resented their exclusion, but for the militants the priority was black self-organization—an essential pre-condition for black advance in a racist society. In this, Black Power echoed the arguments of both Du Bois and Garvey, as well as drawing on the recent and sometimes painful lessons of the civil rights movement.

There was always a sense in which, as Carmichael himself insisted, Black Power was a typically "American" phenomenon—an attempt to organize an ethnic block to secure a better deal within the American system. Eventually, Black Power became the template for particularist interest group politics in general and, ironically, the new white ethnicity that emerged in the next decade. The victories scored by black candidates in big city elections in the late sixties and early seventies were viewed as testimonies to Black Power. A movement that started as a repudiation of black bourgeois leaders and their incorporation within the Democratic party and the white power structure ended up as a rallying cry for a generation of "identity" politicians who used the black vote to parlay themselves into positions of personal influence and affluence. That a craven servant of white power like Clarence Thomas should invoke the name of Malcolm X during his Supreme Court confirmation hearings speaks volumes about the ambiguities of black nationalism, and the ease with which its banner can be hijacked.

• • •

I come to the world with scars upon my soul
wounds on my body, fury in my hands
I turn to the histories of men and the lives of the peoples
I examine the shower of sparks the wealth of the dreams
I am pleased with the glories and sad with the sorrows
rich with the riches, poor with the loss
From the nigger yard of yesterday I come with my burden.
To the world of tomorrow I turn with my strength.

Martin Carter

In its early days, Black Power was a critique of the strategy of symbolic representation favored by the established black leadership. The young militants would no longer accept just any black face in a high place, and especially not any black face that appeared to be colluding with white opinion to stymie black progress. While Black Power emphasized the collective advance of the black community, it was also a search for a new type of symbolic representative, one whose job was not to placate, impress or entertain whites, but to speak up for blacks. The Black Power militants liked to claim that they were more in touch with the streets, with the poor, than the older civil rights leaders. "None of the so-called leaders could go into a rioting community and be listened to," said Carmichael. In a manner characteristic of the era, the critique blended an awareness of the class divisions within the black population with a highly personalized claim of authenticity.

Shortly before his death, Malcolm was asked about appropriate heroes for young blacks. He answered, "Crispus Attucks laid down his life for America, but would he have laid down his life to stop the white man from enslaving black people? So when you select heroes about which black people should be taught, let them be black heroes who have died fighting for the benefit of black people." In answer to this call for a new kind of black hero, Muhammad Ali appeared, ready-made.

Ali straddled all of Black Power's constituencies—the cultural and the political, the anti-imperialists and the black capitalists—and he did it in a forum and language that gripped people in the streets. Ali illustrated a favorite Black Power tactic: the deployment of the black vernacular as a challenge to white assumptions and as a more realistic language than the honeyed words of the civil rights leaders. In the mouths of some, this idiom was to descend into willful coarseness, betraying a brutality that mirrored the forces against which Black Power raged. But Ali himself rarely indulged in obscenity. It's one of his achievements that amidst all the hatred surrounding him, he retained his gentility and generosity, even when suffering fools.

Black Power's striking achievement was that within three years of its birth it had displaced the word *negro* with the word *black*—thus bringing into general usage the terminology preferred by Malcolm,

Ali and the Nation of Islam. Some would see in this shift the first victory of what was later ridiculed as "political correctness," and Black Power was undoubtedly a key precipitate of what has been called "the cultural turn," in which activists and scholars became increasingly preoccupied with questions of identity and cultural difference.

None of Black Power's themes—black pride, economic and political independence, the emphasis on black America's African origins—were new. What was new was their penetration into black popular consciousness. In this context, Ali became a central point of reference, because he had been among the first to articulate the rudiments of black consciousness to a mass audience. In 1968, James Brown followed suit with his soul anthem, "Say It Loud—I'm Black and I'm Proud." Soul food, natural hair, black history, African clothing styles (or what Americans took to be African clothing styles) became the dominant fashions on the streets and among the middle classes. Strikingly, the new assertion of the beauties and values of black culture was shared ground between militants and moderates. Ali, as the first black American male to boast of his 'beauty'—at least, the first to do so without forfeiting public respect for his masculinity—became a hero for both cultural and political nationalists.

The fact that James Brown had been to Vietnam on a US government-sponsored tour shortly before recording his paean to blackness indicates that the cultural impact of Black Power was much wider than the radical politics associated with it. It also highlights Ali's unique stature; he not only sang the song, he led the life. Many found it only too easy to embrace the style of Black Power without the substance. And there is no doubt that Black Power's preoccupation with consciousness and culture made it vulnerable to charlatans and self-publicists. In the end, it was plagued by the same lack of accountability for which it criticized the old civil rights leaders. The very interaction between politics and popular culture that ensured widespread dissemination of the images and rhetoric of Black Power broke the organizational link between leaders and led, substituting for it the mediation of television. In the absence of durable organization and a clearly defined program, rhetoric ruled, along with sectarianism and macho posturing. It's worth noting that Ali, though associated in the minds of many white people with the "violent and angry" stereotype of Black Power, never advocated violence in any form (outside the ring) and made a point of deploring it publicly whenever the subject arose. Thanks to his preference for the language of love and peace, and of course his sense of fun, he drew into his extended family of supporters many people, black and white, with little sympathy for some of the other media-promoted firebrands of the day.

Black Power is often associated with machismo, but it should be remembered that it served as the immediate model for the women's and gay liberation movements, which emerged hot on its heels. Like Black Power, these movements sought to address long-standing and deeply rooted oppressions, viewed self-definition and self-expression as transformative political acts, and promoted a pluralist view of American society. Here, too, you can see Black Power as the first step in the march of the ever-fragmenting politics of cultural difference or, in its insistence on the unique capacity of the oppressed themselves to analyze and transform their condition, as a liberating and humanizing discourse. Speaking as a forty-six-year-old white heterosexual male, I don't buy the facile polarity between "identity" and "class" politics. The African-American freedom struggle, in all its metamorphoses, is a resource for all humanity. It is part of my heritage not only because I choose to make it so, but because it shapes the world I share with others. The critics of Black Power tend to forget that the dominant form of identity politics in the United States remains the politics of a white-identified majority, the politics of American exceptionalism. Critics of the late sixties see Black Power as one of the era's destructive phenomena. They argue that its self-indulgent, violent rhetoric alienated ordinary people, and charge it with substituting the compulsions of self-expression for political strategy. They are even more severe toward Black Power's white allies and would-be emulators on the far left, who are usually portrayed as middle-class narcissists. And, crucially, they charge both the black and white radicals with abandoning the home-grown traditions of democratic change, the traditions and ideals nobly encapsulated by the civil rights movement in its non-violent phase, in pursuit of exotic ideologies and foreign-bred gurus (Marx, Lenin, Mao, Fanon, Che, Ho).

While some of the efforts to adapt the jargon of foreign struggles were far-fetched, the desire to learn from those struggles, and the identification with them, was a positive development whose rarity in American history makes it all the more precious. The internationalism of Black Power was much more than an abstract political ethic. It flowered from a revised and broadened definition of the individual and the community to which he or she belonged. "The masses of black people today think in terms of black," Malcolm X had claimed. "And this black thinking enables them to see beyond the confines of America." Blacks were no longer merely an inferior species of the genus *Americanus*, but part of a global community, a global majority even, and one that had risen from centuries of oppression to stake its claim in the modern world. Black Power was a key vector of the global sixties; it drew inspiration (as well as words and images) from a wide array of anti-colonial and anti-racist struggles, and its impact was felt in the Caribbean, Africa, Asia and Western Europe. As the decade wore on, militant black people in America increasingly identified themselves with the Vietnamese, America's enemy. In 1970, Huey Newton wrote to South Vietnam's National Liberation Front (NLF) offering to send a battalion of Panthers—to fight against American troops. The NLF expressed its gratitude for this expression of solidarity, but declined the Panthers' offer. The exchange was only a small reflection of a wider sentiment, one that was also expressed in Ali's stand against the draft.

Ali's evolution in the sixties paralleled a broader evolution in black (and white) opinion. His assertion of his personal prerogatives led him to embrace a universal cause. Like Malcolm, he emerged from the cocoon of nationalism to spread his wings as an internationalist. But he did so under the pressure of circumstances—the war, the draft, the heavyweight championship, the pull of alternative constituencies. It was Ali's capacity to embody so many of the underlying trends of the time—especially the interaction between personal self-definition and global politics—that made him a representative figure, a hero to the insurgents and a criminal in the eyes of the state.

It is important to remember that the government's pursuit of Ali was only one episode in a wide-ranging campaign of harassment waged by federal agencies against Black Power and its perceived advocates. J. Edgar Hoover had always been hostile to black nationalists and long ago had tangled with both Garvey and Elijah Muhammad. In August 1967, he launched a counter-intelligence program (COINTELPRO) designed "to neutralize militant black nationalists" and "to prevent the rise of a leader who might unify and electrify these violence-prone elements." Within a year, the FBI had recruited more than three thousand "Ghetto Informants" to act as the eyes and ears of the (still overwhelmingly white) bureau in the black communities. They were instructed to ferret out all those "susceptible to foreign influences . . . from African nations in the form of Pan-Africanism," and in New York City to beware specifically of "links between Harlem and Africa." In 1969, Hoover declared the Black Panther party "the greatest threat to the internal security of the country." That year 27 Panthers were killed by police; 749 were jailed. But the enigma of Black Power sometimes befuddled Hoover's efforts. In 1970, his personal list of dangerous "black nationalists" included Jackie Robinson.

• • •

In the wake of the Voting Rights Bill of 1965, SNCC volunteers in Lowndes County, Alabama, had launched an independent Black Panther party to challenge the local whites-only Democratic machine. This early experiment in organizing black political power was a talking point among the Meredith marchers. Especially popular were the new organization's bumper stickers, adorned with a panther silhouette and the slogan, "We're the Greatest." The invocation of Muhammad Ali, at this time the most famously defiant and assertively black male in the country, was by no means accidental. And the casual transition of the first person singular to the first person collective speaks volumes for Ali's transcendence of the confines of the old role models. John Hullet, one of the Lowndes County organizers, explained the panther symbol to Andrew Kopkind: "He never bothers anything, but when you start pushing him, he moves backwards and backwards into his corner, and then he comes out to destroy everything that's before him." The Panther, initially, was not an icon of animal aggression, but of patience, restraint and cunning at the service of hidden power. It's not surprising that the youths who were drawn to this icon would also feel a powerful affinity with Muhammad Ali.

• • •

In his first two years as champion, Ali defended his title twice. In the next year—the year following his remark about the Vietcong—he defended it seven times, demolishing every challenger with an ease and style that had critics invoking ballet, jazz, bullfighting and blitzkriegs. As Hugh McIlvanney observed, strange as it may seem, we may have never seen the best of Muhammad Ali. In 1966 and 1967, he was taking heavyweight boxing into new territory, and he seemed only to have begun to explore his own potential. During the three and a half years of exclusion from the ring that followed, he would have been at his physical peak. But in compensation for this loss boxing fans got something far more precious: the Ali who returned to the ring in what seemed a triumph over the system and over time itself.

Yet throughout this year of extraordinary boxing accomplishment, Ali was under the kind of pressure few if any sports stars have ever faced outside the arena. His views on Vietnam and his determination to stay out of the military were subject to test after test. Training for his rematch with Henry Cooper, Ali walked the Miami ghetto with writer-photographer Gordon Parks. It was clear that the beleaguered champ found the warmth of his reception on black America's mean streets a welcome refuge from the chill wind of hostile officialdom. "These people like me around when they got trouble," Ali told Parks. "Patterson, Joe Louis, Sammy Davis and other Negro bigwigs don't do that. Too busy cocktailin' with the whites. I don't need bodyguards. You don't need protection from people who love you." Parks found Ali confused and troubled, vacillating between denying and embracing the anomaly of his situation and its probable cost, by turns flippant and ferocious.

> I ain't scared. Just show me a soldier who'd like to be in that ring in my place! I see signs saying "LBJ, how many kids did you kill today?." Well, I ain't said nothing about Vietnam. Where is it anyway? Near China? Elijah Muhammad teaches us to fight only when we are attacked. My life is in his hands. That's the way it is. That's the way it's got to be . . . so what if I am the first black athlete to stand up and say what I feel! Maybe I'm like the Japanese flier who sacrifices himself so others can live. Hate! Hate! Hate! Who's got time to go round hatin' whites all day? I don't hate lions, either—but I know they'll bite! What does the white man care if I hate him, anyhow? He's got everything going for him.

The reference to the Japanese kamikaze flier was pure American pop culture, just as the comparison between white people and lions, like the final reminder of the enduring perversity of white supremacy, came straight from the Malcolm X playbook.

• • •

Don't care where you come from
As long as you're a black man, you're an African
No min' your nationality
You have the identity of an African
Cos if you come from Brixton, you are an African
And if you come from Neasden, you are an African
And if you come from Willesden, you are an African

Peter Tosh

We were sitting in the upper tier of a rickety grandstand overlooking a cricket pitch in London's East End. Below, two teams, mostly Asian with a sprinkling of white and Afro-Caribbean players, made the best of the corrugated wicket and patchy outfield. They reflected the new mix of Britain's inner cities and a new strand in the warp and woof of the Black Atlantic. Just as their communities have struggled for a place in British society, so the cricketers themselves are struggling for their place in English cricket. In the grandstand we talked about some of the obstacles they faced: the club secretaries who always discovered their fixture list was full up when an Asian team called; the leagues that required clubhouses, dressing rooms and bars; the umpires who muttered about "over-excitable" Asians. Akram, a Londoner in his thirties, was the manager of one of the teams we were watching. As a day job he worked in his family's business, a halal butchers, but his passion was cricket, and he was a frequent visitor to Pakistan. Soon we were sharing common enthusiasms for the city of Lahore, for the late-swinging yorkers of Waqar Younis, for the hills outside Islamabad and for the high-grade black charas of the Himalayas. Somehow the talk turned to Muhammad Ali and a reverent hush came over our group. With a flickering smile, as if remembering something distant yet intimate, something that could never be taken from him, Akram told us how in 1966 his father, a Punjabi-speaking immigrant, took him to see Ali fight Henry Cooper at the Arsenal in Highbury.

Boxing plays little part in the sporting cultures of South Asia, and Akram's father had never expressed an interest in it before Ali arrived in London. But he splashed out for the tickets (in those days there were still affordable seats at big-time boxing matches) because Ali was a Muslim, and because he was going to give the Englishman Cooper a thrashing. For the young Akram, however, Ali was from the beginning more than an Islamic hero. He was also an ambassador of black America, the embodiment of the bewitching African-American style, as well as of black political defiance. His relevance to the young black cricketers of today's East End, who seek entry to the level playing field on their own terms and without abandoning their own identities, was obvious.

Akram's story is one small example of the way Ali reshaped loyalties and realigned the axes of global sporting partisanship. In banning his fights in America and driving Ali abroad, the authorities inadvertently assisted the complex process that was to turn Ali into a genuinely global champion and thereby provide him with a political leverage deeply resented by the US establishment. Until February

1966, all but two of the post-war heavyweight title bouts had been fought on US territory. Then, in the space of six months, Ali defended his crown in Toronto, twice in London and in Frankfurt.

Ali's early emphasis on his status as "champion of the *whole* world" was in itself anomalous among American sports stars. American popular culture in the form of music, movies, fashion, slang and television has traveled and won acolytes everywhere, but American sports have proved to be less successful exports. Baseball has a mass following in Latin America and Japan, and basketball is now a major game in the Mediterranean and growing rapidly in Africa. But even in these sports the American game (and the American market) remains dominant in a way the English game most certainly does not within cricket, soccer or rugby.

Boxing and athletics are the only two mass sports shared across the Black Atlantic. Soccer reigns supreme as the sport of the black masses in Africa and Latin America. Baseball is confined to one side of the Atlantic, and cricket to the axis joining West Indies, England and to a lesser extent South Africa. In London in 1966, Ali enjoyed a brief interaction with this otherwise alien strand of the Black Atlantic when he was taken to Lord's to see a Test match against the West Indies. "I like cricket. I reckon our baseball must have been based on this game." He was particularly impressed by the master pace bowler Wes Hall, later a politician and diplomat. "Too slow? I don't think so. Running up as fast as Wes Hall would be good training for me." Nevertheless, the champ nodded off as M.J.K. Smith completed a slow century.

The rematch with Cooper was the first heavyweight title contest to be staged in Britain since 1908. When Ali arrived in London on

9 May 1966, the press found him subdued. "I've been driven out of my country because of my religious beliefs, yet every other country in the world welcomes me. It's a strange feeling. All I ask is the same treatment and respect in my country that other boxers and athletes get from Uncle Sam." While in Britain, he didn't want to "be bothered with questions about my personal affairs, such as the draft and my divorce. I'm here to defend my title and that old man Henry Cooper had better watch out." One journalist asked him if he regarded the match as a fight between black and white. Ali shot back, "You look too intelligent to ask a dumb question like that."

Training at the Territorial Army gym opposite the White City tube station in west London, Ali held daily court with British journalists, who found the champion a bewildering figure but gave him a fairer hearing than their American counterparts. "Those who recall the uncomplicated ballyhoo that marked Cassius Clay's training for the first Cooper fight have been struck by the differences in the way Muhammad Ali has prepared for this one," Hugh McIlvanney reported. "Mingling with the predictable callers from the trade . . . there has been a stream of serious-faced negroes."

Among them was Michael X, Britain's most notorious Black Power spokesperson and leader of the militant Racial Adjustment Action Society, whose acronym, RAAS, carried a vernacular insolence unnoticed by most whites. Born in Trinidad as Michael De Freitas, he changed his name after meeting Malcolm X in London in February 1965. The media depicted him as a figure of menace and preacher of hate. In 1967 he became the first person prosecuted for inciting racial hatred under the Race Relations Act of 1965—a law ostensibly designed to protect black people. Later, he was convicted of murder and hanged in Trinidad. Today, some see him as a conman and racketeer, others as a pioneer of black self-assertion in Britain, and others as a mixture of the two. In any case, his encounter with Ali in 1966 was a symbolic moment in the evolution of the Black Atlantic. Together they met with community activists in Notting Hill and visited the local Free School, the creation of white counter-culturalists, and among the first of the self-consciously alternative community institutions which were to proliferate across London in the decade to come. Ali was one of a series of transatlantic visitors who helped infuse the spirit and language of the American black freedom movement into black British communities; he was a participant in the process through which black Britain came to define itself as part of a black diaspora.

In December 1964, stopping in London on his way to Stockholm to collect the Nobel Peace Prize, Martin Luther King met with representatives of the emergent immigrant communities. After the meeting, he told the BBC:

> I think it is necessary for the colored population in Great Britain to organize and work through meaningful non-violent direct action approaches to bring these issues to the forefront of the conscience of the nation wherever they exist. You can never get rid of a problem as long as you hide the problem, as long as you complacently adjust yourself to it.

King's visit helped catalyze the formation of the Campaign Against Racial Discrimination (CARD), the first in a long line of efforts to forge a united anti-racist movement in Britain. CARD split and collapsed within two years, and the initiative passed to groups strongly influenced by Black Power. Malcolm himself visited Britain several times in the last six months of his life, addressing students and community activists. With a BBC camera crew in tow he visited Smethwick in the West Midlands, which had just witnessed the first attempt by a major British political party to "play the race card." During the 1964 general election, the Tory candidate's slogan, "If you want a nigger neighbour, vote Labour," had drawn nationwide attention; with support from white working-class voters, he won the seat. Although Harold Wilson denounced him, in 1965 Wilson's government issued a White Paper proposing to restrict immigration from Asia, Africa and the Caribbean.

When Ali visited in 1966, the Muslim presence, which was to become so pronounced in later decades, was still an unfamiliar one in London. There were only a few improvised mosques, and halal cooking was hard to come by. As a result, Ali, who always followed the Nation's dietary rules more rigorously than any of its other prescriptions, took his meals at a kosher restaurant in Whitechapel, surrounded by photographs of the boxing heroes of the old-time Jewish East End. In those days, Ali often referred to his diet as kosher and suggested that Jews might escape the Armageddon awaiting the white race. His easy interaction with the Jewish, Irish and cockney elements of the London boxing scene helped prepare the way for the acceptance of black British fighters. He took an honored place in the East End's long-established prizefighting tradition, a tradition carried forward today by young Londoners from African, Caribbean and Asian backgrounds.

The mid sixties saw the rise of that distinctively English institution,

"Paki-bashing." In 1965, a Pakistani diplomat reported "a growing mass hysteria against the Pakistanis." In that context, the presence in Britain of Ali, a battling Muslim, was a solace and a stimulus. Unlike black America, the immigrant communities of the sixties shared no common culture, language, music or religion. Precisely because of that, many of the younger generation looked to black America for political and cultural models. Just as Malcolm's visit led to the formation of RAAS, so Stokely Carmichael's brief visit in 1967—he was deported on the order of Home Secretary Roy Jenkins—sparked the formation of the more internationalist Universal Coloured People's Association. The Black House, a refuge for black youth run by Herman Edwards and Michael X, was inspired by Amiri Baraka's Spirit House in Newark, New Jersey. In 1968, a new group calling themselves the Black Panthers appeared on the streets of Brixton in south London selling their *Freedom News* and, like the American originals, excoriating police violence against black people.

However, the impact in Britain of Black Power, and of Muhammad Ali, was never just about blackness or pan-Africanism, as Akram's experience suggests. I think of my friend Suresh, who adopted the Black Panthers as his role models in facing racism as a young man in Lancashire in the sixties, or my friend Achin, spouting Malcolm-style invective on London's street corners in the early seventies, before he returned to a life of political activism in India. Or A. Sivanandan, the Sri Lankan Tamil who arrived in Britain in the late fifties and stayed to help foment, guide and analyze several generations of resistance to racism. Black Power, he argued, "was to alter profoundly our very perceptions of what political struggle was, and how it needed to be waged."

> It was the catalyst which showed up the essential unity of the struggles against white power and privilege—whether in the US itself, in Britain, in Southern Africa, or in the former colonies of the Caribbean. Through it, black became a political color with which other Third World activists and radicals could identify—the Dalit Panthers from among the untouchables of India took their name from the Black Panthers of the US. . . . Black Power is a political metaphor . . . but also, in the terse, explosive precision of its language, a resounding call to arms.

Sivanandan was among the first to insist that Black Power was more than a parochial, nationalist response to American racism. In Britain, it provided an ideology and rhetoric ready-made for a new generation impatient with what he called "the begging-bowl syndrome" of the older immigrant organizations. Younger blacks no longer saw themselves as supplicants in a foreign land. They demanded the right to live and work in Britain on their own terms, while at the same time identifying themselves as part of a world community of the oppressed. Through its linkage of self-discovery and self-assertion with a call to solidarity beyond national borders, Black Power carried many of its adherents—in America, Britain and across the Third World—on a journey toward a new vision of what Fanon called "the universality inherent in the human condition." Here Muhammad Ali, the boxer who did not want to represent anything to anyone, was to prove, yet again, an unlikely pioneer of a global movement.

Black Power's huge overseas resonance was due in part to its transnational ideology and in part to black America's role as a prototype black political culture, the cutting edge of black self-expression. Manthia Diawara recalls growing up in Mali in the sixties:

> You see, for me then, and for many of my friends, to be liberated was to be exposed to more R & B songs and to be au courant of the latest exploits of Muhammad Ali, George Jackson, Angela Davis, Malcolm X, and Martin Luther King, Jr. These were becoming an alternative cultural capital for the African youth—imparting to us new structures of feeling and enabling us to subvert the hegemony of *francité* after independence.

Ali's expanding influence highlights the centrality of the black American freedom struggle to the social dynamic known as the sixties at home and abroad. It was black Americans who dramatized the contradiction between the promise and the reality of America and of the post-war era America dominated.

It is too often forgotten that the American sixties were merely a single facet of a global phenomenon. Ali was one of those who acted as a transmitter between struggles in America and struggles outside. Through his media appearances in every corner of the planet, Ali played a major role in stimulating the worldwide circulation of ideas and images that lies at the heart of the sixties. He became part of a number of overlapping global conversations and movements, linking sports fans, the Black Atlantic, the Third World and the international opposition to America's war in Vietnam. Just as the anti-colonial movement inspired the American black freedom struggle, so that struggle inspired others in Africa, Asia and Europe. Television carried scenes not just of carnage from Vietnam, but also of street demonstrations and battles with authority in Paris, Northern Ireland, Prague, Mexico and Japan. Through this global chain reaction the Black American freedom movement fed and was in turn nourished by events elsewhere. During a student demonstration in response to the King assassination in April 1968, German SDS leader Rudi Dutschke was shot at point-blank range, setting off street fighting which resulted in four hundred injuries and thousands of arrests. One of those involved in the Frankfurt protests was Daniel Cohn Bendit, who was to play a leading role in the explosion in France a month later. The civil rights movement which emerged the next year on the streets of Northern Ireland drew inspiration and tactics from its American namesake.

The key to Ali's story and to the dynamic of the sixties is this meeting and mingling of global currents. Unfortunately, in the historiography of the American sixties, American exceptionalism has prevailed, and as a result the causes, content and consequences of the social movements of the era have been misrepresented. Once liberated from its parochial prison, the sixties seems a lot less about "permissiveness" or "self-indulgence" and a lot more about the growth of a global consciousness from below. For people all over the world, Ali embodied that consciousness. And he in turn was profoundly shaped by his growing awareness of the representative role in which he had been cast. To present him as an American hero acting on an American stage is to miss what made him extraordinary. It was Ali's transgression of American norms—in an American idiom—that enabled him to build his global constituency.

The anti-war movement in Europe adopted what David Widgery called "the weapons of Americanism—the theatricality, the masks, and it pulled in a lot of non-student cultural dissidents." Even as they railed against the American war machine, the insurgent forces in Europe cherished rock and roll, John Ford movies and blue jeans. Ali inadvertently tapped into a widespread ambivalence about America. Many who resented its arrogance and power were fascinated by its vibrant popular culture. For the lovers of jazz and blues and R&B, Hollywood fast talk and Marx Brothers surrealism, Ginsberg and Kerouac, Ali was yet another marvellous example of demotic American energy and invention, along with Bob Dylan, who was also visiting Britain that spring. Here, as in America, there were people on the left who were convinced that Dylan's concerts were sellouts in more ways than one. "Dylan is to me the perfect symbol of the anti-artist in our society," wrote Ewan MacColl. "He's against everything—the last resort of someone who doesn't really want to change the world." Four days before the Ali–Cooper fight, the legendary concert at Manchester Free Trade Hall was interrupted by a cry of "Judas!," to which Dylan replied, "I don't believe you." In the Scottish gigs, the booing was allegedly organized by the local Communist party. The incomprehension of the more puritanical wing of the left seemed only to spur Dylan and his band (which became The Band a year later) to the creation of an ever more ecstatically intense rock and roll. Shortly after his return from Europe in July, Dylan suffered the motorcycle accident that sent him into seclusion and precipitated yet another revolution in his music.

In the year following Ali's visit, anti-war sentiment spread rapidly across Europe. In February 1967, Bertrand Russell's war crimes tribunal began its investigations into American atrocities in Vietnam. Hubert Humphrey was despatched to the capitals of Europe to rally support and was met with angry demonstrations in London, Paris and Bonn. A Gallup Poll later that year showed huge majorities in favor of US withdrawal from Vietnam in Finland, Sweden, Brazil, France, India, Uruguay, Argentina and West Germany. In Britain, the majority was slimmer. The only countries where there was majority support for US policy were Australia and the US itself.

Years later, Ali wrote a letter of thanks to "the people of Great Britain [who] stood with me during the difficult days of my exile from boxing." Many of the communities which had cheered Paul Robeson when he was being reviled in his native land now embraced Muhammad Ali. Certainly Robeson and Ali remain the only African-Americans ever to have had parades staged in their honor through the streets of Tyneside. Nonetheless, when asked by the British press whether he had any plans to escape the draft by going into exile, Ali answered with mournful clarity, "Regardless of the right or wrong back there, that is where I was born. That is where I'm going to return."

• • •

On 23 August, as a result of Ali's appeals, a special judicial hearing was held to review his draft status. Ali's legal team submitted a twenty-one-page statement on his behalf, but the champion also appeared in person to testify in his own words:

> It would be no trouble for me to go into the armed services, boxing exhibitions in Vietnam and traveling the country at the

> expense of the government or living the easy life and not having to get out in the mud and fight and shoot. If it wasn't against my conscience to do it, I would easily do it. I wouldn't raise all this court stuff and I wouldn't go through all of this and lose the millions that I gave up and my image with the American public that I would say is completely dead and ruined because of us in here now.

Much to the dismay of the federal government, and the surprise of mainstream commentators, Judge Lawrence Grauman ruled that Ali was "sincere in his objection on religious grounds to participation in war in any form." Two days later, L. Mendel Rivers, the right-wing chair of the House Armed Services Committee, denounced Grauman's ruling to a meeting of the Veterans of Foreign Wars and threatened to raise hell on Capitol Hill if Ali was deferred. The Justice Department, insisting that Ali's objection to the war was "racial and political," convinced the Kentucky appeal board to ignore Grauman's recommendation and uphold the 1-A classification. The case then proceeded to the national Selective Service Appeals Board, where the Justice Department again opposed Ali's claim, using information obtained by the FBI to show that Ali's motivations were primarily political.

"*I ain't got no quarrel with them Vietcong.*" It sounds so modest, yet it struck people as terrifyingly outlandish. It could be the plaint of any ordinary soldier-citizen. Just how is it that the ostensible enemies of the nation-state to which one is assigned become one's personal enemies? This is a magical process which national establishments have managed with great care and ingenuity since the dawn of the modern era. The counter-process through which Ali broke free of its mystic grip, and defined his own loyalties, is an exemplary voyage of the sixties.

The "I" who had no quarrel with the Vietcong was, first, the highly personal "I" of a young man wondering why he was supposed to kill or be killed by people he didn't know. It was also the "I" of a boxer who wanted to be left alone to be a boxer, a man who had made great efforts to free himself of the burden of representation, a man who only wanted to be an "I." But because of his conversion to the Nation of Islam, and his travels in Africa, this "I" assumed other, collective attributes: black, Muslim, African. Ultimately, it became the "I" of all those who felt they had no quarrel with the Vietcong—and all those who felt they did have a quarrel with America.

Ironically, Ali's reclamation of his selfhood had given his "I" new representative burdens. In retrospect, "I ain't got no quarrel with them Vietcong" seems a characteristic sixties declaration, highly personal yet charged with political import. In it, the various vectors of the sixties—individualist and collectivist, particularist and universal—intersected.

Muhammad Ali refused complicity in one of the atrocities of the twentieth century. Against this, the fact that he didn't know Le Duc Tho from Nguyen Kao Ky, Haiphong from Hué, is nothing. After all, there were many bright and well-informed people who could list every strategic hamlet, but who remained blind or indifferent to the welfare of the human beings who occupied those hamlets. Jeremiah Shabazz emphasizes that Ali made up his own mind, without pressure from the Nation of Islam. "He never studied day-to-day current events like the thousands of white kids who opposed the war. But even though he was unsophisticated in his thinking, he knew it was a senseless, unjust war." In opposing the draft and the war, and paying the price for that opposition, he reached beyond America and "Americanism," beyond blackness and Islam. Ali's stand against the draft was one of the most piquant expressions of that broadening of human sympathies that was the best of his era.

• • •

When he finally fought Terrell in Houston in early 1967, Ali's ferocity shocked the pundits. Terrell, a powerful hitter, probably Ali's most dangerous opponent since Liston, had made the mistake of calling him "Clay" during a pre-fight press conference. "What's my name?" Ali roared again and again as he pummeled Terrell. "Uncle Tom! What's my name?" The *New York Daily News* called the fight "a disgusting exhibition of calculating cruelty, an open defiance of decency, sportsmanship and all the tenets of right versus wrong." Jimmy Cannon called it "a kind of lynching." Arthur Daley called Ali "a mean and malicious man whose facade has crumbled as he gets deeper into the Black Muslim movement." Another veteran boxing correspondent, Milton Gross, confessed: "One almost yearns for the return of Frankie Carbo and his mobster ilk."

Rarely has the hideous hierarchy of boxing's values been made so explicit. Ali's violence in the ring (and within the rules) was declared reprehensible by the very people who condemned him for not engaging in much more deadly violence in Vietnam. Even the violence of organized crime was considered less discrediting to the sport of boxing than Ali's crime of conscience. As in the Patterson fight, it was argued that somehow Ali had stepped over the ill-defined line demarcating the permissible limits of aggression in the ring. When Mike Tyson bit Evander Holyfield's ear, he was clearly breaking the rules and making a mockery of a sporting contest. But what exactly was Ali's offense? That he allowed his anger to become visible? That he was in uncompromising mood? Even one of his admirers has described the Patterson and Terrell fights as the "only times he deliberately inflicted pain" in the ring. Surely Ali, like every other boxer, deliberately inflicted pain every time he stepped into the ring. In both these fights Ali had hyped the symbolic character of the contest; in each one he was fighting more than his opponent. His critics saw these fights through this lens as much as Ali did. It's hard to resist the conclusion that what really rankled was the spectacle of an uncompromising Ali glorying in his opposition to—and momentary triumph over—"the American way." Neither Patterson nor Terrell ever complained about Ali's treatment of them in the ring.

• • •

On a rare holiday in the first week of January 1967, Martin Luther King contemplated photographs of napalm-scorched Vietnamese children published in the latest issue of the radical journal *Ramparts*. Over the last year, he had grown increasingly distressed by American violence in Vietnam, but his sense of responsibility to the civil rights movement had caused him to refrain from outright opposition. Now he resolved to break what he was later to call "the betrayal of my own silences." On his return from holiday, he informed SCLC colleagues of his determination to make anti-war activity his priority. Some were uneasy with their leader's new course, and feared it would alienate both the government and white liberal supporters. On

25 February, in a speech in Beverly Hills, King argued that "the promises of the Great Society have been shot down on the battlefield of Vietnam." Yet more controversially, he claimed that US policy in Vietnam "seeks to turn the clock of history back and perpetuate white colonialism."

On 6 March 1967, the national Selective Service Appeal Board unanimously upheld Muhammad Ali's 1-A classification. That same day, President Johnson told Congress, "The knowledge that military service must sometimes be born by—and imposed on—free men so their freedom may be preserved is woven deeply into the fabric of the American experience." On 14 March, Ali received his induction notice. Thanks to the rapid intervention of his lawyers, the call-up was postponed until 28 April so that he could fight Zora Folley at Madison Square Garden on 22 March. In his last appearance in the ring for more than three and a half years, Ali was at his most dazzling and dominant, finishing off the challenger with a knockout in the seventh round. That month's issue of *Ring* magazine declined for the first time to designate a fighter of the year because "Cassius Clay," the obvious candidate for the award, "is most emphatically not to be held up as an example to the youngsters of the United States." That week saw 274 US deaths in combat, the highest tally since the war began.

On 29 March, a federal judge rejected Ali's three draft appeals, including his objection to Louisville's all-white draft board. Induction became inevitable. Only now did Elijah Muhammad come to his disciple's support in the pages of *Muhammad Speaks*. All Ali wanted, Muhammad insisted, was to "go his own way . . . but he is being blown up as one of the greatest criminals in America, a country in which he does not even belong." More significantly, on that same day, Martin Luther King arrived in Louisville for an SCLC board meeting. Following the meeting, the board issued a statement condemning the "morally and politically unjust" war and the draft which "discriminates against the poor and places Negroes in the front lines in disproportionate numbers and from there to racially segregated cemetery plots in the deep south."

While in Louisville, King took time out to meet privately with Ali, who was visiting his home town. Afterwards, the two men met the press, and King praised the boxer's stance against the draft. "As Muhammad Ali has said, we are all victims of the same system of oppression," King told the newsmen. Ali nodded, gave the older, shorter man's rounded shoulders an affectionate squeeze and called him "brother." In private, King's humor was as irrepressible as Ali's and the two men seem to have hit it off. More importantly, Ali's stand gave King a focus for his appeal to young men caught in the draft, and King's increasingly vocal critique of the war and direct support for Ali reduced the champion's isolation.

The SCLC had chosen to meet in Louisville, where King's brother, A.D. King, was a leading pastor, partly in order to support the bitter and protracted open-housing campaign waged by local blacks. Marchers through segregated white residential areas were greeted by white mobs throwing rocks and bottles, while police stood passively to one side. After meeting with King, Ali toured the city's black neighborhoods. "In your struggle for freedom, justice and equality, I am with you," he told the protesters. "I came to Louisville because I could not remain silent in Chicago while my own people—many of whom I grew up with, went to school with and some of whom are my blood relatives—were being beaten, stomped and kicked in the streets simply because they want freedom, justice and equality in housing." It was an extraordinary statement from the man who had told the world he didn't want to "carry a sign" or live in a white neighborhood, who only three years before had publicly renounced both the integrationist program and political methods of the civil rights movement. Revealingly, hardly anyone seemed to notice the shift; supporters and opponents alike saw Ali's increasingly political explanation of his attitude to the war as a logical extension of the man's personality, and in keeping with the changing temper of the times. Both Ali's turn to the Nation and his support for the integration struggle in Louisville had their roots in his personal identification with a larger constituency. It was his abiding sense of responsibility to that constituency that compelled him to re-define again and again the parameters of the role model, to reconstruct who and what he represented, independently of the powers that be, even as he exploited their media in order to do it.

In Louisville, Ali visited churches and schools and was dogged by reporters. Later that day, he made his most explicitly political statement yet about the war and his refusal to participate in it:

> Why should they ask me to put on a uniform and go ten thousand miles from home and drop bombs and bullets on brown people in Vietnam while so-called Negro people in Louisville are treated like dogs and denied simple human rights? No, I am not going ten thousand miles from home to help murder and burn another poor nation simply to continue the domination of white slavemasters of the darker people the

> world over. This is the day when such evils must come to an end. I have been warned that to take such a stand would put my prestige in jeopardy and could cause me to lose millions of dollars which should accrue to me as the champion. But I have said it once and I will say it again. The real enemy of my people is right here. I will not disgrace my religion, my people or myself by becoming a tool to enslave those who are fighting for their own justice, freedom and equality. . . . If I thought the war was going to bring freedom and equality to twenty-two million of my people, they wouldn't have to draft me, I'd join tomorrow. But I either have to obey the laws of the land or the laws of Allah. I have nothing to lose by standing up for my beliefs. So I'll go to jail. We've been in jail for four hundred years.

The confused young fighter who merely wanted to avoid the unpleasantness of military service had matured into a hero of global solidarity. In Louisville, Ali testified to the tranformative power of the experience of struggle, one of the keynotes of the sixties. Circumstances, personal and historical, had locked him in conflict with authority; in the fire of that conflict, new and powerful links between the inner self and a broader community were forged. Undoubtedly, Ali received help in drawing up statements such as the one he issued in Louisville, though probably more from Chauncey Eskridge than from the Nation of Islam. Nonetheless, however shaky his grasp of geography, his understanding of the moral dimension of the choice before him was now deeply informed. Significantly, much of the rhetoric and many of the arguments he deployed derived from

Malcolm X, whose shadow, unacknowledged, seems to have hovered over Ali during these years of challenge and change.

• • •

The resistance to open housing in Louisville was one of several events in 1966 and 1967 which fed King's growing pessimism about the prospects for peaceful social change. Returning to Louisville in July, he told a crowd, "The vast majority of white Americans are racists"—he had arrived at a position little different from that held by Malcolm in the last year of his life. Five days after meeting Ali, and exactly one year before his assassination, on 4 April 1967, King delivered his magnificent oration at the Riverside Church in New York. In this speech, his most uncompromising indictment of the war to date, he wove together the themes of racism, war, poverty and America's global role. Responding to those who pressed him to condemn ghetto rioters, he explained, "I could never raise my voice against the violence of the oppressed without first having spoken clearly to the greatest purveyor of violence in the world today"—the American government. "Every man of humane convictions must decide on the protest that best suits his convictions," he declared, "but we must all protest." Describing himself as "bound by allegiances and loyalties which are broader and deeper than nationalism," he recommended conscientious objection to "all who find the American course in Vietnam a dishonorable and unjust one."

Only three years before, when he received the Nobel Peace Prize, King had been fêted by the media and acknowledged as the preeminent leader of black Americans. But his militant turn against the Vietnam War infuriated many former allies. Roy Wilkins, Whitney

Young, A. Philip Randolph and Bayard Rustin all publicly distanced themselves from King, as they had from Robeson twenty years before. "Dr. King has done a grave injury to those who are his natural allies," lectured the *Washington Post*. "He has diminished his usefulness to his cause, his country and his people." The *New York Times* rebuked his "reckless" attacks on America and described his opposition to the war as "wasteful and self-defeating." *Life* magazine characterized the Riverside speech as "a demagogic slander that sounded like a script for Radio Hanoi." Hoover wrote to Johnson: "He is an instrument in the hands of the subversive forces seeking to undermine our nation." The NAACP board described King's attempt to link Vietnam and civil rights as "a serious tactical mistake."

Alarmed at the growth of anti-war sentiment among blacks, the government and the military launched a counter-offensive. General Westmoreland told reporters in Saigon, "I have an intuitive feeling that the Negro servicemen have a better understanding than whites of what the war is about." Westmoreland also repeated his racial view of the conflict: Orientals valued human lives, including their own, less than Americans, and were therefore harder to beat on the field of battle. Briefed by the military, the *New York Times* reported, "In Vietnam the Negro for the first time has been given the chance to do his share of fighting for his country" and concluded, "The Negro's performance in battle is in every way the equal of his white comrades." But among black youths such assurances rang hollow. At a Senate hearing on the draft, the editor of the Howard University newspaper told the politicians that black people saw little reason to risk their lives. "Those people who benefit most from the society should be those people who will lay down their lives for it." On

5 April, the day after King's Riverside speech, an anti-draft caravan toured New York City schools; the *Times* reported with some bemusement that interest in the caravan's message was keenest among young blacks and Puerto Ricans. The next day, a draft-card burner was sentenced to two and a half years in prison for refusing to accept a replacement card.

On 11 April, Ali was ordered to report for induction. On 15 April, Manhattan witnessed the largest anti-war demonstration yet staged in the United States. One hundred and twenty-five thousand gathered in Central Park and later heard speeches from King, CORE's Floyd McKissick and Stokely Carmichael (who described Selective Service as "white people sending black people to make war on yellow people in order to defend land they stole from red people"). A columnist in the *New York Times* complained that the protesters smelled bad and dismissed them as frustrated misfits, but the unprecedented size of the demonstration made it clear that the misfits were becoming a force in the land.

On 25 April, Ali's lawyers filed a petition in federal court stating that their client would not agree to induction and requesting exemption on religious grounds. The Justice Department contested the petition; a spokesman argued, "If he wins, all the Muslims will refuse to take the oath, and where will we get the soldiers?" The next day, Johnson intensified the bombing of North Vietnam. His supporters argued that domestic criticism was undermining the war effort and accused dissenters of disloyalty. A letter to Secretary of Defense Robert MacNamara from one thousand seminarians urged an extension of the conscientious objection criteria to include moral objection to a particular war, thus "easing the coming confrontation between the demands of law and those whose conscience will not permit them to fight in Vietnam." Neither the government nor the judiciary was prepared to contemplate such a concession to the anti-war movement. The federal court rejected Ali's petition and he was ordered to report for induction.

On 28 April, Westmoreland assured a joint session of Congress that the war was just, necessary and winnable. That morning, Ali reported, as ordered, to the Federal Customs House in Houston. Outside, a small group of demonstrators, including SNCC's notorious Rap Brown, cheered the champion. Students from Texas Southern University appeared with a banner reading "Stay Home Muhammad Ali." Others held placards urging "Draft Beer—Not Ali." The heavyweight champion, along with twenty-five others called for induction that day, spent the morning filling out forms and undergoing routine examinations. The induction ceremony took place at 1:05 P.M. Three times the sergeant in charge called the name, "Cassius Marcellus Clay," and three times Ali refused to step over the yellow line marked on the floor. After being formally advised by a Navy lieutenant that his refusal was a felony offense and made him liable to imprisonment, Ali submitted a written declaration claiming exemption as a minister of Islam. He then issued a four-page statement to the media:

> I am proud of the title "World Heavyweight Champion" which I won in the ring in Miami on February 25, 1964. The holder of it should at all times have the courage of his convictions and carry out those convictions, not only in the ring but throughout all phases of his life. It is in light of my own

> personal convictions that I take my stand in rejecting the call to be inducted into the armed services. I do so with full realization of its implications and possible consequences. I have searched my conscience and I find I cannot be true to my belief in my religion by accepting such a call. My decision is a private and individual one. In taking it I am dependent solely upon Allah as the final judge of these actions brought about by my own conscience.

Although Ali still claimed the right to act and speak as an unrepresentative individual, he also now appealed explicitly to his obligations as a role model, which he had radically re-defined. To the boxing authorities, his use of the heavyweight title as a platform for protest was an intolerable affront. One hour later, before Ali had been charged with any offense, the powerful New York State Athletic Commission suspended his boxing license and stripped him of his title. Within a month, other state commissions had followed suit, as had the WBA, Madison Square Garden, the British Boxing Board of Control (at this time, Harold Wilson's Labour government was still backing Johnson in Vietnam) and the European Boxing Union. It was the beginning of his three-and-a-half-year exile from the ring.

Boxing promoters welcomed his removal from the scene, and quickly announced plans to stage an elimination contest for the "vacant" title among a wide array of contenders. "There is more money to be made in a tournament among these men than in a continuation of Clay's one-sided fights," reported Robert Lipsyte. When asked about the champ who had made him a fortune, Bob

Arum, who was promoting the eight-man eliminator, responded jokingly, "Cassius who?"

Ali's refusal to cross the yellow line was front-page news, not only in America, but around the world. In Guyana, Cheddi Jagan led a picket of the US embassy. In Karachi, a young Pakistani fasted outside the US consulate. There was a demonstration in Cairo. An editorial in the *Ghana Pioneer* deplored what it called the "concerted efforts" to strip Ali of his championship. During the first major British demonstrations against the war in April 1967, among the host of leaflets handed out in Grosvenor Square was one reading "LBJ Don't Send Muhammad Ali to War." Bertrand Russell congratulated Ali on his courage and assured him, "The air will change. I sense it." Incensed by the hypocrisy of the American government, an Irish boxing fan named Paddy Monaghan, a hod carrier who lived on a council estate in Abingdon, began a long and lonely picket of the US embassy in London. Over the next three years, he would collect more than twenty thousand signatures on a petition calling for the restoration of Muhammad Ali's heavyweight title.

Lionized abroad, Ali found himself a prisoner in a society increasingly polarized over the issues he stood for. In an editorial entitled "Clay v. the Army," the *New York Times* argued that to exempt "Clay" would "chip away the foundation of universally shared obligation on which the Selective Service system rests. Citizens cannot pick and choose which wars they wish to fight any more than they can pick and choose which laws they wish to obey. Moreover, if Cassius Clay and other draft-age objectors believe the war in Vietnam is unjust, they have the option of going to prison on behalf of their beliefs." The latter argument was one which Ali refused to accept: "If justice prevails, if my constitutional rights are upheld, I will be forced to go neither to the army nor jail."

Black opinion on Ali remained divided. An editorial in the *Amsterdam News*, headed "American Tragedy," linked Ali's draft defiance to King's Riverside protest. It noted that Ali's objections to military service "stem ultimately from our centuries of racial injustices" but was careful not to endorse his stand. A survey of Harlem opinion in the same paper revealed contrasting perceptions. A black Rockefeller aid declared, "It's a tragedy. It is being blown up out of all proportion. He's not Ralph Bunche or Roy Wilkins, whose views on foreign policy would carry weight as far as Negro opinion is concerned." But a community activist in a local youth project disagreed: "It should encourage every black man in the new generation to follow in his footsteps." In his syndicated column, Jackie Robinson criticized King's statements on the war and in particular his support for Ali. "I admire this man as a fighting champion and a man who speaks his mind. I can't help feeling he wants to have his cake and eat it too. I can't help wondering how he can expect to make millions of dollars in this country and then refuse to fight for it." He asked King: "What values do you have in mind when you praise him [Ali] and say he has given up so much? I think all he has given up is his citizenship. I think his advisers have given him a bum steer. I think the only persons who will come out well in this situation are his lawyers."

Robinson's views, however, no longer carried great weight among younger blacks, and among the most politically conscious it was Ali and not Robinson who now epitomized black aspirations. Those who had placed the burden of symbolic representation on black sports stars now found the tables turned. A writer in *The Liberator* relished their discomfort:

> By refusing to obey, Ali poses a problem of disastrous potential. How can the government overcome? Can "responsible negro leaders" be called upon to quell the redoubtable Muhammad Ali's influence over black youth? But Messrs Roy Wilkins, Whitney Young, A. Philip Randolph, and Ralph Bunche are scorned as paid buffoons of white liberalism! And the Reverend Dr Martin Luther King has defected to the peace movement! In short, Muhammad Ali has become the establishment's domestic Vietcong: his impact far outweighs his size.

Two days after Ali refused induction, King preached a sermon in his Ebenezer Baptist Church in Atlanta. With the atheist Stokely Carmichael sitting ostentatiously in the congregation, King urged "every man in this country who believes that this war is abominable and unjust" to take the path of conscientious objection. And once again he singled out Ali for praise. "He is giving up even fame. He is giving up millions of dollars in order to stand up for what his conscience tells him is right." The following day, 1 May, Ali's lawyers moved to politicize his conflict with the government by filing an appeal in federal court on the exclusion of blacks from draft boards. In the two states dealing with Ali's case, Kentucky and Texas, only 0.2 percent and 1.1 percent of draft board members were black, although blacks made up 7.1 percent and 12.4 percent of their respective populations. On Ali's behalf, the lawyers asked that all draft boards in Kentucky be restrained from functioning until more blacks were appointed. The appeal was denied.

A week later, a hitherto little-known group of Oakland militants calling themselves the Black Panther Party for Self-Defense burst on to the national scene when they invaded the California state legislature in a protest over what they saw as an attempt to restrict their constitutional right to carry arms. "As the aggression of the racist American government escalates in Vietnam," their press statement declared, "the police agencies of America escalate the repression of black people throughout the ghettos." Their analysis was echoed by an increasingly indignant James Baldwin, who argued, "A racist society can't but fight a racist war—this is the bitter truth. The assumptions acted on at home are the assumptions acted on abroad, and every American negro knows this, for he, after the American Indian, was the first 'Viet Cong' victim."

In Washington, DC, a week after refusing induction, Ali toured the ghetto and spoke to inmates at a federal penitentiary. At Howard University he was welcomed by a huge and enthusiastic crowd comprising the majority of the student body. At the invitation of the newly formed Black Power Committee, Ali spoke from the steps of Frederick Douglass Hall (university officials had denied the committee permission to hold the meeting inside). "We have been brainwashed," Ali told the crowd. "Even Tarzan, king of the jungle, in black Africa, is white." When a heckler offered to take his place in the army for $1000, Ali shot back, "Your life is worth more than a thousand dollars, brother." Unprotected, Ali immersed himself in the throng. According to local newspapers, a "carnival atmosphere" prevailed. Students said they were impressed by Ali's "lack of arrogance" and his "positively black" presence.

Days later, Ali addressed another student crowd at the University of Chicago's Stag Field. "I have lost nothing," he told the students, a mix of black and white. "I have gained the respect of thousands worldwide, I have gained peace of mind." In a call-and-response routine that was to become a stock-in-trade in the coming years, he bellowed, "Who is the heavyweight champion of the world?" and the packed stadium roared back the indisputable answer, "Ali! Ali! Ali!"

• • •

On 8 May 1967 Ali was indicted by a federal grand jury in Houston. Of the twenty-one citizens on the jury, one was black. Ali was photographed, fingerprinted and released on $5000 bail on condition he did not leave the US.

In early June, Herbert Muhammad brought together a number of black sports stars for a private meeting with Ali in Cleveland. Some observers were convinced Herbert wanted the stars to persuade Ali to make a deal with the government. If that was so, Herbert had seriously underestimated his fighter's determination. The stars, including football players Jim Brown and Willie Davis and basketball heroes Bill Russell and Lew Alcindor (who later converted to the Hanafi brand of Islam and changed his name to Kareem Abdul-Jabbar), found Ali in a mood of quiet determination. Many left the meeting deeply moved by Ali's sincerity and courage. "Ali didn't need our help," Jabbar recalled, "because as far as the black community was concerned, he already had everybody's heart. He gave so many people courage to test the system." For Bill Russell, Ali in 1967 was "a man accepting special responsibilities." He told *Sports Illustrated*:

> I'm not worried about Muhammad Ali. He is better equipped than anyone I know to withstand the trials in store for him. What I'm worried about is the rest of us.

Years later, Russell told Thomas Hauser, "Philosophically, Ali was a free man. Besides being probably the greatest boxer ever, he was free. And he was free at a time when historically it was very difficult to be free no matter who you were or what you were. Ali was one of the first truly free people in America." But at this moment this truly free man was facing not only the threat but the likelihood of jail. Gerald Early claims that Ali was no "martyr" because "he never went to jail." But this is to substitute hindsight for history. In 1967, and for the next three years, Ali had every reason to believe he would end up in prison and never fight again. After all, in those days there were few, if any, precedents for a black person defying federal authority and getting away with it. Robeson and Du Bois had been effectively silenced and forced into exile for merely articulating the ideas that Ali was now acting upon.

In Houston, on 19 June 1967, Ali was tried by an all-white jury. His attorneys raised a host of objections, including a protest against the all-white make-up of the draft board that had classified him, but the Justice Department and the judge insisted the only relevant factor was Ali's refusal to obey the induction order. The black attorney prosecuting the case for the government argued that if Ali escaped the draft, large numbers of black youths would be encouraged to join the Muslims. He also noted that, in the course of his dealings with the Selective Service, Ali had claimed exemption on a variety of grounds, and that therefore there was reason to suspect that his claim to conscientious objector status was insincere. (Under the law, sincerity was a crucial test for all CO applicants.) The illustrious defendant listened to the arguments in bored silence. After deliberating for twenty minutes, the jury found him guilty. Ali asked the judge to pass sentence quickly. "I'd appreciate it if the court will do it now, give me my sentence now, instead of waiting and stalling for time." The prosecution told the judge that "Clay" had a record of good conduct but "he got into trouble when he joined the Black Muslims, which are just as much in politics as religion." For the first time in the proceedings, Ali objected. "My religion isn't political in no way."

The judge handed down the maximum sentence of five years in prison and a $10,000 fine. The usual sentence in these cases at the time was eighteen months, and even the US attorney seemed surprised at the severity of the judgement. Ali was released on bail pending appeal. His passport was confiscated.

In Washington, on the day of Ali's conviction, the House passed a bill to extend the draft for another four years. The vote was 337 to 29. The House also passed a law—by 385 to 19—making it a federal crime to "desecrate" the flag. The following week, on 23 June, Ali appeared at his first and only anti-war demonstration. Johnson was scheduled to speak at a $500-a-plate fund-raising dinner at the Century Plaza Hotel in Los Angeles. In response, local anti-war activists organized a rally at the Cheviot Hill Playground. Twenty thousand turned out for the largest anti-war gathering yet held in southern California. The speakers included Benjamin Spock and Rap Brown. Ali arrived in a Rolls-Royce and mounted a garbage can to address the crowd. "Anything designed for peace and to stop the killing I'm for one hundred percent," he told them. "I'm not a leader. I'm not here to advise you. But I encourage you to express yourself." And he launched into his now familiar refrain, "Who's the champion of the world?" The *Los Angeles Times* noted suspiciously that the crowd replied with "Clay's Black Muslim name." The demonstrators then marched (without Ali) to the hotel, where the Supremes were performing for the president (their boss, Berry Gordy, regarded this as a sound commercial move). Governor Ronald Reagan had placed the National Guard on stand-by. When some of the demonstrators began a non-violent sit-in in front of the hotel, 1200 LAPD officers attacked the crowd with clubs. After an hour of mayhem, fifty demonstrators had been arrested and at least two hundred injured. A shocked (white) demonstrator commented, "I saw Mississippi in Los Angeles last night." The city council condemned the demonstrators and refused to hear the organizers' well-documented complaint about police misbehavior. It was to be several years before anti-war activists attempted to stage another mass demonstration in Los Angeles.

The violence outside the Century Plaza may have deterred Ali from future participation in large-scale anti-war protests. Certainly, from that moment on, without in the least diluting his anti-war stand, Ali preferred to speak as an individual, from his own platforms. Not that it made any difference to the forces of law and order. On 25 July, an FBI memorandum recommended intensified surveillance of "Clay," who, the anonymous author complained, has "utilized his position as a nationally known figure in the sports world to promote through appearances at various gatherings an ideology completely foreign to the basic American ideals of equality and justice for all, love of God and country."

• • •

In August 1967, Ali's appeal against the confiscation of his passport was heard in Houston. Talking to Hugh McIlvanney before the hearing, Ali was at pains to distinguish himself from other black power figures and to assert his belief in non-violence:

> Rap Brown and these boys can say what they like because they're nobody. Nobody gives a damn. With me it's different. If I went to a negro district they'd come runnin'. It would just take some young fool to throw something and that would be it. He don't care anything about race. He wants publicity. He wants to see a nice fire. I want to keep away from that stuff.

Ali's lawyers presented recordings of Ali's appearances on television to support their client's contention that he had said nothing anti-American or inflammatory. Ali himself promised to inform local police chiefs before he visited black areas. But this belated attempt to persuade the courts that Ali really was a role model of the old school came to nought. The judge decided that his presence at the Los Angeles peace rally revealed "a ready willingness to participate in anti-government and anti-war activities." He told Ali he should consider himself lucky not to be confined to one state or district.

The second half of 1967 witnessed an intensification of domestic anti-war protest, climaxing in the spectacular demonstration outside the Pentagon and militant anti-draft actions in Oakland. Yet as protests swelled, so did the ferocity of the war. By the end of the year, there were half a million US troops in Vietnam, who were, according to the Department of Defense, killing or seriously injuring one thousand non-combatants a week. In early 1968, the CIA launched Operation Phoenix, in the course of which tens of thousands of Vietnamese civilians were kidnapped and tortured. In March, US troops slaughtered 347 civilians in the hamlet of My Lai, an atrocity concealed from the American public until November 1969. The war was costing the US taxpayer some $2 billion a month and leaving some one hundred US troops dead each week. The Pentagon Papers reveal that one of MacNamara's assistants characterized US war aims at this stage as "70 percent to avoid a humiliating US defeat" and only 10 percent "to permit the people of South Vietnam to enjoy a better, freer way of life."

• • •

A sad old soldier once told me a story
About a battlefield that he was on
He said a man should never fight for glory
He must know what is right and what is wrong

So I'm headin' for the nearest foreign border
Vancouver may be just my kind of town
Cause they don't have the kind of law and order
That tends to keep a good man underground

Flying Burrito Brothers, 1968

Of the 350,000 men who received induction notices in 1967, 952 were subsequently convicted under Selective Service legislation, among them Muhammad Ali. Ninety percent of those convicted received jail sentences. In the next three years, this trickle of defiance swelled into a great wave. The number of appeals against 1-A classification multiplied from only four per thousand in 1965 to seventy-nine per thousand in 1968 and one hundred and two per thousand in 1969. In 1970, more than 100,000 applications for conscientious objector status were submitted to local draft boards—more than in all of World War I and World War II combined. By the end of the war, 22,000 men had been indicted for draft law violations. Only 7 percent of them claimed traditional pacifist allegiances. A total of 50,000 sought sanctuary abroad.

The first draft-card burnings took place in late 1964. In October 1965, SDS chapters organized sit-ins outside draft boards (in a punitive response, General Lewis Hershey, director of the Selective Service system, altered the status of some student demonstrators from 2-S to 1-A). In December 1966, the SDS national council called for non-compliance with the draft laws and adopted the slogan "from protest to resistance"—an evolution which Ali himself was undergoing at that time, albeit unwillingly. That month a national anti-draft conference at the University of Chicago attracted five hundred participants. Student-body presidents warned Johnson: "A great many of those faced with the prospect of military duty find it hard to square performance of the duty with concepts of personal integrity and conscience."

April 1967 witnessed the first mass burning of draft cards. In San Francisco, David Harris (husband of Joan Baez and, after Ali, the most well-known draft resister in America) announced the formation of The Resistance.

> There are many ways to avoid the draft, to stay clear of this war. Most of us now have deferments . . . but all these individual outs have no effect on the draft, the war, or the consciousness of this country. To co-operate with conscription is to perpetuate its existence, without which the government could not wage war. We have chosen to openly defy the draft and confront the government and its war directly. . . . Our hope is that upon our example every young man in America will realize that he must decide whether to resist or acquiesce to the draft and the war.

During Stop the Draft Week in October 1967, demonstrations were staged across the country. "Before, we talked. Now we must act," urged an SDS leaflet. "We must stop what we oppose." In Oakland, thousands of white demonstrators battled with police in a forlorn effort to close down the local induction center. An SDS strategist called the event "a watershed in the course of the anti-draft and white student movement analogous to Watts for the black movement." Conspiracy charges were brought against seven individuals alleged to have organized the Oakland actions.

In Washington, as demonstrators encircled the Pentagon, Yale chaplain William Sloane Coffin and Benjamin Spock tried to return one thousand draft cards to the Justice Department, which refused to accept them. A week later, Daniel Berrigan and colleagues invaded the Baltimore Customs House and poured blood on draft records. In December, during the second Stop the Draft Week, attempts to close induction centers and draft boards (rarely successful) led to hundreds of arrests. A sit-in led by Spock in Whitehall in lower Manhattan was broken up by mounted police. In January 1968, Spock, Coffin and others were arraigned for "conspiracy to counsel, aid and abet" draft evaders.

Despite government reprisals, direct actions against the draft proliferated over the next two years. In May 1968, the Catonsville Nine raided a draft board in a Baltimore suburb. In September, activists in Milwaukee followed their lead. In 1969, the Pasadena Three took 600 1-A files and burned them in a field (an offense for which they received three years in federal prison); the Silver Spring Three threw paint on files and destroyed equipment; the Chicago Fifteen stole files and burned them; and on 4 July, the New York Five shredded 6500 1-A files and damaged the "1" and "A" keys on draft-board typewriters. In October, two activists set fire to draft records in Akron. Records were shredded in Indianapolis, Minneapolis and Boston. That year, student-body presidents sent another letter to the White House. Its explicit call for resistance is a measure of how the mood had changed since their last appeal in 1966:

> We must make an agonizing choice: to accept induction into the armed forces, which we feel would be irresponsible to ourselves, our country, and our fellow man; or to refuse induction, which is contrary to our respect for law and involves injury to our personal lives and careers. Left without a third

> alternative, we will act according to our conscience. Along with thousands of our fellow students, we campus leaders cannot participate in a war which we believe to be immoral and unjust.

Among the numbers who resisted the draft, none was even remotely as famous as Muhammad Ali, and his defiance is surely worth more than the footnote it's usually assigned in accounts of the growth of the anti-war movement. As the principal public role model for conscientious objectors and draft resisters, he gave courage to thousands of young men, many of them isolated from the organized movement. He made dissent visible, audible and attractive.

In this era of youthful celebrities, it is remarkable how few seemed to have grappled with the dilemma that Ali faced—and how few were prepared to make the choice he made and take the consequences. Although the mass, self-ordained counter-culture was intimately linked, at least in the public's mind, with protest against the war, the politics of the war and of anti-war activism rarely intruded upon the nebulous celebration of "love and peace." Popular music provided the counter-culture, and the anti-war-movement, with a unifying ethos, but scarcely any popular musicians took the kind of stand, either in their lyrics or their lives, that Ali did. To the extent that the music of the late sixties referred to Vietnam, it did so mainly in reference to the draft, which directly affected the lives of many in its audience. In spring 1967, Country Joe and the Fish released their "Feel-Like-I'm-Fixin'-to-Die-Rag." Its morbid sarcasm offended some older peace movement veterans, but delighted teenagers. That year also saw the release of Arlo Guthrie's "Alice's

Restaurant" and the Byrds' "Draft Morning," in which the sound of bombs and gunfire punctuates the mellow country harmonies:

> Today
> was the day for action
> leave my bed
> to kill instead
> why should it happen?

As in other songs of the time, the draft here was resented primarily as a personal intrusion. The next year, Creedence Clearwater Revival recorded "Fortunate Son" (a reflection on the class inequities of the draft system); Steppenwolf, the forgettable "Draft Resister," and the Burritos (including Chris Hillman, who co-wrote "Draft Morning"), the ballad "My Uncle," the best song by a white group about the draft and one of the few that treats it as a moral choice. In 1969, John Lennon and the Plastic Ono Band released "Give Peace a Chance," a song utterly void of politics but carrying, in the circumstances, a huge political punch. At the November Moratorium march in Washington, Pete Seeger led a million demonstrators in repetitive chorus after chorus. Indeed, as a popular-culture hero, only John Lennon even comes close to rivaling Ali in his forthright opposition to American policy in Vietnam. In 1971, Lennon paid thousands of pounds to Michael X for the bloodied boxing shorts Ali had presented him in 1966, then donated the shorts to an anti-war fund-raiser. Because of his statements on Vietnam, Lennon, like Ali, was targeted by the FBI.

The rise of rock and roll coincided with that of the anti-war movement, and both attracted a vast constituency of white youth. As a result, some radical critics came to see the new music as an instrument of social revolution. The "guitar army," in John Sinclair's phrase, would storm the bastions of American power. But there was always a fundamental distinction between rock music, which treated radicalized youth as consumers, and protest politics, which treated rock-loving youth as participants. It was a distinction easily overlooked by many of the media-designated spokespersons for "the younger generation," though not by record company executives.

Strikingly, Vietnam and the draft largely vanished from white popular music after 1969. An ostensibly revolutionary album like Jefferson Airplane's (execrable) *Volunteers* makes no mention of it. On New Year's Eve 1970, Jimi Hendrix, with his new all-black Band of Gypsies, recorded "Machine Gun" before a live audience. "I'd like to dedicate this one to the draggin' scene that's goin' on," Hendrix told the crowd, "all the soldiers that are fightin' in Chicago, Milwaukee and New York . . . oh yeah, and all the soldiers fightin' in Vietnam." The ambiguity of the dedication was matched by the song:

> machine gun
> tearing my body all apart
> evil man make me kill ya
> evil man make you kill me
> evil man make me kill you
> even though we're only families apart
> well I pick up my axe and fight like a bomber

(you know what I mean)
hey and your bullets keep knocking me down

In its fusion of military, sexual and musical metaphors, the Hendrix song exemplified what David E. James called "the ambiguity of the ecstatic energy of destruction which allows rock and the war to become interchangeable metaphors for each other." Hendrix (who was the same age as Ali) was a black American R&B virtuoso who had recreated himself in mid-sixties England as a prophet of psychedelia. In this context, his blackness became exotic and erotic. At the end of January 1970, the Band of Gypsies played their second concert—at an anti-war fund-raiser in Madison Square Garden. Hendrix's manager disapproved of the overtly political gig and, some say, slipped the guitarist an overdose of LSD to prevent him appearing on stage. Whatever the truth, during the band's second song Hendrix stopped and announced, "I'm sorry but we just can't get it together," and walked off. It was the last performance of the Band of Gypsies.

Rock music offered emotional cohesion and a sense of cultural mission to the anti-war movement, but it also inculcated quietism and consumerism. The sixties witnessed a momentary intersection between capital and mass resistance in the global media marketplace, an intersection which Ali's career helped generate. It was discovered that gestures of defiance could be commodified and marketed, and the profits recycled to bolster precisely those forces which were allegedly being defied. "We found out, and it wasn't years later till we did," Keith Richards noted, "that all the bread we made for

Decca was going into making little black boxes that go into American air force bombers to bomb fucking North Vietnam."

Popular culture became simultaneously a vehicle of protest and a vehicle of incorporation. The impact of this paradoxical development on the rapidly evolving social movements—especially in America where they lacked roots in organized labor or a socialist tradition—was overwhelmingly deleterious. The radical students of the late sixties found themselves in the same dilemma that had faced America's black community for generations: the people recognized by the establishment as their representatives were not in any way accountable to the constituency they were alleged to represent. What made Ali different from other popular-culture heroes of the day was his powerful sense of accountability, not to the media he used so skillfully, but to a burgeoning global army of supporters.

• • •

In exile, Ali found himself without finance and without organizational support. The white promoters and lawyers had fled from his camp; the Nation of Islam continued to manage his affairs from a distance, but offered no money and little political backup; after Los Angeles, he kept his distance from the organized anti-war and anti-draft movements. He was alone, as he never was during his fighting years, but at the same time he found himself embraced by an international constituency comprising hundreds of millions. Despite the press attacks and the threat of jail, Ali rarely expressed a bitter thought during these years. Reporters found him quietly determined, but ready, as ever, to lighten the mood with jokes, pranks and surreal monologues.

In August 1967, Ali married the seventeen-year-old Belinda Boyd, who had been raised in the Nation of Islam. After his bruising experience with his first wife, Sonji, Ali may have sought someone more compliant, or at least more willing to conform to the Nation's definition of Muslim femininity. Certainly Belinda was to play a key role in helping Ali manage the more modest lifestyle imposed by his exclusion from the ring—even as she gave birth to four children (including the twins, Jamillah and Rasheeda) in four years. To meet his mounting legal expenses and feed his family, Ali took to the college lecture circuit. In 1968 alone, he spoke at some two hundred campuses. Black or white, Ivy League or A & M, Ali didn't care. His appearances were festive occasions, his speeches laced with jokes, poetry and political brio. "Talking is a whole lot easier than fighting," he said, though he did spend time preparing his speeches and even rehearsing routines in front of a mirror. The students found his conservative homilies against drugs, sex, alcohol and intermarriage quaint, but they always responded with one voice to the exhortation with which he finished his talks: "Can my title be taken away without my being whupped?" "No!" "One more time!" "NO!" "Who's the heavyweight champion of the world?" "You are!"

In his college talks, Ali invoked the classic themes of black nationalism—separatism, black pride and the need for a black homeland—often using analogies and formulations favored in the early sixties by Malcolm X. "When are we going to wake up as black people and end the lie that white is better than black? We've been down so long we can't even imagine having our own country." Like Malcolm, Ali linked the discovery of racial pride to a new internationalist perspective: "I'm expected to go overseas to help free people in South Vietnam and at the same time my people here are being brutalized and mistreated and this is really the same thing that's happening over in Vietnam." Mostly, Ali talked about the call of conscience and his own need to "speak truth to power," those great underlying themes of the sixties. In the colleges, the draft issue struck close to home, and Ali's defiance was inspirational, all the more so since he had never been able to shelter under a student deferment.

> Damn the money. Damn the heavyweight championship. I will die before I sell out my people for the white man's money. The wealth of America and the friendship of all the people who support the war would be nothing if I'm not content internally and if I'm not in accord with the will of Allah.

During the years Ali was touring the campuses, a new wave of black student activism washed across the country, fired by Black Power and frequently centering on the demand for black studies. The concerns with black identity and culture that had seemed so extreme and eccentric when articulated by Malcolm in the early sixties had become the common currency of black youth, not least because of the high-profile and highly appealing example of Muhammad Ali, who was, at the same time, a physical presence on the campuses. It was a confrontation between the local Black Students' Union and the white editor of the college newspaper over a derogatory remark the latter had made about Ali that lit the fuse of the conflict that was to engulf San Francisco State University in 1968 and 1969. Here, the struggle for a black studies department and more minority admissions led to a bitter 134-day student strike, ending with a total police occupation of the campus and year-long jail sentences for the strike leaders.

• • •

In the wake of the assassination of Martin Luther King in April 1968, black ghettos in more than one hundred and twenty cities across the country erupted. Sixty-five thousand National Guardsmen and federal troops were summoned. Fifteen thousand were arrested and thirty-eight killed, including Bobby Hutton, the seventeen-year-old treasurer of the Black Panther party. In Washington, DC, the Black Anti-War Anti-Draft Union led a march from a local high school to Howard University, where a crowd of one thousand cheered as the US flag was lowered and the black nationalist colors raised in its place.

Ali's draft case was to play a coincidental but critical role in the historical evaluation of King. The ACLU had filed a plea in Ali's case challenging the exclusion of blacks from draft boards (an issue it had already raised in the case of SNCC activist Cleveland Sellers). In its submission, the ACLU noted that Ali's Selective Service file was crammed with letters and newspaper clippings of a prejudicial nature. One item included in the official dossier was a letter from a member of the public saying simply, "Send that nigger away." In June 1968, the circuit court of appeals confirmed Ali's conviction. While accepting that there was, as Ali's lawyers charged, "systematic exclusion of negroes from draft boards," the court nonetheless upheld the draft board's decision on Ali's classification. However, during the course of the hearings, it was revealed that information on Ali's views had been gleaned from FBI wiretaps of his telephone conversations with Martin Luther King and others. This was the first time any hint of the FBI's extensive and often illegal surveillance operation against King and the civil rights movement had surfaced in the public domain. Hoover at first denied everything, but on 30 August 1968 the Justice Department acknowledged it had recorded Ali's conversations with five individuals under surveillance. It was later revealed that the FBI had kept a file on Ali since he was first sighted with Malcolm X. One FBI agent was even detailed to tape-record Ali's late-night appearances on chat shows. As a result, his encounters with the likes of Johnny Carson appear alongside those with King and Elijah Muhammad in the files.

In response to the revelations, the Supreme Court ordered the district court in Houston to conduct a special hearing to determine if illegal wiretaps had any bearing on Ali's conviction under the draft laws. At the hearing, an FBI agent testified about the surveillance of King, and the ACLU attorney read into the record the details of four of Ali's five recorded conversations. The fifth conversation, conducted with an unidentified individual said to be working for "foreign intelligence," was not disclosed in court but was read in private by the judge, who ruled, in June 1969, that the wiretaps had no impact on Ali's conviction.

• • •

Besides inspiring thousands to resist the draft, Ali ignited a wave of protest among black sports stars. At a Black Power conference held in Newark, New Jersey, in the summer of 1967, a resolution was passed urging black athletes to boycott the 1968 Olympics unless Ali was reinstated as heavyweight champion. During the 1967/68 academic year, black athletes at thirty-seven white-dominated colleges and universities raised demands for more black coaches, facilities, cheerleaders and trainers. Bob Beaman, the future long-jump record-setter, was dropped by his university coach for refusing to compete against Brigham Young University, where the Mormon orthodoxy of white supremacy was still upheld. That year, black sports people came together to form the Olympic Project for Human Rights (OPHR). In its list of demands, the first was "the restoration of Muhammad Ali's titles." The second was the removal of the racist Avery Brundage as head of the United States Olympic Committee, and the third was the exclusion of South Africa and Rhodesia from competition. The demands reflected both the internationalism of Black Power and Ali's symbolic centrality. His exclusion from the ring represented the global exclusion of blacks, and his capacity to challenge and resist that exclusion made him, in the words of Harry Edwards, one of the key organizers of OPHR, "the warrior saint in the revolt of the black athlete in America."

Initially, OPHR advocated a black boycott of the Olympics, but it proved difficult to mobilize support for this tactic among black competitors for whom the Olympics were the chance of a lifetime. Attention turned, instead, to subverting the event from within. The potent symbolism of the Olympic podium—a celebration of individual excellence at the service of the nation-state—was diametrically opposed to the tenets of black consciousness. The militant athletes wanted to compete, and to win, but no longer on behalf of an America which excluded their brothers and sisters. On 16 October 1968, at Mexico City, a supporter of OPHR, Tommie Smith, the twenty-four-year-old son of a migrant laborer, captured the gold medal in the 200 meters with a world-record-breaking run. In third place was another OPHR supporter, John Carlos, a twenty-three year old from Harlem. On the winners' podium, before a global audience of hundreds of millions, the two athletes bowed their heads and raised clenched fists during the US national anthem. Smith explained their gesture:

> I wore a black right-hand glove and Carlos wore the left-hand glove of the same pair. My raised right hand stood for the power in black America. Carlos's raised left hand stood for the unity of black America. Together they formed an arch of unity and power. The black scarf around my neck stood for black pride. The black socks with no shoes stood for black poverty in racist America. The totality of our effort was the regaining of black dignity.

The need to overthrow the old role models had driven Smith and Carlos to invent a complex new symbolism. The tropes of individual victory and national glory were replaced by those of racial solidarity. American Olympic success, which in 1960 Ali himself had portrayed as a Cold War triumph, had been turned on its head, reshaped into nothing less than a public repudiation of the United States and all its works. In a counter-gesture, the authorities persuaded George Foreman, the new Olympic heavyweight boxing champion, to wave a small American flag during his medal ceremony. An FBI report claimed that Foreman's victory over a Soviet fighter and subsequent patriotic display "gave every American an emotional lift." The FBI also noted the "sharp contrast with the earlier, despicable Black Power black-gloved demonstration of Tommie Smith and John Carlos and the anti-Vietnam stand of Cassius Clay." After the Olympics, the FBI arranged for Foreman to receive an award from the Freedom Foundation, which was linked with the J. Edgar Hoover Foundation.

Smith and Carlos were ejected from the Olympic village, banned from the Games and vilified at home, as were other black athletes who backed their protest. "Doing my thing made me feel the freest I ever felt in my whole life," Carlos later recalled, "but I came home to hate." In the *Chicago American*, Brent Mussberger railed at the protest:

> One gets a little tired of having the United States run down by athletes who are enjoying themselves at the expense of their country. Protesting and working constructively against racism in the United States is one thing, but airing one's dirty clothing before the entire world during a fun-and-games tournament was no more than a juvenile gesture by a couple of athletes who should have known better.

Smith and Carlos had committed a new variant on the old offense for which Robeson had been hounded. As a result, the careers of both men were truncated. But there was one asset which the authorities could never take from Smith and Carlos. As far as the public was concerned, they remained the world's number one and number three 200-meters men, just as Ali remained the world heavyweight champion. All three had won these distinctions in fair and open competition. Ali's support grew not only because the tide of opinion swung against the war, but also because he could appeal to sport's egalitarian autonomy:

> I have the world heavyweight title not because it was given to me, not because of my race or religion, but because I won it in the ring through my own boxing ability. Those who want to take it and hold a series of auction-type bouts not only do me a disservice but actually disgrace themselves. I am certain that the sports fans and the fair-minded people throughout America would never accept such a title holder.

In August 1968, Ali toured Times Square with Adam Clayton Powell, then campaigning for his twelfth consecutive term in the House. Following charges of impropriety, Powell had been barred from taking his seat by a vote of his fellow congressmen. "We're here to shake hands with the people and show them what the land of the free and the home of the brave has done to two champions," Powell explained. "I'm not in the Congress and he's not in the ring."

When they staged the elimination bouts for his "vacant" title, Ali warned: "Everybody knows I'm the champion. My ghost will haunt all the arenas. I'll be there, wearing a sheet and whispering, 'Ali-e-e-e! Ali-e-e-e!'" Protesters did appear outside Madison Square Garden during the bouts (with placards reading "Hell No We Ain't Goin" and "Fight Racism, Free Muhammad Ali") but they were dismissed by the boxing moguls, who were happy with the ringside attendance and impressive television ratings. For several years, they remained unaware of how deeply they had compromised their sport when they stripped Ali of his title. Not least among Ali's growing band of supporters were the sports fans, in America and around the world, who recognized the logical integrity of his claim to the heavyweight championship. Carlos and Smith had been castigated for importing politics into the pure realm of sport. But in Ali's case, it was the authorities who had imported the politics; they turned Ali into a martyr not just to the anti-war cause, but to the cause of fair play and pristine sport. Ironically, as a result of the authorities' reaction to his politics, some sports fans—including many in boxing's huge working-class base—began to give those politics a serious hearing. Ali was able to use the specific injustice inflicted upon him to raise awareness about broader and more contentious questions.

• • •

In December 1968, Ali served ten days in Dade County jail, Miami, for driving without a valid license. He seemed to take both the harsh sentence and his first experience of prison life with equanimity. "I'm not scared about going to jail," he said after his release. "Somebody's got to do something to knock the fear out of these negroes. Somebody's got to stand up."

He was often asked, "Do you miss boxing?" and his usual answer was, "No, boxing misses me." But when Howard Cosell inquired about his future plans during a television interview in early 1969, Ali said he hoped to fight again—because he needed the money. The casual remark infuriated Elijah Muhammad. On 4 April 1969, *Muhammad Speaks* carried a statement by the Messenger:

> We tell the world we're not with Muhammad Ali. Muhammad Ali is out of the circle of the brotherhood of the followers of Islam . . . for one year. . . . Mr. Muhammad Ali has sporting blood. Mr. Muhammad Ali desires to do that which the holy Qur'an teaches him against. . . . Mr. Muhammad Ali shall not be recognized with us under the holy name of Muhammad Ali. We will call him Cassius Clay.

Only the year before, Ali had been one of the keynote speakers at the Nation's annual Savior's Day convention in Chicago. Now he was to be spurned by the people for whom he had sacrificed so much, at the time when he needed them most; he was even to be stripped of the "original name" over which he had fought so many battles. Backing his father's verdict, Herbert Muhammad announced he was no longer "at the service of anyone in the sports world." John Ali, the Nation's national secretary, remarked that the former champ was short of money because he "did not follow the wise counsel of Messenger Muhammad in saving himself from waste and extravagance."

What made Elijah Muhammad suddenly re-discover his old prohibition against boxing? Why, of all the weird and wonderful public declarations made by Ali during these years, did the Messenger take such offense at this one? It was hardly in the same league as Malcolm's crack about JFK. Claude Clegg suggests that "along with the declining tithes and loss of the heavyweight title, the draft controversy probably convinced Muhammad to minimize his losses while he was ahead. In essence, Ali had become a liability for the Nation, which was already feeling the sting of enhanced counter-intelligence operations launched by the FBI in 1967." By disciplining his organization's most famous and best-loved member, the old man may also have wished simply to assert his authority. In his last decade, Muhammad governed the Nation of Islam by ostentatiously putting dynamic disciples back in their place while promoting unimaginative henchmen (and in some cases FBI plants).

John Ali was eager to deny reports that the Nation of Islam had bled the fighter dry. However, in early 1970, Muhammad Ali publicly accused Main Bout, the company formed by Bob Arum and the Nation to manage and promote him, of mishandling his finances; as a result, John Ali, one of Elijah's closest associates, was dismissed from his post as the Nation's financial director (two years later, he was reinstated). For three years, *Muhammad Speaks* included not a single reference to the once and future champ.

But the mood of black America, and of large parts of white America, was changing, and at the end of the decade Ali found himself less alone than at any time since he had publicly embraced the Nation of Islam. In late 1969, the National Baptist Convention, the largest black religious organization in the United States and for years a bulwark of anti-Communist conservatism, urged the government to show clemency for Ali in order to "lesson domestic tensions," even as it was careful to remind militant black youth that "the future of Americans is with America."

Among the grunts serving America in Vietnam, Ali found new partisans. According to Wallace Terry, whose book *Bloods* chronicles the black experience in the war, many black soldiers initially believed Ali "had given up being a man" when he refused induction; within a few years, assumptions had been turned upside down. "If you asked black soldiers in 1969 who was his leader in America," Terry reports, "they'd list the late Martin Luther King and Malcolm X, Eldridge Cleaver of the Black Panther Party, and then Muhammad Ali." *Newsweek* reported that 56 percent of blacks now opposed the war because of its impact on their own communities. To black people, Vietnam was "their own particular incubus—a war that depletes their young manhood and saps the resources available to healing ills at home." From 1968, battlefield resistance and indiscipline among American troops escalated sharply. By 1971, for every US solider being treated for combat wounds four were being treated for drug abuse.

Disillusionment was rife at home as well. In October 1969, one million marched in Washington and millions more joined local demonstrations across the country. By early 1970, the proportion of the American public disapproving of the original decision to enter combat had risen to 57 percent. In the face of domestic division and economic downturn, big business also began to register dissent. The *Wall Street Journal*, *Fortune* and *Business Week* expressed increasingly sharp criticism of both the handling and objectives of the war. A cover feature in *Esquire* declared, "Muhammad Ali deserves the right to defend his title." Among the luminaries assembled in a group photo of Ali supporters were Howard Cosell, Michael Harrington, Roy Lichtenstein, Sidney Lumet, George Plimpton, Budd Schulberg, Jose Torres, Truman Capote and James Earl Jones (at that time enjoying Broadway success in the role of Jack Johnson in *The Great White Hope*).

The acme of the anti-war movement was its response to the invasion of Cambodia on 30 April 1970. A spontaneous wave of student protests rolled across the country. At Kent State University in Ohio, four white students were shot dead by the National Guard. Within days, 350 universities were on strike and there were demonstrations at 500 others. The entire California State University system was closed. The National Guard was sent to twenty-one campuses. After a 3000-strong protest at Jackson State University in Mississippi, trigger-happy police fired on a small group outside a dormitory, killing two and wounding fourteen. To honor the victims (and contain the new wave of black anger) New York City officials closed the school system for a day. Howard University suspended regular courses and for the remainder of the semester the campus was dedicated to the study of black liberation.

An estimated four million US students (60 percent of total higher education enrollment) took part in the protests of May 1970, which also spread to high schools and junior highs. No corner of the country was unaffected. It was clear that concessions had to be made—or at least to appear to be made—if control was to be retained. By the end of the year, the number of American troops in Vietnam had declined to 280,000, combat fatalities had dropped sharply, and Muhammad Ali had returned to the ring.

• • •

For years, the government strove vainly to demarcate the "religious" from the "racial" and "political" in Ali's resistance to the draft. And Ali himself rarely succeeded in convincing anyone (other than himself) that his refusal to serve in the military was entirely and exclusively religious. The difficulties in disentangling Ali's motives ought to give pause to those who would, in retrospect, segregate the elements that form the composite moment of the sixties, in an effort to reclaim some and renounce others. Ali's journey through the decade illustrates the inter-relationship of the early and late sixties, of self-expression and collective action, the cultural and the political, the margins and the mainstream, personal identity and global solidarity. The only interpretations of the sixties that can illuminate the period, and provide guides for the future, are those which can account for these inter-relationships, and for Muhammad Ali.

5

At the Rendezvous of Victory

> And no race holds the monopoly of beauty, of intelligence, of strength
> and there is room for all at the rendezvous of victory and we know that the sun turns around our land shining over the plot chosen by our will alone and that every star falls from the sky at our limitless command.
>
> *Aimé Césaire*, Cahier d'un retour au pays natal

In August 1970, Atlanta became the first American city to license an Ali fight since 1967. It was a testimony to the growing political and economic clout of the city's black elite, among them Martin Luther King, Sr. and Maynard Jackson. They forced through the measure despite the enraged opposition of Governor Lester Maddox, who tried to get the Justice Department to intervene. It had been hoped that Ali would fight Joe Frazier for the title, but in light of the continuing uncertainties surrounding Ali's legal position, Frazier's camp remained noncommittal and Ali signed to fight Jerry Quarry.

Meanwhile, the NAACP legal defense fund filed a suit against the New York State Athletic Commission on Ali's behalf. On 28 September, a federal judge, noting that convicted rapists, robbers and army deserters were currently licensed by the commission, ruled that Ali's rights under the Fourteenth Amendment had been violated and ordered his license restored.

In the run-up to the Atlanta bout, the Ali-haters made their presence felt. Gunshots were fired outside Ali's cabin in the Georgia woods. In the mail, he received a box with the severed head of a black chihuahua and the message: "We know how to handle black draft-dodging dogs in Georgia. Stay out of Atlanta!" On 26 October, Ali made his return to the ring. After the years in exile he seemed more aware than ever of his peculiar representative burden: "I'm not just fighting one man. I'm fighting a lot of men, showing them here is one man they couldn't conquer. Lose this one, and it won't just be a loss to me. So many millions of faces throughout the world will be sad." A 90 percent black crowd watched Ali knock out Quarry (the first white American he'd fought since 1962) in the third round. In attendance were Bill Cosby, Sidney Poitier, Ralph Abernathy, Andrew Young, Coretta King, Whitney Young and Mary Wilson. "Because of that fight," Julian Bond recalled, "Atlanta came into its own as the black political capital of America."

The era of Ali's return to the ring witnessed an efflorescence of black pride and black culture. The themes of Black Power were echoed in soul and funk music. White performers had turned their backs on the Vietnam conflict and the music of social protest, but black singers, composers and arrangers spoke more passionately and directly about the war than ever before. In 1970, Edwin Starr released his thunderous "War," and in "Ball of Confusion" the Temptations stormed, "People all over the world shouting end the war, and the band played on." The next year Marvin Gaye released his musical mosaic of social realism and redemptive religious aspiration, *What's Goin On*:

> Crime is increasing
> Trigger-happy policing
> Panic is spreading
> God knows where we're heading

Graphic references to black poverty and oppression, invocations of racial awareness, the call for community responsibility—all regarded as the commercial kiss of death in the early sixties—now became staples of commercial black cultural production. In the hands of Gaye, Curtis Mayfield, Smokey Robinson, Stevie Wonder, Bobby Womack and others, social consciousness was transmuted into an art at once sensuous and reflective. Overt political partisanship, Ali-style, remained rare. Nonetheless, in these years, black popular music articulated, disseminated and legitimized themes and feelings that had long been present in African-American culture, but which only a few years before, when broached by Malcolm X or Muhammad Ali, had been regarded as entirely alien to American public discourse. And, of course, it did so under the aegis—and for the profit—of a white-dominated recording industry.

This was also the era of the rise of reggae, a unique effusion of the Black Atlantic. The Wailers began by re-working American R&B and soul with Caribbean rhythms and instrumentation, themselves the product of a composite culture that had matured over centuries. Their generation felt the impact of Black Power across the West Indies, where it answered the need for a post-colonial analysis of racial oppression. Influenced by Garveyism, pan-Africanism and the revolts in the Third World, as well as the ferment in North American ghettos (not to mention the transnational mysticism of ganja), Marley and Tosh chronicled the experiences and voiced the yearnings of the Jamaican poor, but placed them in a world context. Like the Nation of Islam, they expressed the desire for collective and individual redemption through the Biblical language of exile and return. Like Ali, in speaking of and for a diaspora, they invoked a vision of universal social justice underpinned by human love. From the margins of the world economy, out of a parochial vernacular, they created a vanguard modern sound which proved hugely influential on both sides of the Atlantic and in northern and southern hemispheres.

Even as reggae radiated outward from its home base, the same spirit of Caribbean pride, the same diaspora identity, was carried abroad by the great West Indian cricketers of the 1970s. Under the leadership of Clive Lloyd, they left deference and division behind, and became icons of style and success wherever cricket has a hold on the popular imagination. Viv Richards, the master batsman from Antigua, whose exploits on English wickets gave huge pleasure to Britain's black communities, was the self-conscious personification of black pride, and openly associated himself with both Rastafarianism and Black Power. Not surprisingly, he frequently cited Muhammad Ali as his inspiration and "role model."

In America, however, this era of ever more dramatic assertions of black pride and identity was accompanied by a retreat from political organization and engagement. The anti-war movement had peaked. The reduction of American ground troops in the wake of Nixon's Vietnamization policy blunted domestic opposition, even as US bombers rained destruction on Southeast Asia with unprecedented ferocity. On the civil rights front, legislative progress had ground to a halt. From the late sixties, unemployment was on the rise in the ghettos, which never recovered from the Vietnam War, a war whose reality was receding even then from American consciousness. Amidst the gritty street observation and social criticism, the songs of the time also include wild celebrations of hedonism and invocations of a racial-musical utopia. Funk's great theme became funk itself—"One nation under a groove." More and more, the initiative was being surrendered to representations and representatives. It was the era of Hollywood blaxploitation and the rise of elected black officials. In this contradictory environment the second career of Muhammad Ali—from 1971 to 1978—unfolded, coinciding with the zenith, fracturing and decline of Black Power.

• • •

Six weeks after his comeback fight in Atlanta, Ali knocked out Oscar Bonavena in the fourteenth round at Madison Square Garden. On 30 December he signed to fight Joe Frazier for the undisputed heavyweight championship of the world. Whether measured by the amount of money involved or the scale of global interest, it was at that time the biggest fight in boxing history. Ironically, the promoters and the media owed this bonanza to Ali's defiance of the draft and exile from the ring. Officially, Frazier was the champion and Ali the challenger; in reality, as Frazier himself acknowledged, he would not be recognized as the true titleholder until he beat Ali. For the fans, the fight promised to resolve one of the most hotly debated questions in world sports: Who was really the best heavyweight?

However, it was not only Ali's long absence from the ring, but also its causes and context that made this fight compelling to huge numbers of people otherwise indifferent to boxing. By now, Ali had mastered both the rhetoric of race and the symbolic power of the ring. He knew better than anyone how to combine the two to mobilize popular support (and sell tickets).

> Frazier's no real champion. Nobody wants to talk to him. Oh, maybe Nixon will call him if he wins. I don't think he'll call me. But 98 percent of my people are for me. They identify with my struggle. Same one they're fighting every day in the streets. If I win, they win. I lose, they lose. Anybody black who thinks Frazier can whup me is an Uncle Tom.

Sixty years earlier, when Du Bois had declared "the blacker the mantle the mightier the man," it had seemed, even in the black community, a shocking statement. Now, Ali reclaimed the idea in the common parlance of boxing promotion. The irony was that Frazier had grown up among the poorest of the black poor in South Carolina and his skin, as he himself pointed out, was blacker than Ali's. In calling Frazier "an ignorant gorilla," Ali used language which, had it come from a white fighter, would have provoked a bitter reaction among black people. "Joe Frazier is too ugly to be champ. Joe Frazier is too dumb to be champ. The heavyweight champion should be smart and pretty like me. Ask Joe Frazier, 'How do you feel, champ?'

He'll say, 'Duh, duh, duh.'" Frazier resented being cast by Ali as another Liston and, these days, is one of the few people willing to say anything uncomplimentary about Ali in public. "Calling me an Uncle Tom; calling me the white man's champion. All that was phoniness to turn people against me. He was helping himself, not black people. Ali wasn't no leader of black people. . . . A lot of people went to the fight that night to see Clay's head knocked off and I did my best to oblige them." But this was precisely Joe Frazier's dilemma: the people who wanted him to beat Ali were the die-hard racists, the love-it-or-leave-it brigade, the people who resented everything Ali stood for. Frazier was a magnificent boxer whose tragedy was that he came along at a time when his only public profile was as a foil to Ali. His bitter complaint against Ali—that the latter stole his blackness from him—reveals how much had changed since the days of Liston and Patterson, not to mention Joe Louis and Jack Johnson. Blackness had become a positive attribute, a selling point for professional sports figures, a key to success on and off the level playing field. It was a tremendous achievement and one that belonged in no small measure to Muhammad Ali.

The poet Larry Neal, one of the key figures in the black arts movement of the time, felt the polarization between Ali as the blacks' black and Frazier as the whites' black obscured a much more interesting dialectic between the two men, both of whom, he believed, were necessary expressions of black style. "Frazier is stomp-down blues, bacon, grits and Sunday church. . . . But Ali is body bebop." In the event, the fight proved a contest not only of styles, but of will and staying power. It was a brutal battle, the first of three they would contest over the next four years, and after fifteen rounds Frazier emerged victorious. For the first time since 1964, Ali could no longer claim even the unofficial world championship. He had finally been "whupped" in the ring. It was his first professional defeat, and he accepted it with calm dignity. In Pakistan, however, an Ali fan died of a heart attack, the only known occasion, apart from its cricket matches with India, when sporting partisanship has proved fatal in that country. In London, Sivanandan lamented:

> Tonight the black world weeps that their king has passed away. But tomorrow and tomorrow and tomorrow . . . every black man will become his own king—for that is the legacy that Muhammad Ali leaves. . . . The civil rights movement had only served to cordon off the black athlete in a Bantustan of sport. It was left to Malcolm X and the Black Power movement to threaten the total release of the negro. Muhammad Ali is the epitome of that release. And it is this that bugs white society. He is not just a prizefighter, he is not even one man. He is many men—and all of them black.

• • •

Through all this, the threat of jail still hung over Ali's head. In July 1970, the federal appeal court had upheld his conviction, and during his fights with Quarry, Bonavena and Frazier he was technically out on bail pending a final appeal. In April 1971, his case finally came before the Supreme Court—the same court which had recently refused to sanction conscientious objection on the grounds of opposition to a particular war. Pressure for Ali's imprisonment was still coming from southern congressmen, and the Justice Department never relented in its insistence that Ali's objections to military service "rest on grounds which are primarily political and racial." The chief justice was Warren Burger, a Nixon appointee, and Ali, as Jackie Robinson said, was Nixon's "pet peeve." Back in 1969, when the case first came before the Court, only one judge, Brennan, had been prepared to hear it, but the wiretap revelations had given the judges the excuse to defer the matter by sending it back to a lower court. Now, Brennan and others felt that there was no room for further evasion. Given the mood in the country, Ali had to be accorded a hearing in the Supreme Court before he could be jailed.

Thurgood Marshall, who had been solicitor general when the Justice Department initiated the case against Ali, recused himself. Of the remaining judges only three, Douglas, Brennan and Stewart, supported Ali's appeal; the other five voted to uphold his conviction and send him to jail. Harlan, in his last year on the bench, was sent away to write the majority opinion. His clerk was persuaded by another clerk, who had read *The Autobiography of Malcolm X*, to reconsider Ali's claims. At his instigation, Harlan read Elijah Muhammad's *Message to the Black Man in America*, and as a result became convinced that the Justice Department had misrepresented Ali's and the Nation's beliefs. Since Ali was sincerely opposed to all wars, Harlan decided, he should be exempt. The vote was tied four to four. An outraged Burger told a clerk that Harlan had become an "apologist" for the Black Muslims.

A deadlock in the Supreme Court would mean that the lower court judgement would stand. Ali would still go to jail. But Stewart remained anxious about the implications of jailing Ali in the absence of a final decision by the Supreme Court. A compromise was agreed.

It appeared that in its arguments to the Court, the government had subtly altered its position. It now accepted both that Ali was "sincere" in his opposition to the Vietnam War and that this opposition was based on religious beliefs (the first two tests of conscientious objection), but it still claimed that he did not oppose all wars (the third test) because he had stated he would fight for his own people in a Holy War. However, that was not what the Justice Department had told the draft board when it considered Ali's initial appeal against 1-A classification. As a result, it was possible for the Court to rule that the government had given the draft board incorrect advice (as to the sincerity and religious basis of Ali's objection), which was sufficient grounds for overturning the conviction stemming from that draft board's decision. The Court could set Ali free, without setting a dangerous precedent. With some reluctance Burger fell into line, conceding the deal "would be a good lift for black people."

On 28 June 1971, the Supreme Court reversed Muhammad Ali's conviction and the Justice Department dropped all criminal charges against him. His passport was returned. Ali's reaction was revealing:

> I don't really think I'm going to know how that feels until I start to travel, go to foreign countries, see those strange people in the street. Then I'm gonna know I'm free.

In August he traveled to Caracas and Trinidad to fight exhibitions. In November he was in Buenos Aires. In early 1972, he flew to Libya with Herbert Muhammad to meet Qaddafi, who in his student days in London had visited Ali's dressing room in search of an autograph. They negotiated a $3 million interest-free loan for the construction of a new mosque in Chicago. Ali re-emerged as a major spokesman for the Nation of Islam. In December, the cover of *Muhammad Speaks* featured photographs of Ali and Elijah Muhammad under the headline, "Two Spotlights of the World!"

The Nation of Islam was no longer the dynamic force it had been in the early sixties. The leadership of the black nationalist tradition had passed to other, more radical forces. Yet in the meantime it had become an accepted and even respected institution within the black community. Elijah Muhammad emerged as a kind of grand old man of black pride. Thanks to his status in black America, his wealth and his conservative politics, he even gained the belated recognition of white America. Mayor Richard Daley declared 29 March "Honorable Elijah Muhammad Day in Chicago." The Messenger told FBI agents that "he believed in law and order . . . and loved America very much." But he remained on guard against schismatic factions. One of these was the Hanafi sect, which Kareem Abdul-Jabbar had joined, following Ali's example in his own way. In January 1973, Nation of Islam members brutally executed five members of the family of the sect's founder, Hamas Abdul Khaalis.

In 1972, Bob Arum approached Ali with a proposal for a fight in Johannesburg. Initially, Ali and Herbert Muhammad considered the deal favorably, but were dissuaded by anti-apartheid campaigners. The Nation of Islam saw little difference between selling Ali's talents to white Americans and selling them to white South Africans. At this time, despite the upsurge of black consciousness, black America remained only peripherally aware of South Africa. The Soweto uprising and Olympic boycott of 1976 changed that. Had Ali fought in South Africa in 1972, he would have been profoundly compromised in the long run. That may have meant little to Herbert Muhammad, but, even at his most confused, Ali was aware of the power he drew from his unique symbolic status. Certainly, in retrospect, it's worth contemplating how much would have been forfeited for the sake of a single big payday.

After his loss to Frazier, many boxing pundits wrote Ali off as a spent force. It was indeed an arduous climb back. Ali fought fourteen bouts between his first and second fights with Frazier, losing only to Ken Norton, who broke Ali's jaw. (Ali won the rematch six months later.) He fought in Zurich, Tokyo, Vancouver and Jakarta. In Dublin he told reporters that his great-grandfather was an Irishman named Grady (which was true). In January 1974, he once again faced Joe Frazier, who in the meantime had been deposed as champion by the awesome George Foreman. After another twelve grueling rounds, Ali won a unanimous decision. The stage was set for his meeting with Foreman.

• • •

In Kinshasa, Ali lived up to and beyond every boast he had ever made. The Rumble in the Jungle is the stuff of legend, and thanks to *When We Were Kings* the legend has been passed down to new generations. As a feat of athletic genius and a heart-stopping drama, Ali's against-the-odds victory over George Foreman before a huge crowd of partisan Africans and a global television audience has few rivals in the history of sports. But it was also a symbolic triumph par excellence, a Rasta-style allegory of redemption through suffering, of exile and homecoming. Kinshasa echoed with the most triumphal verse of Ali's own redemption song, but it was also, in disturbing ways, a triumph of representations over realities.

• • •

In 1966, Cleveland numbers runner and part-time club owner Don King beat a man to death with a pistol. He was charged with second-degree murder but the judge, whose links with the Mafia were revealed after his death, reduced it to manslaughter. When the same judge ran for the state court of appeals in 1976, Ali, at King's request, endorsed his campaign on local black radio stations.

King had listened to the first Ali–Frazier fight in his prison cell. After his release, he met up with Ali's R&B hero and one-time mentor, Lloyd Price, who had known King since his days on the road in the late fifties and had visited him in prison. The forty-year-old King had resolved to make himself into the first big-time black boxing promoter. He started by staging a fund-raising exhibition for an ailing Cleveland hospital serving a black neighborhood. As a favor to King, Price convinced Ali to spar a few rounds; somehow, King also talked Lou Rawls and Marvin Gaye into singing. Jackie Prosser, the Teamster leader, bought up reams of tickets and appeared at King's side during press conferences. The event helped clean up King's post-prison image and won him praise in the local media. The hospital, however, never received most of the cash King claimed to have raised and was forced to close in 1978.

Boxing needed a black promoter. King pushed himself through the door, happy to be what he gleefully called "the token nigger." The chief obstacle to black entrepreneurship—in sports or elsewhere

—has never been a shortage of entrepreneurial skills, but of capital. King solved that problem by persuading other people to advance the cash (among them, Mobutu, Marcos and the Mafia). This he managed largely through his uncanny ability to convince fighters to consign their fates to him. In *The Life and Crimes of Don King*, Jack Newfield recounts King's outlandish efforts to secure the Ali–Foreman fight. In the end, he managed to bypass Bob Arum, who had the inside track in both fighters' camps, by sheer bravado, and not least by an appeal to shared blackness. "You're two super athletes, both black," King told the hesitant Foreman. "You've got to forgo the pettiness. This event is bigger than both of you as individuals. It's monumental, not just in revenue but in the symbolic impact that will reverberate throughout the world—from a black perspective. This is my promotion! And I'm BLACK!"

In the end, King signed both Ali and Foreman by a process of bluff and double bluff. It's possible neither fighter thought he'd ever have to honor his signature, because it seemed so unlikely King would ever be able to put together the finance. In fact, King's search for a bankroll was beginning to seem hopeless when he was contacted by Fred Weymer, who had been implicated in the recent Bernie Cornfeld investment scandal (and as a result barred from the United States). Weymer was now managing Mobutu's Swiss bank accounts and negotiated with King on his master's behalf. In return for a commitment to stage the fight in Kinshasa, Risnelia, a Panama-chartered shell company used as a front for Mobutu's overseas holdings, provided King with two $4.8 million letters of credit, one for each fighter. The deal proved to be Don King's passport to the top of the boxing business.

By staging the fight Mobutu hoped to strengthen his regime,

attract foreign capital and win global prestige. Since his installation as dictator in 1965, ruling through repression and cronyism, he had transformed the Congo into a paradigm of post-colonial civic disintegration. Infrastructure deteriorated, the countryside was depopulated, the cities swelled. In the late sixties, he inaugurated a policy of Africanization, and in 1972 changed his own name to Mobutu Sese Seko, the name of his country to Zaire and the name of its capital, Léopoldville, to Kinshasa. Meanwhile, hunger became endemic in rural areas as Kinshasa swallowed up food supplies and mineral wealth flooded out of the country. Between 1969 and 1976, less than 1 percent of state expenditure was invested in agriculture, the mainstay of the majority. With support from western capital and western governments, Mobutu treated Zaire as a private empire, exploiting it as ruthlessly as the Belgians in the days of Leopold II's Congo Free State. As his country went to hell, he amassed one of the world's largest private fortunes.

• • •

> When as a singer I walk on to the platform, to sing back to the people the songs they themselves have created, I can feel a great unity, not only as a person, but as an artist who is one with his audience.
>
> *Paul Robeson*

At the age of thirty-two, Ali once again found himself the underdog against an unstoppable powerhouse. "This man is supposed to annihilate me, but ten years ago they said the same thing about

Sonny Liston," Ali reminded the press. "George Foreman don't stand a chance. The world is gonna bow down to me, because the stage is set." Responding to a question about Foreman's daunting punching power, he observed, "What you white reporters got to remember is, black folks ain't afraid of black folks the way white folks are afraid of black folks." Still, only the most dedicated wishful thinkers gave the ex-champ any chance against Foreman. Like many Ali fans, I too saw the Rumble in the Jungle as a last, probably forlorn, attempt by my hero to recapture past glory.

In the decade since he had announced "I don't have to be what you want me to be," Ali had accrued enormous symbolic capital and a genuinely global constituency. In promoting the Foreman fight, he set about mobilizing that capital and that constituency. Foreman had set himself up for his role in Ali's allegorical drama when he waved that little American flag in Mexico City in 1968. Like Frazier, Foreman became, in Ali's typecasting, another "white hope," another inferior specimen of the black male, graceless and witless. In contrast, Ali promoted himself as a representative of all those forces that had risen up over the last decade to challenge white American domination. And he happily linked his fate to theirs.

> You think the world was shocked when Nixon resigned?
> Wait till I whup George Foreman's behind.

While training in America for the fight, Ali playfully warned reporters, "When you get to Africa, Mobutu's people are gonna put you in a pot, cook you, and eat you." Mobutu's foreign minister complained to Herbert Muhammad, "Mr. Ali's remarks are damaging our image." When he arrived in Africa with his personal entourage of thirty-five, Ali acted as if he'd never been there before, waxing lyrical about the cars, skyscrapers, television sets and airplanes flown by black pilots. "I used to think Africans were savages. But now that I'm here, I've learned that many Africans are wiser than we are. They speak English and two or three more languages. Ain't that something? We in America are the savages." Throughout his career, Ali was always happy to repeat and reshuffle his old routines. It was a method of performance derived from a formulaic oral tradition, but it was also Ali's way of shaping his own message and communicating it to a vast audience. Sometimes the press complained they'd heard it all before, but this time they didn't even notice that Ali had said much the same thing about Africa on his first visit, ten years earlier.

Eight days before the scheduled fight, Foreman sustained a cut above the eye while sparring. The bout was postponed from 25 September to 30 October. Both fighters were advised by Mobutu's regime not to leave the country. Ali put a bold face on his disappointment, but told Howard Bingham he missed America, especially ice cream and pretty girls in miniskirts. The music festival, a celebration of the African diaspora organized by Lloyd Price, could not be postponed. The first night was poorly attended, but the government gave away tickets and the final night drew a huge crowd. When Price himself mounted the stage to perform "Stagger Lee," Ali was on his feet for one of his old favorites.

Price was never paid for his efforts and learned, as so many did, that his trust in Don King had been misplaced. James Brown thought King a hustler from the start, but played along with the black rhetoric for the sake of the show. In private, Ali squabbled with King, but in public he declared, "Don King is the world's greatest promoter and if it wasn't for him we wouldn't be fighting here in Africa."

Inadvertently, in Kinshasa, for the first time since the 1960 Olympics, Ali allowed somebody else to manipulate and package his symbolic value. It was Muhammad Ali's status and history that charged the African venue with popular significance, but it was Don King who orchestrated this symphony of black representations. Kinshasa became a self-consciously African affair, the acme of what might be called "dashiki-ism" among the black American middle class. Yet there was a disjunction between the Africa embraced by the Americans and the Africa the Africans wanted to project. At one press conference, King appeared in African robes, while Mobutu's ministers wore suits and ties. The official pre-fight publicity emphasized the city's gleaming new hotels, freshly painted government buildings and wide, spotless boulevards, as well as the country's mineral wealth (diamonds and copper) and bright economic prospects. Later, David Frost, hired by King to emcee the closed-circuit TV coverage, was to invoke the dynamism of technological advance by breathlessly repeating at every opportunity that the fight was being broadcast "live via satellite from Zaire, Africa." But it was through song, dance and above all the physical presence of Muhammad Ali in the streets that the real connections between black America and black Africa were made in Kinshasa. Of all the memorable moments in *When We Were Kings*, the most haunting are those when Ali is at leisure to interact freely with the African poor, especially the children.

Over the years, reporters who observed Ali with children often remarked that he was a politician in the making. Ali kissed babies, however, not to court popularity, but because among children he could indulge his softness, his delight in play and his love of fantasy. Best of all, among children he could slough off the burden of representation; no one would be trying to read between the lines. His generosity of spirit could be expressed without reserve. In return, the generosity of strangers—the African children, the people in the ghetto streets—sustained and empowered him. Ali liked to say he found "strength" in "the love of the people." That was more than poetic license. By some complex psychological process, he brought this love into the ring with him, and converted it into strength. He turned the burden of representation into an inexhaustible reserve of patience and determination.

In the scenario Ali constructed for the Rumble in the Jungle, he was not only the underdog, but the representative, in Dylan's phrase, of all the "underdog soldiers of the night." Shortly before the fight, he spoke directly to Leon Gast's camera. Along with much else of value, this footage never found its way into the final film, but it reveals that at this moment of ultimate trial, the consummate test of his career, Ali remembered the teachings of his dead friend, Malcolm X. "I'm fighting for God and my people," he said. "I'm not fighting for fame or money, I'm not fighting for me. I'm fighting for the black people on welfare, the black people who have no future, black people who are wineheads and dope addicts. I am a politician for Allah." Then, recalling Malcolm's great hero even as he prepared to fight under the patronage of one of his murderers, he added wistfully, "*I wish Lumumba was here to see me.*" Not for the first time, Ali may have said much more than he realized.

• • •

> Though't be a sportful combat,
> Yet in the trial much opinion dwells

No one will ever know exactly how much of his country's treasury Mobutu plundered to stage this spectacle. Jack Newfield has chronicled the extravagance. Within four months, the stadium on the outskirts of the city was entirely rebuilt, one hundred phone lines were installed to link the stadium to the satellite station fifty miles away, a new runway was built at the airport and a four-lane highway was laid from the airport to the hotels in downtown Kinshasa. Along the way, billboards obscured the view of squatters' camps. One of them read, "BLACK POWER IS SOUGHT EVERYWHERE IN THE WORLD, BUT IT IS REALIZED HERE IN ZAIRE."

Fifteen thousand people turned up to witness the weigh-in, where Foreman tried to steal Ali's thunder by entering in an African robe. The fight itself was preceded by a lengthy exhibition of state-sponsored "tribal" dancing. The Mobutu regime presented this as an affirmation of African tradition on the new global media stage; but it was also, like the fight that followed it, a commercial display of black bodies for the entertainment of a largely white television audience. Over the renovated stadium hung a forty-foot-high portrait of Mobutu, the "lion of Zaire."

A crowd of 62,000 (overwhelmingly Africans) watched Ali come out attacking in round one. After that, he spent most of his time leaning against the ropes—the "rope-a-dope," he called it later—and covering his face as Foreman punched away at his body to little effect. Between rounds, Ali led the crowd in its deafening chant: "Ali! *Bomaye!*" (Ali! Kill him!). Taunting Foreman throughout, soaking up punishment that would have finished off almost anyone else, Ali blunted Foreman's offensive. Among other things, Ali's performance in Kinshasa was an astonishing display of canny ringcraft and total ring vision. Contrary to his pre-fight predictions, he hardly danced at all after the first round, but somehow managed to lead the ever-advancing Foreman from one corner of the ring to another. Even as ringside critics puzzled over his tactics, he remained in control. At one point, after taking a fearsome battering in the ribs, he seemed to wink at the TV camera. Never was Ali's supreme gamesmanship—holding, clinching, pushing, tying up and frustrating Foreman, while always staying just the right side of the law—utilized to better effect. He launched and landed fewer punches than Foreman, but they counted for more: swift, economical and accurate. One might almost call them delicate, were it not for the telltale swellings on Foreman's face.

With thirty seconds left in round eight, Ali moved out from the ropes and suddenly nailed the tiring Foreman with a perfectly executed left–right combination that sent the champion tumbling to the floor. For a moment, Ali stood over him, bouncing on his toes, fists cocked to deliver more punishment if needed, snarling and supreme, eyes afire with victory. The crowd, the writers, the broadcasters were beside themselves. For once, David Frost got it right when he described the jubilant chaos as "the most joyous scene in the history of boxing!" Years later, the Nigerian poet, novelist and human rights activist Wole Soyinka combined African and American idioms to explain Ali's strategy and success in Kinshasa:

> Mortar that goads the pestle: Do you call that
> Pounding? The yam is not yet smooth—
> Pound, dope, pound! When I have eaten the yam,
> I'll chew the fibre that once called itself
> A pestle! Warrior who said, "I will not fight,"
> And proved a prophet's call to arms against a war.

In exile Ali had learned faith in himself and in the future; he had learned to suffer and to wait, and he had learned that he could prevail against the odds. The early lessons of the Nation of Islam, of self-reliance and group solidarity, had matured into a spirit made indomitable by a combined confidence in himself and in the love of the people. The terrifying fortitude Ali displayed in Kinshasa, and later in Manila, was rooted in the experience of exile and persecution. His sixties tribulations hold the key to his seventies triumphs.

Robert Lipsyte called the Rumble in the Jungle "probably the most mythic moment in world sports." Ali himself explained its appeal: "People like to see miracles. People like to see underdogs that do it. People like to be there when history is made." But thanks to Ali's struggles over the years outside the ring, there was much more to Kinshasa than the thrill of a sporting upset. This was a triumph of intelligence and sheer intensity of personality over impersonal brawn.

It was also a triumph for everything and everyone that Ali had stood for and with. All over the world, people—black and white—felt Ali's triumph as their triumph, the vindication of a historical epoch, "the baby figure of the giant mass / Of things to come at large."

But it must be remembered that there were others present at this rendezvous of victory. One was Don King. Thanks largely to Ali, he was now set on a fantastically lucrative twenty-year career as the heavyweight division's premier promoter and possibly the most ruthless exploiter of black talent boxing has ever known. Another was Mobutu Sese Seko, who, fearful of any large gathering of his own people, did not attend the fight in person. Instead, he watched the action on closed-circuit TV with his house guest, Idi Amin. Even as the world's media swarmed around his capital, the price of copper was plunging, and with it the Zairean economy. "The thirst for money transforms men into assassins," lamented the Archbishop of Kinshasa, "and whoever holds a morsel of authority or means of pressure profits from it to impose on people and exploit them."

Mobutu was to retain power for another two decades. And the hopes that the Rumble in the Jungle would herald a new era of reciprocity between America and Africa, mediated by African-Americans, were betrayed. The fight in Kinshasa proved a staging-post in a path of development that would leave Africa at an ever greater economic and political disadvantage. Between 1975 and 1995, debts rose, commodity prices fell, and transfers of wealth from sub-Saharan Africa to the United States grew larger by the year. To Basil Davidson, Mobutu's Zaire exemplified "a degradation which seemed unthinkable during the early years of post-colonial independence."

He cited the murder of Lumumba as a "turning point" in the "downfall."

• • •

The Rumble in the Jungle was one of several events which fomented a renaissance of black American pride in African origins. Another was the publication, in 1976, of Alex Haley's *Roots*. Reviewing the book for the *New York Times*, James Baldwin found it quite natural to link Haley's chronicle of enslavement and liberation to the values represented by the heavyweight champ.

> Even way up here in the twentieth century, Muhammad Ali will not be the only one to respond to the moment that the father lifted his baby up with his face to the heavens, and said softly, "Behold—the only thing greater than yourself."

The following year, the television series adapted from the book projected black America's African identity to a huge and highly diverse audience. Themes that had been quietly nurtured by black intellectuals and activists for more than a hundred years suddenly found a place in the mainstream of popular culture. Ali helped prepare the way for this momentous development, which was to give rise to conflicting passions and programs over the next two decades. The popularization of radical pan-Africanism—a response to the global crisis of the seventies—was a resource for the oppressed, but it also provided a cloak for the privileged. It led to a commodification of African culture for the black American market, and at the same time inspired funk and hip-hop artists, poets, dancers and painters. It led to the black American mobilization in solidarity with the South Africa freedom struggle in the eighties, as well as to Louis Farrakhan's deals with the military despots of Nigeria in the nineties. It was behind the rediscovery (and naming) of the Black Atlantic, and the reification of the "black essence" in Afrocentrism. And all these phenomena are foreshadowed in the career of Muhammad Ali.

• • •

In the wake of the Kinshasa fight, even Ali's old enemies had to admit he was truly "the Greatest." *Ring* magazine finally named him Fighter of the Year. *Sports Illustrated* declared him Sportsman of the Year. In December 1974, he was invited to the White House, where Gerald Ford welcomed him in what was widely seen as a symbol of post-Vietnam, post-Watergate national reconciliation. For the first time since he seized the title from Sonny Liston, Ali began to receive substantial endorsement offers. America had failed to break him, so now it accommodated him.

As it turned out, Ali's victory in Kinshasa set the stage for his reappropriation by the establishment and ultimately his own physical decline. The zenith of Ali's career, in and out of the ring, coincided with the beginning of the retreat of the black freedom movement and the reversal of the gains made by the black community. Saigon may have fallen to the Vietcong, but in Boston and other cities across the country white people were mobilizing against bussing with vigor and venom. Integrated and equal education—the starting point of the modern civil rights movement back in 1954—remained one of America's empty promises. In the decade following the Rumble in the Jungle, average real earnings for young black males fell by 50 percent, as did the proportion of black males in full-time employment. From the mid seventies, de-industrialization, white flight and cuts in public services pounded away at the social and economic base of the black community, which was further eviscerated by the movement of middle-class blacks out of the ghetto (a movement made possible by the gains of the previous era). The income gap between whites and blacks, which had closed over the previous twenty years, began to widen.

As the wave of protest receded and the drive toward black liberation stuttered to a halt, Ali cut a less threatening figure. "The Ali that America ended up loving was not the Ali I loved most," Jim Brown told Hauser. "The warrior I loved was gone. In a way, he became part of the establishment." Ali's new respectability owed much to events in the Nation of Islam following the death of Elijah Muhammad in February 1975. Days later, at the Savior's Day convention, Ali and senior figures in the Nation publicly pledged allegiance to Wallace Muhammad, the one-time apostate, as the new supreme minister. Ali was also a member of the five-man board appointed to assist Wallace, along with Herbert Muhammad and Louis Farrakhan. Over the next year, Wallace transformed the Nation. Seats were removed from the mosques. Paper-sale quotas were dropped. The paramilitary Fruit of Islam was abolished. Members were urged to register and to vote. Wallace called for a "new sense of patriotism" and for blacks to "identify with the land and the flag." Mosque No. 7 in Harlem was renamed for its former minister, "Malcolm Shabazz." Most shockingly of all, whites were admitted.

In October 1976, Wallace announced to his followers that they were no longer the Nation of Islam, but the World Community of Islam in the West. Seven months later, he publicly renounced his father's claim to divine messenger status and brought the organization's theology into line with Sunni orthodoxy. Publicly and privately, Ali welcomed Wallace's reforms. He had always been uncomfortable with the "white devil" theory and through his travels had become aware of the gulf between world Islam and the teachings of Elijah Muhammad. However, his old mentor, Jeremiah Shabazz, was appalled and left the Nation in disgust, as did Louis Farrakhan, who founded a second Nation of Islam, re-emphasizing Elijah's black nationalism and conservative social philosophy. The liquidation of the Nation of Islam proved in the end an occasion for its rebirth, not because of any master strategy on the part of Farrakhan, but because the underlying conditions of poverty and exclusion that gave rise to the first Nation have endured.

• • •

After Kinshasa, Ali defended his title eleven times in three and a half years, in the course of which he took his road show to Kuala Lumpur, Puerto Rico, Munich, Bogotá and, most famously, Manila, which staged his third and final meeting with Joe Frazier. The bout was preceded by Ali's now familiar dramatics—he was still "the Greatest" and Frazier was still "the gorilla"—but in the ring the contest was distilled into one of the purest and most testing boxing encounters in the sport's history. Both fighters exceeded themselves in dishing out and soaking up punishment. In the end, Ali prevailed only by once again summoning hidden reserves of strength and guile. It was to be his final display of boxing genius, and it took a physical toll from which he never recovered.

Among the fifty-strong entourage which accompanied Ali to Manila (compared to the seventeen who came with Joe Frazier) was the young and beautiful Veronica Porche. They had met a year before when Veronica had been chosen as one of the four "poster girls" to promote the Rumble in the Jungle. One evening in Kinshasa, Belinda discovered her husband returning late to the hotel with Veronica, and smacked him. Nonetheless, he continued the affair, and a year later Veronica escorted him to Manila, while Belinda remained at home with the children. The press knew about the liaison, but in those days sports stars' private lives were protected by unwritten laws. It was only after Ali took Veronica with him to meet Ferdinand and Imelda Marcos at the presidential palace that the ill-kept secret reached the public. Marcos assumed Veronica was Ali's wife and, in the presence of the media, complimented him on her beauty. *Newsweek* then broke the story of the long-running affair. In uncompromising mood, Ali decided to confront the media's hypocrisy:

> I know celebrities don't have privacy. But at least they should be able to sleep with who they want. Anybody who worries about who's my wife, tell them, you don't worry who I sleep with and I won't worry about who you sleep with. . . . The only person I answer to is Belinda Ali, and I don't worry about her.

The next day, an aggrieved but composed Belinda flew out to Manila, confronted Ali in private (though the shouting echoed through the hotel corridors), then flew straight back to the US. A year later, she filed for divorce, citing desertion, adultery and mental cruelty. In June 1977, Ali married Veronica. They already had one baby and were expecting another. As Ali's illness grew visible in the early eighties, this marriage also foundered, and the two were divorced in July 1986. That November, Ali married for a fourth time.

In an interview with the champ after the Thrilla in Manila, *Playboy* had the gall to criticize the Nation of Islam's double standards toward women. Defending himself and his religion, Ali was angry and confused:

> If you can't protect your women, you can't protect your nation ... if you put a hand on a Muslim sister you are to *die* ... horses and dogs and mules walk around with their behinds out. Humans hide their behinds ... showing our women disrespect—a man should die for that. And not just white men, black men too.

Ali's closest friends claim his womanizing began after his break-up with the feisty Sonji. Belinda blamed the Nation's pervasive hypocrisy for corrupting her husband: "some of them were married and fooling around themselves. ... They tried to make him like they were, and they were successful." Ali himself, like Elijah Muhammad, sometimes cited the Qur'an in defense of his promiscuity. Looking back, however, Ali acknowledges, "It hurt my wife. It offended my religion. It never really made me happy." He now recognizes as his own two children whose mothers he never married.

As Jeffrey Sammons, one of Ali's most insightful celebrants, sadly concluded, "Ali did not transcend the sexism of his times, his profession or his chosen faith." It is also true that black sexism continues to be more harshly judged—at least by many whites—than white sexism. In David Burner's account of the sixties, JFK's serial adulteries are passed over as "not uncommon among politicians and men of wealth," while the offenses of Huey Newton and Stokely Carmichael are dwelt upon at length and presented as fatal political flaws. Nonetheless, the racial double standard is no excuse for the sexual one. The reaction to Mike Tyson's rape of a black, teenage beauty contestant in 1991 demonstrated that in many minds blackness, boxing and violence against women remain frighteningly intertwined, a historic legacy for which Ali must share some blame. Tyson was backed not just by Farrakhan but also by a bevy of Christian ministers, who held him up as the victim and castigated Desiree Washington as the embodiment of feminine wiles, a svelte seductress who got what was coming to her. As with Clarence Thomas and Anita Hill, the Tyson affair showed how "black pride" could be deployed to crush black women.

• • •

As the promoter of the Thrilla in Manila, Don King took credit for the awesome spectacle, though it was Ferdinand Marcos who put up the money (as with Mobutu, it was hard to know which funds were coming from the Marcos family and which from the national treasury). Shortly after the fight, King made an audacious bid to supplant Herbert Muhammad as Ali's manager, but like everyone else who tried to pry Ali loose from the Muhammad family over the years, he failed and in the process antagonized not only Herbert but Ali himself (not least by bribing people in Ali's training camp). In May 1976, Ali signed with Madison Square Garden to promote his title fight against Ken Norton at Yankee Stadium. An outraged King claimed he was the "financial victim" of the Nation's new-found fondness for white people and denounced Herbert Muhammad as a "Judas."

The young militant Al Sharpton emerged as a champion of King (later, he informed on him for the FBI). Describing the boxing promoter as a hero "of Third World youth," Sharpton urged blacks to boycott the Ali–Norton fight and even staged a sit-in at the MSG offices. "Has Ali forgotten that it was we who stood by him when he was stripped and vilified? Has Ali forgot that we crowned him the people's champion when they took his title? Has he forgot that this black promoter brought him and other brothers more money than ever before? Has Ali forgot that the Garden endorsed his demise? His rhetoric says black but the bottom line reads lily white." But when it came to black rhetoric, no one could challenge King, who described Ali's deal with MSG as "a case of the slave hurrying back to the slavemaster." Although the black community ignored King and Sharpton, their stunt demonstrated how Black Power had become detached from its living roots in a black movement for power.

King's real relationship with the black community he claimed to represent is best revealed by the black fighters he ripped off. Larry Holmes said that King "looks black, lives white and thinks green." Tim Witherspoon observed, "Don's speciality is black on black crime." In the twenty years following his breakthrough in Kinshasa, 100 law suits were filed against King by disgruntled fighters and managers. But the real question about King is not how he managed to swindle and manipulate heavyweight fighters, but how he managed to do the same to the government and the judiciary. It has to be remembered that King prospered not in defiance of but in collusion with the white establishment, from boxing boards to television executives. There was no one who was not prepared to deal with King, if the price was right. In the end, he merely represents in extreme form the malaise that has always infected boxing.

• • •

Shortly after signing for the Norton fight, Ali visited Tokyo, where he took part in a hybrid boxing–wrestling match against a Japanese champion. This adventure was primarily a money-spinning gimmick, but it was also one of Ali's many efforts to make the *world* in world champion mean more than the *world* in baseball's World Series. It proved an undignified spectacle, a humiliating falling-off from the rigor required by a true sporting contest. Curiously, here was Muhammad Ali, the man who had remade the image of the black sports hero, reduced to the depths of Joe Louis's wrestling exhibitions or Jesse Owen's races against horses. Ali was better paid, and treated with greater personal respect, but, even so, he ended up compromising his sport and his image.

Ali had always walked the fine line between self-projection and self-parody, but in his later years as champion he grew more careless about the distinction. In this era, the icon of Ali—in books, on posters and magazine covers, in the movies or on television—was ubiquitous. There were suddenly a lot of people making money out of representations of Ali, not least Ali himself. His autobiography, *The Greatest*, appeared in late 1976. The accuracy of the book is disputed by most chroniclers of Ali's life today, and Ali himself claims to have read it only after it was published. It is by turns an artful and tedious composition, and it rarely sounds like Ali. But despite the embarrassing paean to Herbert Muhammad with which it begins, it is the last expression of the radical and angry Ali, thanks probably to its writer, Richard Durham, a black nationalist (but not a Muslim), and its editor, Toni Morrison. In the film of the same title, which came out a year later, Ali played himself. Watching him reprise past scenes of defiance, I think of Sitting Bull in Buffalo Bill's Wild West Show, re-enacting the Little Bighorn for the titillation of an audience ensconced in safety and comfort, an audience no longer threatened by his antagonism.

A curiously revealing avatar of Ali's personality is to be found in Sylvester Stallone's *Rocky*, which was directly inspired by Ali's first post-Kinshasa title defense, against Chuck Wepner in Cleveland in March 1975. Don King promoted the low-rated Wepner as a "white hope" and himself as "an equal opportunity employer who wants to give the white race a chance." Here, the racialization of boxing, so intense and volatile in earlier decades, has become cheap decor, a mere selling point, and a flimsy one at that. (The fight was a box-office flop.) But Wepner's doomed challenge provided Stallone with raw material for his story of Rocky Balboa, plucked from obscurity to face Apollo Creed, the flamboyant black champion and master of braggadocio, obviously modeled on Muhammad Ali (the film even invokes his rivalry with Frazier). Here, it is the white fighter who is inarticulate, who relies on brute force, and the black fighter who is quick-witted and quick-footed. The transposition of the old stereotypes is a tribute to Ali and a measure of the changes he had wrought in public perceptions. But the film is also a measure of the increasing adaptability of his icon. The drama is set during America's bicentennial celebrations and the climactic title fight is presented as a celebration of American nationalism. The Apollo Creed character enters the ring in an Uncle Sam hat, bedecked with the stars and stripes (it is Rocky, the "Italian Stallion," whose ethnicity comes to the fore). Departing even further from reality, the sequels which followed the first film showed the white hero winning and retaining the title, while Apollo Creed was reduced to a standard-issue Hollywood black sidekick.

In 1977, Ali sat for an Andy Warhol silk-screen portrait, thus joining Marilyn and Elvis among the artist's gallery of American "icons." The champ was astounded to learn how much Warhol was being paid for "an hour's work," and Warhol dryly agreed that it was an easy life. In retrospect, the Warhol portrait marks the moment of symbolic appropriation, the transition of Ali from a divisive to a consensual figure. In Warhol's iconography, Ali became one among an infinite series of celebrity images, all equivalent, all interchangeable. For the best part of two decades, the boxer used the electronic conduits of the burgeoning global media industry to project his personal identity and the messages that sprang from it to a vast new audience. At the same time, this industry used Ali to project its messages, to sell itself and its products. The icon of Ali could not but be transformed in the process.

• • •

In February 1978, Ali was vanquished by the young, inarticulate and inelegant Leon Spinks. The fight had been promoted by King's rival, Bob Arum, who found himself unexpectedly holding the options for the new champion's next three fights. Arum immediately arranged for a rematch with Ali. King, who needed a way back into the heavyweight title stakes, then conspired with the WBC to strip Spinks of his new title—for the crime of giving Ali, rather than Larry Holmes or Ernie Shavers (who were in King's camp), first crack at it. A series of eliminator bouts for the "vacant" title was then staged (under King's aegis). It was a key moment in the fragmentation of boxing authority, which in time would lead to the proliferation of putative heavyweight champions and the decline of the sport's competitive integrity.

Bob Arum approached Ali about fighting his rematch with Spinks in Sun City, the resort-style capital of the South African puppet state of Bophuthatswana. With South African backing, Arum guaranteed Ali a mind-bending $14 million. Ali was tempted. Despite protests from Arthur Ashe and Jesse Jackson, Herbert Muhammad proceeded with negotiations for the fight, which were only abandoned in the face of tax complications and threats of a closed-circuit television boycott. Ali expressed his own thoughts on the issue in a late-night ramble to Hunter S. Thompson, who tried to persuade the champ that he should take on and beat a white South African in South Africa. Ali considered the proposal. Yes, he was attracted to the idea of the fight, provided that "on that day there'd be equality in the arena." Then he added another, crucial rider: "If the masses of the country and the world were against it, I wouldn't go." He was intrigued by, but also wary of, the symbolic dimensions of such a fight. "What worries me is getting whupped by a white man in South Africa. . . . That's what the world needs . . . me getting whupped by a white man in South Africa." On the other hand, "If I beat him too bad and then leave the country, they might beat up some of the brothers." He concluded: "I wouldn't fool with it. I'm a representative of black people. . . . It's too touchy. . . . it's more than a sport when I get involved."

Many thought Ali should have retired after Manila. Many more thought he should have retired after losing to Spinks. Instead, Ali returned to defeat an under-trained Spinks in a poor excuse for a heavyweight title fight. True, Ali had won the world championship for an unprecedented third time, but the triumph seemed a low-rent, recycled imitation of earlier glories. Most Ali fans breathed a sigh of relief when he announced his retirement in June 1979, at the age of thirty-seven. He had been fighting professionally for nearly nineteen years and had been defeated only three times—by Frazier, Norton and Spinks—in fifty-four bouts.

Ali returned to Africa in early 1980. For the first time, he visited the continent as an official emissary of the United States, despatched by President Jimmy Carter to drum up support for Washington's proposed boycott of the Moscow Olympics in response to the Soviet invasion of Afghanistan. Ali may have thought his devotion to Islam and his obligations to America had at last coincided, but in Africa he was quickly disabused. In Tanzania, Kenya, Nigeria and Senegal, local politicians and journalists sharply questioned the logic of his stand and his willingness to be deployed as a propaganda tool in the renewed Cold War. Under pressure, Ali backtracked, "Maybe I'm being used to do something that ain't right," he admitted at a press conference. "You're making me look at things different. I'm not a traitor to black people." At this point, the State Department minder closed the press conference and hustled Ali out the door.

In sharp contrast to previous trips to the African motherland, this mission was a disaster. Ali returned to America perplexed and embarrassed. He had often mused about assuming a leadership role in retirement, and it may be that his disappointment in Africa was one of the factors which drove him back to the ring. It may also have been a need for money, an addiction to the theater of the fight game, or some desire to compensate for the three and a half years he'd lost defying the draft. Most likely, it was a combination of all these factors and others which led Ali to sign with Don King for a comeback bout against world champion Larry Holmes, his former sparring partner. For once, King was forced to put up his own money to finance the fight, which may be one reason it proceeded despite mounting concerns about Ali's health. Holmes worshipped Ali and tried his best to keep the thirty-eight-year-old living legend upright through eleven rounds without inflicting permanent damage. King was less considerate. He paid Ali $1,170,000 less than his contract stipulated. Ali was forced to sue. King, under pressure to repay the Mafia money he'd borrowed to set up the Wepner fight, could not afford to meet Ali's claim in full and was desperate to settle out of court. He located Jeremiah Shabazz, now preaching in Philadelphia, and paid him to visit Ali, who was in hospital, undergoing treatment for the mysterious nervous symptoms which had already begun to plague him before his first retirement. Shabazz handed Ali $50,000 in cash, and in return Ali signed a paper releasing King from the remainder of the debt. A few years later, Wole Soyinka described the ageing ex-champ sitting at the ringside watching lesser fighters battle for the title that once was his:

A brief salute—the camera is kind,
Discreetly pans, and masks the double-talk
Of medicine men—"Has the syndrome
But not the consequence." Promoters, handlers
It's time to throw in the towel—Parkinson's'
Polysyllables have failed to tease a rhyme
From the once nimble Louisville Lips.

The shocking thing is not that Ali persisted in fighting, obsessively seeking out the money, glamor and success he had been willing to forfeit in earlier years, but that others allowed him to do so. Without the media, the boxing and licensing authorities, the promoters and investors, Ali would never have had the chance to do such terrible damage to himself. And whenever I hear pundits aver that it was Ali himself who insisted on returning to the ring, that Ali himself would have it no other way, that Ali considers parkinsonism a price worth paying, I am reminded of an early Dylan song (recorded by Pete Seeger in 1963), "Who Killed Davey Moore?," in which the singer asks an unanswerable question of referees, managers, promoters, spectators, gamblers and writers:

Who killed Davey Moore,
Why an what's the reason for?
"Not me," says the boxing writer
Pounding print on his old typewriter,
Sayin', "Boxing ain't to blame,
There's just as much danger in a football game,"

Sayin', "Fist-fightin' is here to stay
It's just the old American way.
It wasn't me that made him fall.
No, you can't blame me at all."

The lesson of the final phase of Ali's career is an old one. Just as defeats may contain the seeds of victories, so victories may contain the seeds of defeats. For so many years, Ali embodied what C.L.R. James called the "future in the present." The tragedy is that his body carried the injuries of the past into the future, and that tragedy is inseparable from the institutions and traditions of boxing.

• • •

In January 1980, Ali visited Bombay with his then wife, Veronica, on a promotional tour sponsored by Air India and Amul butter. In his suite at the Taj hotel, he expounded his views on religion and politics to two young reporters from the India *Times*:

> "Muhammad went to the Arabians, Krishna to India, Buddha to China, Jesus to the Jews and Gentiles they say. Man has through his intoxication and misunderstanding fought with others. But in reality there's only one message, the message of wisdom. It was not man's message, it was God's message. One reason I converted to Islam was because it was the only religion that I heard say all people are equal and that a man can go to heaven if he lives right and believes what God said."

"But," interjected one of the reporters, "Marx said that all men are equal."

"I don't know him," said Ali. "Was he a religious man?"

"No."

"Was he doin' good for the people?"

"He wanted to, yes."

"Then I'd say, he'd go to heaven."

• • •

As I finished work on this book, Ali appeared in two new roles on British television screens.

In the first, he was advertising a retirement pension. The advert begins with images of the young Ali, eye-catching as always, the expressive vivacity and verbal energy somehow even more striking than ever in an era of de-valued, over-hyped celebrity. Then we are presented with the speechless figure of Ali today, awkwardly tapping a black boy on the shoulder. "So you can still be the Greatest," the voice-over insists, "even when you retire." Yet the tottering Ali of the advert's final images is clearly no longer the Greatest, and I wonder if the sponsor's real intention was to make people who remember the sixties feel old and insecure.

The second role was as a silent yet somehow eloquent champion of the campaign to cancel Third World debt. It was hard to imagine a celebrity advocate more suitable to the cause. Watching Ali in this latest guise, I thought: they haven't quite tamed him yet—either the icon or the man. Just by being there, he had brought the struggles of the sixties where they belong, into the present, as aid and support for the global resistance of the future.

Conclusion: Crowns and Garlands

Make a garland of Leontynes and Lenas
And hang it round your neck
    Like a lei.
Make a crown of Sammys, Sidneys, Harrys,
Plus Cassius Mohammed Ali Clay.
Put their laurels on your brow
    Today—
Then before you can walk
To the neighborhood corner,
Watch them drop, wilt, fade
Away.
Though worn in glory on my head,
They do not last a day—
Not one—
Nor take the place of meat or bread
Or rent that I must pay.

Great names for crowns and garlands!
Yeah!
I love Ralph Bunche—
But I can't eat him for lunch.
Langston Hughes, 1967

In Palermo, amid the World War II rubble which (thanks to five decades of Mafia mismanagement) still clutters the precincts of the old city, I came upon a West African street vendor. He had spread his wares along the pavement in front of the bombed-out façade of a baroque palace and there, next to the pocket knives and plastic binoculars, he displayed an assortment of posters, some new, some old, many printed in garish colors, others curling at the edges. Among the latter was an image of Muhammad Ali dating from the mid seventies, nestling cozily alongside Madonna, the Pope, Leonardo DiCaprio, the Spice Girls and various Italian and African footballers. The only other African-American in this exalted company was Michael Jordan, who had recently completed his last season of professional basketball.

When Jordan announced his retirement, the media celebrated him as a "global symbol of America," and the event was noted even in countries where basketball ranks beneath cribbage as a popular pastime. Inevitably, comparisons were drawn with Muhammad Ali. Yet Jordan's retirement will merely remind any student of world sports that Ali remains incomparable.

To some extent, the US media delude themselves about the global sway of basketball. True, compared to other American sports it has at least established a toehold abroad, but it still enjoys only a fraction of the inter-continental reach of boxing, not to mention soccer.

Outside the United States, and outside the basketball enclaves, Jordan is famous, first, for making more money out of sports than any athlete in history, and, second, for his association with the Nike corporation. The America of which he is a symbol is corporate America and its winner-takes-all ethic. His blackness has been deliberately submerged within his Americanness, which is reduced, in the end, to his individual wealth and success.

Since Ali's day, the advance of blacks in big money sports has gone hand in hand with the impoverishment of the communities they come from. The escalating rewards at the highest levels—epitomized by Michael Jordan—have made black sports stars ever less representative of the black community as a whole, 45 percent of which lives below the poverty line. In *Darwin's Athletes*, John Hoberman has argued forcefully that black success in sports has re-enforced "the myth of race" and distorted the development of both black individuals and their communities. Black sports heroes long ago demolished the nineteenth-century myth of the white man's physical superiority. But its place has been taken by the equally insidious myth of black physical superiority—with its unspoken concomitant, black intellectual ineptitude. Sport, for Hoberman, has become a racial prison, though for many it still looks like a Promised Land. When Jackie Robinson broke the color bar, it was often said that major league baseball became a true mirror of American society. However, the high-profile affluence of a small number of black sports stars has now turned sports into a distorting mirror and in some ways an outright lie about a society in which, for example, white Americans enjoy a six-year advantage in life expectancy over blacks. Sports, which did so much to force whites to acknowledge the black presence in America, now contribute to the invisibility of both the real hardships suffered in black communities and the persistence of racism.

Nothing could be further from the ethos of Muhammad Ali than the no-risk business acumen of Jordan. When campaigners trying to draw attention to the plight of low-paid workers in Nike's Southeast Asian sweatshops appealed to Jordan for help, they got the brush off. So did black Democrats in Jordan's home state of North Carolina when they asked him to endorse their efforts to defeat the racist, homophobic tobacco champion, Jesse Helms. Ali said he didn't want "to carry a sign"; Jordan only wants to carry the signs he gets paid for carrying. Ali's embrace of an alternative nationality, in the form of the Nation of Islam, evolved under the pressure of events into a humanist internationalism, a sense of responsibility to the poor and powerless of all nations. Jordan's subordination of himself to "America" made him an emblem of "globalization," a form of rule from above by multi-national corporations. His astonishing achievements on the basketball court, and the huge rewards he has reaped from them, are advanced as justifications for "the American way," the capitalist way. Jordan has become the embodiment of the Social Darwinism of the new world order.

Having learned nothing from history, the media hailed Jordan throughout his career as a role model. Exactly how are wealthy celebrities like Jordan supposed to set an example for those who are neither rich nor famous? Most poor people can work as hard as Jordan has, can be as law-abiding, self-disciplined and self-effacing, and will still reap little reward for their efforts. There is, in short, no way we can emulate Michael Jordan, unless we are among the minute fraction of the population with the physical attributes required by big-time professional sports. In contrast, we can all emulate at least some of what Ali did outside the ring, not the verbal fireworks, perhaps, but certainly the adherence to conscience in defiance of social pressure, the expression of the self through a commitment to a higher cause and a wider community. It was the willingness of the Greatest to link his destiny with the least and littlest that won him the devotion of so many.

America wants to forget what it did to the people of Vietnam, and has yet to pay a penny in war reparations. Yet America also wants to embrace Muhammad Ali and even convert him into a symbol of national identity. Perhaps I've lived abroad too long, but for me what makes Ali a role model is precisely his rejection of American national identity in favor of a broader, transnational sense of selfhood and social responsibility. Ali's career is a standing reminder to us all that national affiliation—in sports, in politics, in life—is not natural or God-given; it is constructed and can therefore, as Ali demonstrated, be deconstructed.

There are some who have discovered belatedly and with shock that Ali was an imperfect hero. Perfect heroes, however, are not only implausible but also useless. They can only be admired, not imitated. Ali's flawed humanity reminds us that role models are always incomplete and contradictory. Commenting on the revival of black nationalist icons in the 1990s, Angela Davis has warned, "Where cultural representations do not reach out beyond themselves, there is the danger that they will function as surrogates for activism, that they will constitute both the beginning and end of political practice."

In his heyday, Ali was like a computer virus, reversing polarities, short-circuiting connections, infiltrating the marginal into the mainstream. But in the long run he became a prisoner of the electronic conduits, and today the virus guards have grown more sophisticated and more vigilant. The inflation of wages, prize-money and endorsements may have liberated sports stars from their serf-like status of the past, but it has also made them more dependent on and integrated with corporate power, and intensified the pressures for conformity. Michael Oriard has dubbed Ali "an anachronism, a kind of hero perhaps no longer possible in the age of the spectacle," and it is true that the prospects for resistance seem more limited than in Ali's time. Yet Ali's story proves that those who write off such prospects are in danger of falling into the trap Bob Dylan warned about in a song released the week after Ali declared "*I don't have to be what you want me to be.*"

> Come writers and critics
> who prophesize with your pen
> and don't speak too soon
> for the wheel's still in spin
> and the loser now will be later to win.

If one day we're lucky enough to live through a sporting revolution in which the domination of finance is overthrown and sport is at last permitted to come into its own, not as an instrument for monetary gain or national aggrandizement, but as an exercise with no end but itself, I have no doubt the revolutionaries will draw inspiration from Muhammad Ali. His example of personal moral witness, of border-crossing solidarity, belongs not to sixties nostalgia, but to the common future of humanity.

Note on Sources

The foundations for the current Ali renaissance were laid by the publication of Thomas Hauser's biography in 1992. This book is a glorious work of oral history, imbued with both a sense of proportion and a deep love for its subject. Like others who have written about Ali, I have plundered Hauser's master-work for facts and quotations. Nonetheless, it must be said that, like any account of a great individual, the Hauser biography is a product of its time and place. It cannot be the final word.

In an attempt to fill out the details of Ali's political career and reactions to it, I have researched the contemporary newspaper records (especially the black press) and as many accounts of the black freedom and anti-war movements as I could lay my hands on. I have also corresponded with sports fans and political activists in various countries. Apart from Bob Dylan's lyrics, all the song transcriptions are my own.

The books listed on the following pages are only a selection of those consulted.

Angelou, Maya, *The Heart of a Woman*, 1981

—, *All God's Children Need Traveling Shoes*, 1986

Armstrong, Scot, and Bob Woodward, *The Brethren: Inside the Supreme Court*, 1979

Ashe, Arthur, *A Hard Road to Glory* (three volumes), revised edition, 1993

Bak, Richard, *Joe Louis, the Great Black Hope*, 1996

Baldwin, James, *Collected Essays*, 1998

Bergreen, Laurence, *Louis Armstrong, An Extravagant Life*, 1997

Branch, Taylor, *Parting the Waters: America in the King Years, 1954–63*, 1988

Branch, Taylor, *Pillar of Fire: America in the King Years, 1964–1966*, 1998

Cleaver, Eldridge, *Soul on Ice*, 1968

Clegg, Claude Andrew, *An Original Man: The Life and Times of Elijah Muhammad*, 1997

Davidson, Basil, *The Black Man's Burden: Africa and the Curse of the Nation-State*, 1992

Davison, Geoffrey, "The Cold War and the Evolution of Sports Consciousness in America," *Sporting Heritage*, 1, 1995

Duberman, Martin, *Paul Robeson: A Biography*, 1988

Du Bois, W.E.B., *Souls of Black Folk*, 1903

—, *An ABC of Color*, 1963

—, *The Autobiography*, 1968

Early, Gerald, *The Culture of Bruising*, 1994

Early, Gerald, ed., *The Muhammad Ali Reader*, 1998

Essien-Udom, E.U., *Black Nationalism: A Search for an Identity in America*, 1962

Evanzz, Karl, *The Judas Factor*, 1992
Fraser, Ronald, *1968: A Student Generation in Revolt*, 1988
Freedman, Suzanne, *Clay v. United States: Muhammad Ali Objects to War*, 1997
Fryer, Peter, *Staying Power: The History of Black People in Britain*, 1984
Garrow, David J., *Bearing the Cross: Martin Luther King Jr. and the Southern Christian Leadership Conference*, 1986
Gilroy, Paul, *The Black Atlantic: Modernity and Double Consciousness*, 1993
Gorn, Elliott J., ed., *Muhammad Ali: The People's Champ*, 1995
Halstead, Fred, *Out Now! A Participant's Account of the American Movement against the Vietnam War*, 1978
Hartmann, Douglas, "The Politics of Race and Sport: Resistance and Domination in the 1968 African American Olympic Protest Movement," in *Ethnic and Racial Studies*, vol. 19, no. 3, July 1996
Hayden, Robert, *Collected Poems*, 1996
Haygood, Wil, *King of the Cats: The Life and Times of Adam Clayton Powell Jr.*, 1993
Hoberman, John, *Darwin's Athletes*, 1997
Hughes, Langston, *Collected Poems*, ed. Arnold Rampersad, 1994
James, C.L.R., *Nkrumah and the Ghana Revolution*, 1977
Johnson, Jack, *The Autobiography of Jack Johnson*, reprinted, 1992
Kelley, Robin D.G., *Race Rebels, Culture, Politics and the Black Working Class*, 1994
—, *Yo' Mama's Disfunctional*, 1997
King, Martin Luther, Jr., *A Testament of Hope: Essential Writings and Speeches*, ed. James M. Washington, 1988

Kopkind, Andrew, *The Thirty Years War*, 1995
Lewis, John (with Michael D'Orso), *Walking with the Wind: A Memoir of the Movement*, 1998
Malcolm X, with the assistance of Alex Haley, *The Autobiography of Malcolm X*, 1965
Marable, Manning, *W.E.B. Du Bois, Black Radical Democrat*, 1986
—, *Race, Reform and Rebellion*, 1991
Marcus, Greil, *Invisible Republic, Bob Dylan's Basement Tapes*, 1997
McIlvanney, Hugh, *McIlvanney on Boxing*, 1996
Newfield, Jack, *The Life and Crimes of Don King*, 1995
O'Reilly, Kenneth, *Racial Matters: The FBI's Secret File on Black America, 1960–72*, 1989
Perry, Bruce, *Malcolm: The Life of a Man Who Changed Black America*, 1991
Remnick, David, *King of the World*, 1998
Roberts, Randy, *Papa Jack: Jack Johnson and the Era of White Hopes*, 1983
Robeson, Paul, *Here I Stand*, 1958
Rower, John Carlos, and Rick Berg, eds, *The Vietnam War and American Culture*, 1991
Sammons, Jeffrey T., *Beyond the Ring: The Role of Boxing in American Society*, 1988
Shelton, Robert, *No Direction Home: The Life and Music of Bob Dylan*, 1986
Sivanandan, A., *A Different Hunger: Writings on Black Resistance*, 1982
Soyinka, Wole, *Mandela's Earth and Other Poems*, 1989
Steen, Rob, *Sonny Boy: The Life and Strife of Sonny Liston*, 1993

Tanner, Michael, *Ali in Britain*, 1995

Terry, Wallace, *Bloods: An Oral History of the Vietnam War by Black Veterans*, 1984

Thompson, Hunter S., *The Great Shark Hunt*, 1979

Tygiel, Jules, ed., *The Jackie Robinson Reader: Perspectives on an American Hero*, 1997

Ward, Brian, *Just My Soul Responding: Rhythm and Blues, Black Consciousness and Race Relations*, 1998

Wolff, Daniel, *You Send Me: The Life and Times of Sam Cooke*, 1995

Young, Andrew, *An Easy Burden: The Civil Rights Movement and the Transformation of America*, 1996

Index